International series on the quality of working life

Vol. 4

A choice of futures

A choice of futures

Fred Emery and Merrelyn Emery
Centre for Continuing Education, ANU, Canberra

Martinus Nijhoff Social Sciences Division
Leiden 1976

ISBN 90 207 0635 7

Printed by Mennen, Asten, the Netherlands.

Preface

Exploration of the nature of *human* communication and the media is a prerequisite to any assessment of the likely future role of communications.

We cannot assume that the nature of these things is transparently obvious to everyone and therefore commonly understood. Three developments in recent decades should adequately warn against such an assumption. First, we had the fiasco of social scientists trying to apply Shannon's mathematical theory of information as if it were a theory of human communication. 'In Shannon's use of information we cannot speak of how much information a person has only how much a message has.' (Ackoff and Emery, 1972, p. 145). They would not have wandered into that blind alley if they had stopped to think about the nature of human communication. Second was the belated but wholehearted acceptance of the Heider theory of balance and its subsequent wane. Its wane had nothing to do with its inherent merits. It waned because it could not survive on the Procrustean bed of the psychologists' theory of choice. It did not occur to the psychologists to question their assumptions about how people made the choices that lead to purposeful communication (Ackoff and Emery, 1972, p. 58). The last example has been the bitter and unended furore about McLuhan. This time the psychologists and sociologists have been strangely quiet but we can be sure this does not imply acquiescence in McLuhan's views. It would seem rather that they cannot find enough common ground about the nature of human communication to start debating.

As envisaged in several documents prepared by the N.T.P. team we have had to outline a model of man that accounts for how man can communicate with distal parts of his environment, with his fellow man (ABX systems) with himself (pox systems) and via the environments created by communication technology. This has taken us far afield into biology and neuro-physiology etc. but there has been no other choice in the absence of a suitable existing model. 'For not only is human communication a system too great to permit its parts to be understood in isolation from one another, but it is also a *sub*system too great to be treated fruitfully in isolation from other aspects of human behaviour.' (Ackoff and Emery, 1972, p. 8). Fortunately, chapters IX to XI of that book have relieved us of a major part of the necessary groundwork.

Very detailed attention was given to the television medium because of its centrality in telecommunications and the uncertainty about its modus operandi as a medium of human communications.

We then chose to test our model against McLuhan's theses. This brought us into consideration of the future role of telecommunications.

In the final part we have used the model of societal development that appeared in *Futures We're In*. This model was only recently completed and we feel that subsequent evidence only further supports the major features of the model. Experts we knew who where then laughing at the notion of a two child family as the norm have now publicly declared that this is what is happening. Chile has gone the way that we expected. France is seriously involved in the democratization of work. Our assumption that energy would become cheaper was sharply set at abeyance by the oil producers' move, late 1973. This was a move, however, that went a long way to resetting terms of commodity exchange that had reflected the older imperial-colonial era. It provided an immediate impetus to conservation and to nuclear energy to achieve the scale required for much cheaper energy.

One of the outstanding features of the oil price-hike was that there was no military retaliation. This degree of stability in international relations augurs well for even more such peaceful adjustments of resource control and pricing to the benefit of the developing nations.

The continued strengthening of positive adaptive responses can be seen in such diverse matters as the new liberal family legislation in France and Italy and the successful conclusion of the Watergate affair.

Futures We're In thus provided us with a framework for developing positive and negative social scenarios. Within these scenarios we have tried to untangle the role of telecommunications.

The most critical guidelines derived from this model were that

1. communication is a secondary property. It is and has been always a *necessary* condition for human beings to act socially. Not, however, a *sufficient* condition. Many situations have existed where increased communication has increased conflict. Many situations can be observed where communication channels are in existence but not used for social ends.
2. The most important of the sufficient conditions for social communication

lie in a society's choice between the two basic designs for social organization.

With these guidelines we attempted to identify the emergence of new requirements for human communication as people's behaviour becomes more
purposeful, as their organizations become democratized, and as the cultural
patterns evolve around transformed ideals.

Throughout the course of this study we suspended any judgement about
what kinds of telecommunication technology might be required, with the one
exception of a detailed study of video-access centres in Australia. Only in the
final months did some sort of a picture begin to form.

Most readers will be well advised to start from Part II, and return to Part I
only when difficulty is experienced with the use of concepts such as medium,
affect, communication and such like. Part I is difficult technical reading but
then some of the basic issues required this treatment.

Contents

Part II

The modern media and man

Part III

Human communication and the adaptive response

A model of man as communicator

Introduction

This part constituted a major part of the theoretical scaffolding used to construct the later parts.

We felt it desirable to separate off this theoretical material but nevertheless to make it publicly available, both to assist critical appraisal of what was built with its aid and to aid further building or reconstruction.

It seeks to make more explicit several major theses used in the later parts:

1. that communication, and the use of communication to inform, instruct, enlighten and persuade, are critically dependent on the informational characteristics of the environment within which such efforts are pursued;
2. the concept of the social field as distinct from social organizations taken singly or collectively;
3. that too much information may be as destructive to adaptation as too little.

Each chapter represents a strand of thought, each makes some contribution to the following chapter. And yet each is incomplete. In some cases successive drafts have spread over the last decade or more. They have not achieved finality in the past and we have had no intention of conveying an air of finality now.

1. Persuasion and communication

Persuasion is inseparable from communication in that it implies that someone does something in the environment of another person, even if only to
produce sound waves, that these changes are somehow registered or perceived by that person, that the psychological processes thus set up influence
other psychological processes, and that the individual in turn acts on the
environment to produce further changes. There are processes of persuasion,
like pushing the learner into the water, that are not mediated by changes in
the mind of the person, but we have excluded these. There are processes of
communication that are no more than pushing a button, and we have excluded these (Ackoff and Emery, 1972, p. 142). The overall process thus
starts outside the individual and ends up outside. It is therefore reasonable
to precede an analysis of what goes on 'inside' by an analysis of what can
take place *outside* that could communicate with what takes place 'inside'.

The minimum set of elements that we can take to represent the outside
situation is two people and an environment that permits some physical contact. For our purposes we will refer to this as an ABX system where A and B
represent people and X the environment. From a practical viewpoint, it seems
commonsense to take these as the minimum set because there is nearly always an actual or presumed communicator and what a person is being per-
suaded to do is nearly always felt to have some relevance for others. There is,
however, a historical bias in psychology toward taking AX as the minimum
set, the individual and such stimuli as are actually impinging upon his sense
organs; the outside is not thought to be relevant except insofar as it is represented by such proximal stimuli. At this level of discourse we insist that
there is a prior question of what is outside that can be represented. The outside world is not entirely chaotic, but has structural features and processes
that may be considered to carry more or less information regardless of
whether their offshoots of vibrations and particles impinge on someone's
sensory organs. The communicator must be guided by such considerations
both in deciding on what he does in the other's environment and in deciding

what change he wishes the other to make as a result of the communication.

The next step in our argument is that the way people handle information tends to be influenced by general assumptions they make about the structural and informational properties of their environment, including assumptions about the information-handling abilities of other persons. If we did not postulate the existence of such assumptions it would be difficult to understand the consistency with which perception and cognition are adapted to the distal objects and structural characteristics in the environment despite great variation in the proximal stimuli. Clear examples of this adaptation are to be found in size constancy, moon illusion etc. As we see in such examples these assumptions may not be conscious.

The problem of what is 'out there' is therefore relevant not only to the practical problem of what can be done 'out there' but also to what takes place at the sensory boundary of the inner processes, to whether different stimuli will be taken to convey the same information, the same stimuli different information, and so on.

For the above reasons analysis will proceed at several different levels. We shall consider first the properties that belong to the environment and to individuals and which allow for certain possibilities of interaction. Then we shall proceed to interactions that occur between individuals and, only after this, to the processes that occur within individuals.

An extended treatment of human communication was only recently published by Ackoff and Emery (1972). That is only partially drawn on in the following because our concern is with a different question. There the concern was with systems and their capabilities; here our concern is with environments, their evolution and the consequent evolution of human populations with communication characteristics. For the same reason we have chosen to use the older terminology of Sommerhoff's directive correlation model rather than the terminology of producers, co-producers and product. The lesser generality of the former actually served our purposes best by stressing the special role of the environment as co-producer and highlighting the potential role of environment in defining the coenetic or starting variables.

2. Informational structure of the physical world

Organisms adapt to a much wider environment than that with which they are immediately interacting causally. We do not live in a world which is bounded by our sense organs, but communicate with, influence and are influenced by outside things and events, many of which are far removed from us.

This is only possible because there is an information flow from the wider environment. The physical basis of this information flow rests in the structural difference between *things* and *media*, and the effects these differences have on the flow of light, sound, smell etc. (Heider, 1926). Things have a unitary character which we recognize in the way their parts are interdependent. The parts tend to retain their position with respect to each other; they are more closely tied to each other than each is tied to what is immediately outside and, although a unit can be taken apart, this usually takes more energy than it would take to move the whole. As a result, when light etc. strikes the surface of a thing, it is reflected in a way which is largely conditioned by the free vibrations of that thing. We speak of these processes taking place on the surface of a thing as *internally conditioned*.

Media, like air, tend to be composed of parts that are to a high degree independent of each other. As a result, the events carried in such a medium are composite events made up of an aggregate of parts that have been, individually and independently, *externally conditioned.* Man-made communication systems such as languages, have, it will be noted, these medium characteristics. It is important to bear in mind that this property of mediating, by which we hear, see, smell, recognize meanings through words, 'cannot be attributed entirely to the properties of our perceptual equipment. Something can be a mediator only if it occupies a particular place in the structure of the environment, and if it possesses the characteristics of a mediator *independent of whether or not is is used by an organism as such.*' (Heider, 1930, p. 36, our emphasis). The properties of things can be grasped only through the media that surround them. There are also static traces that are left after interaction with other things (like glacial scars) or are offshoots which become fixed as a medium loses its mediating properties (as with the fixing of photographic film).

Offshoots and traces enable the variety of properties possessed by things to be represented at a distance in space and time. They also enable things to be represented by other things, such as drawings, which while structurally quite different, send out a manifold of offshoots that correspond with some that are given out by the original thing. *But as a composite event, it could not communicate the unitary nature of the thing unless its parts could be traced back to their common origin.* That it is possible to trace these manifolds back to their origin is primarily due to the lawful characteristics of the mediating processes. Thus eyes can see objects and not just register light patterns because of the 'projective capacity of light'. When light is many times reflected in all directions from an array of surfaces – when it 'fills the environment' as we say – it has the unique property that reflected rays will converge to any point in the medium. The objective environment is projected to this point (Gibson, 1958, p. 183). If the solid surfaces vary in reflectance, a projection of these differential reflectances is obtainable at any point in the medium. Textured light in the manifold indicates the differentially reflecting structure of a solid surface. Homogeneity or lack of texture indicates an unobstructured medium. A textured cone in the manifold with a distinct boundary indicates a solid object or thing. In a natural environment (*i.e.* one untouched by man) there will be few copies of things and stable objects will be represented at each point in observation by a unique manifold of offshoots. The physical properties of light also enable higher order and more distinguishing properties of objects to be transmitted, *e.g.* internal pattern as well as texture, shape as well as contour, colour, and of great importance, the invariant features that identify an invariant object through a flow pattern of a manifold, whether this flow pattern be due to saccadic movements of the eye, head movements or change in relative position of object and organism.

How much information the manifold of offshoots and traces convey will depend upon how far they remain co-ordinated to the original core-events and structures and do not become co-ordinated to the processes and structural characteristics of the meda. *A 'good' mediator[1] will be one which is highly docile, a property that tends to go with being homogeneously composed of a large number of elementary parts, with a high degree of independence.*

1. Like a national communications service.

Thus, for example, dry sand will more closely follow the contours of a casting mould than will large stones, and the restricted vocabulary of Basic English renders it a poorer linguistic medium than the Queen's English. The informational content will depend also upon how unambiguously the offshoots can be traced back and attributed to their original core-events rather than to other core-events that might send off similar offshoots.

These two restrictions on information flow require comment.

Regarding the first, no medium can be perfect, and hence some 'noise' will always be present, *i.e.* to some extent the offshoots or traces will be co-ordinated to properties of the medium (*e.g.* refraction, diffusion, bias and style). This gives some positive informational function to 'noise' because if no media are perfect, and different media can be involved, it is more frequently necessary to identify the medium and its special characteristics. If the 'noise' can be traced to the medium, it is theoretically possible to make allowance for the effects of the mediating processes, and for a more accurate reconstruction of the core-structures or events. Thus in spearing fish, the target will be more correctly located if allowance is made for the *refraction that occurs at the surface*. In following political events allowances can be made for the bias of one's sources of news, if we know their politics and integrity. We are here referring to objective possibilities that arise from the causal texture of the environment. *If an organism is to adapt to such an environment it must to some extent be able to perceive and make allowance for the media differences that are relevant to its world.* The human organism has evolved specialised apparatus for sensing some of the major differences such as light, sound and smell. Within these media the organism also senses in a gross non-analysable way differences in brightness, loudness etc. It is likely that where other radically new media differences become relevant, as in the extended social world of man, there will be a tendency to evolve (learn) similar gross but reality-oriented indicators of 'noise' level.

The second restriction on information arises from the fact that the offshoots arrive together at the sense organ, not because they are causally tied to each other, but because they have a common source. Furthermore, *although they look like the thing they come from, they cannot act causally in the same manner as the thing, and in themselves have no relevance to the organism as obstacles, food, or the like – only as potential information about things.* Organisms do not usually interact behaviorally at the physical level at which waves and particles have effects, but live in a world of things, where by 'things' we mean objects like trees, chairs, and stones that are in the size range between astronomical and molecular units. Only very rarely do organisms interact behaviourally with astronomical bodies or with molecular or atomic particles in a way which enables individual events to be co-ordinated; the usual interaction between levels is mass action and is non-specific, as we see in the case of gravity or when a wind blows. For the spurious units, which are carried as a composite of events at the molecular or atomic level, to produce behavioural effects at the level of things there has to be some apparatus that will transform them into unitary processes that are co-ordinated to the source events rather than to the offshoots or traces, and to the actual source, not other possible sources. *Without some success in this co-ordination to the correct source-events, organisms would not be able to adapt as they do to distal objects.* This is the function of the perceptual apparatus, the sensory organs plus the central nervous system. The mechanisms by which this feat of co-ordination is achieved are unclear, but not the fact of achievement. That it is at all possible to trace back from a manifold of offshoots to the source is due to the causal properties of the environment that we have discussed above, and to the conservatism of things relative to the spatio-temporal scale of things, not to the other levels. This conservatism is such that 'any complex event tends to be followed by other complex events identical, or approximately identical with it in structure, and distributing themselves from next to next throughout a certain region of space-time.' (Russell, 1949, p. 467).

While the possibility of correct attribution is rooted in the above features, there is an aspect of the physical environment related to the last-mentioned feature which may well be essential in keeping the probability of correct attribution at survival level for the organism. This is the *redundancy* of offshoots that come from the majority of things that are vitally relevant to man under the ordinary conditions of his waking life. Organisms live in a sea of energy only a fraction of which would be necessary to uniquely identify objects if there were no competing source-events with similar offshoots. It seems that the evolution of organisms has been in the direction of adapting to parts of the environment – and to evolving mechanisms – that offer greatest redundancy of offshoots. In using the English language, a man-made medium, redundancy is estimated at 70-80 per cent. The notion of redundancy can be illustrated by a simple example. Many many millions of offshoots are continuously given off by a table in a lighted room, but a single glance is sufficient to prevent one walking into it. Redundancy of offshoots makes the perceptual task easier (more likely to be achieved) because the individual offshoots are only spuriously correlated. The more variety there is in the source, the less reliably one can trace a given fixed number of offshoots back to that source, rather than another.

Experience in systems engineering suggests that this unreliability increases exponentially with increase in variety or complexity (Ellis and Ludwig, 1962). It is possible that an increase in redundancy of the same order enables the perceptual function to cope with more complex core-events and structures without significant loss of reliability.

In the above discussion we have sought to show that the environment not only sets the primary task for the perceptual apparatus – co-ordination with distal core-events and structures – but also guides the way these taks are carried out.

A somewhat similar set of results arises when we consider the other essential side of adaptation, which is how the inside unitary events issue forth to produce definite unitary changes in environment or the position of the organism in the environment. In practically anything more than a sneeze, the action has to be mediated by a multitude of subsidiary actions in order to produce a unitary effect in the complexly structured environment. Once again we find that the key to adaptation lies in the correspondence that is achieved between a unitary event inside, and a unitary event outside the organism. This correspondence is in fact achieved despite variations in the mediating sub-actions and subsidiary changes in the environment. The pattern of mediating sub-actions form a spurious unit as they are determined independently of each other and their apparent unity derives from their common directing source. The degree of actual interdependence between the action parts is an unavoidable consequence of the imperfections of the medium. Two aspects of this process of co-ordination need noting. The complex structuring of the environment necessitates a complex structuring of tools and physical supports to the forces emanating from the organism. These physical parts play the part of media. The second point is that the offshoots from the organism's own actions are available to it as information although not to other things that do not have special apparatus corresponding to a perceptual apparatus.

Certain of these offshoots are undoubtedly internal to the organism as kinaesthetic and other such sensations, but an important part is mediated by the environment and carries information about the organism-in-the-environment. Thus changes in the organism's path can be manifested in the flow pattern of the manifold of offshoots at the same time as the manifold carries a static pattern (Gibson, 1958, p. 185). The informational value of this external feedback is enhanced by the fact that action in the physical environment shares many of the properties of other physical events – things move if a force is exerted on them, they tend to move in the direction of the force imparted, and effects tend to occur in the region and at the time of the action. That is, the environment which the organism encounters when it acts is structurally similar to that which is mediated by its sensory organs. *It is not necessary to infer any special mental mapping procedure to account for the way information gained in the first perceptual phase is used in conjunction with, and is 'corrected' by, information gained in the action phase.*

We have traced out a chain of connections from environmental core event:

→ 'spurious' unit of stimuli → sensation → central neural event → spurious unit of sub-actions → environmental core event.

'Thus the organism does not stand in the causal texture like a thing that is pushed and pushes other things; it lives between two spurious units of composite process. This peculiar kind of causal connection makes possible new events in the world of things . . . This kind of causal connection involving two spurious units, one on the perceptual and one of the motor side, frees the organism from gross physical relationships.' (Heider, 1926, p. 33).

However, our concern was not simply to discover the facts that underlie the organism's freedom from immediately impinging gross physical relationships. We were as much concerned with how, given this degree of freedom, the organism managed to relate itself to the wider environment. It was only possible to trace out a sensible causal chain by invoking the notion of adaptation and the criterion of adequate adaptation.

The points in the causal chain from source event to organismic action where the argument of adaptation is critical are:

1. the formation from sensations of a central neural event corresponding to the distal event *in order that* eventual action would bear a certain relation to those distal events and
2. the patterning of sub-actions *in order to* create an end result in the environment that would correspond to certain central neural events.

The role attributed to adaptation in the second phase, *i.e.* the mediation through sub-actions, is primary. Given this, the preceding steps constitute a causal chain that is theoretically determinate and it involves nothing that could not theoretically be accomplished by apparatus obeying physical laws. The conceptual difficulty does not therefore lie in the notion of a structure which, like an organism, is disposed to register certain distal but physically mediated changes in an environment to which it is physically coupled. The conceptual difficulty lies in the 'intentionality' or 'purposiveness' of action. We would be stupidly negligent of real life to proceed as if the biological and physical systems were not coupled in a way that justifies the concept of purpose. However, concepts of intention and purpose have not been required by the more highly developed sciences and do suggest an appeal to the common deeply-rooted belief that a qualitatively different kind of determination is involved, one that is incommensurate with physical causality. If this were so, then we would have failed in our present attempt to interpret the organism as 'open with respect to its environment' and we would have merely re-asserted that the organism is 'free of its environment'.

To account for the relevant observations and theoretical requirements, we do not have to assume that adaptation refers to any such incommensurate principle of determination. In the first place we can assume that structures which obey physical laws can be 'time binding'; that is, are able to integrate, with respect to time, information received from other independently determined processes. We can safely assume this to be possible, because we now construct physical apparatus that does just this. Given this much, there is no difficulty, again in terms of physical causality, in such a structure being arranged to act on some extrapolation of the information it receives and to 'correct' its 'memory' (probability of acting in way x, at t_1 to information y, gained at t_0) according to information subsequently received from these processes. Thus the first steps in the causal chain from source event to organismic action start to become comprehensible in a causal sense by referring them to a broader system in which there are at least some other causal chains arising from and determined by an independent system. The next stage seems to imply teleology when we find the sub-actions being varied *in order to* achieve a certain end result. A solution which avoids teleological implications begins to emerge if we again start from the fact that the end result has a double reference – it refers to something in the organism and to something in environment. Although each sub-action causally contributes to the end-result, the relation is indeterminate if it is studied simply in terms of the organism because there is no necessary one-to-one relation between sub-actions and the end result: different sub-actions 'lead to' the same result, similar actions 'lead to' different results. There have been attempts to understand this property of equifinality as a special case of equilibrium properties to be found in some physical systems. Such a physical system would be a ball in a hemispherical container – wherever the ball is placed it will roll back to the same end position at the bottom. However, this thought-model seems more likely to lead to confusion than understanding. The variables in such physical models are not conceptually independent whereas we are here dealing with couplings between independent systems, and the equilibrium characteristics shown in equifinality of behaviour cannot be attributed simply to the mechanical stability of the organism.

The relation becomes determinate only if we take into account the two systems, organism and environment, and examine the way in which they are coupled. In adaptation the coupling takes the following form:

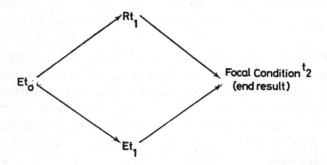

An initial state of affairs in the environment sets off a causal chain in the organism and at the same time a causal chain in the environment. The two causal chains proceed independently to produce an organismic response (Rt_1) and at the same time a physical setting (Et_1). Response and setting interact to produce a change in the environment (what we have termed the Focal Condition).

Two important features emerge from this system of coupling:

1. The end change in the environment is something which would not have happened if Rt_1 had not occurred, and hence it is in a real sense independent of the initial environmental state. 'The peculiar property of any focal condition is that the directive correlation with which it is associated imparts to it a kind of independence from the effects of events which have entered into its history.' (Sommerhoff, 1950, p. 60).

2. The independence of the focal condition does not imply a lack of causal determination (or teleology) but it is an emergent product of *joint causation*. 'It is an independence which is not based on the absence of causal chains between Focal Condition and Et_0 but in the fact that there are at

least two such chains (the one involving Rt_1 and the other involving Et_1) and that the partial effects of these two chains exactly compensate or offset each other.' (Sommerhoff, 1950, p. 64).

This adaptive coupling is but a special case of the broader concept of 'directive correlation' (Sommerhoff 1950). In directive correlation there is no assumption that the initial independent variable, the coenetic variable, is in the environmental system but allows for either system to be the 'leader'. For our purposes we have spoken of only two coupled systems but additional systems would make no difference to the apparent purposiveness that emerges from such joint causation.[2]

How far an organism can bring about or maintain the focal conditions appropriate to itself is determined by its ability to match the potential environmental states (Et_1) suggested by the initial states with a range of potential responses so that for each Et_1 there is an Rt_1 which would produce the same, jointly caused, end result. A simple example may illustrate this last point.

If two people play a game of calling numbers, the point of which is that one will call any number between 0 and 6 and the other, to win, has to simultaneously call another number which together with the first call will total six. If the first person has a rule such as smallest odd number to largest, then smallest even number to largest (1, 3, 5; 0, 2, 4, 6), and if the second person knows this, then he can always react to the last number used by his opponent to call a number that ensures that the total is always 6. In this situation we can say that the second person's behaviour is fully adapted to the behaviour of the other and we can use the end result, the total of the two calls, as a criterion of adaptation.

So far we have considered what it is about the physical environment that enables a human organism to gain information about it and to behave adaptively. Certain of these features are so important that they almost certainly have to be represented in the behavioural assumptions of the organism. We may now raise a further question. How is an environment changed when it contains a system, an organism, that is able to use the natural information flow and to establish directive correlations with parts of the environment?

2. When Heider considered the coupling of personal and environmental systems in his 1930 paper, he noted that 'With these considerations we have found an approach to the concept of 'purpose'. A function is called purposeful if it can be meaningfully referred to two different systems – or, if we want to use a more cautious formulation, to two systems which at first sight seem to be separate.' (p. 52).

The kind of changes that take place in the causal texture of the environment may be more readily grasped if we compare a stone rolling down a hill with a man running down a hill for a bus. At each instant the stone's path will be determined by the reaction of its inherent qualities upon the forces immediately acting upon it. The man's path will be a near constant function of the distant bus; if it moves off, he may change direction so as to intercept it. His mode of procedure will be some function of the immediate setting so that he will step over holes and stones, but if he hurts his foot, he may proceed by hopping; if he hears the bus horn tooting, he may quicken his pace. If he stops and sits down, we are inclined to think he has given up, not that he has run into an impassable field of forces, as may, however, happen to the rolling stone. The causal sequence in the case of the stone is not localised in the stone – we no longer say that it is in the nature of the stone to roll – but in each of the physical settings in which it was placed. If there were any apparent choice points in the course of the stone, such as teetering on an edge, we would rightly ascribe these to random fluctuations in physical forces, not to choice. In contrast to this the man is seen as the *localised source* of the actions at each stage, he exhibits *equifinality* in that he hops if he cannot walk, crawls if he cannot hop and his behaviour is in some ways a constant function of the distant bus.[3] The environment of the man might be represented as some sort of field of psychological forces but this field could have little in common with any physical concept of field.

This example points to a general change in the causal texture with the emergence of apparent discontinuities as aspects or parts are chosen by the organism as focal conditions and persist in relative independence of the ordinary chains of physical causation. The more such changes are made in an environment, the more that environment takes on the characteristics of a *habitat* for the organisms concerned. Things that emerge as a focal condition for one directive correlation, *e.g.* a shelter, become involved in further directive correlations, *e.g.* persisting population clusters and storage of reserves. The more the environment is transformed in this way, the greater is the role played by directive correlation and the more the organism's survival

3. The fact that it is the organism alone which has the power to establish directive correlations gives rise to what has been described as 'local causality' (Heider, 1958, p. 105) – the convergence on the focal condition is controlled and guided by a localised part of the total setting. The fact that the directive correlation is maintained by a range of differing responses has been described as 'equifinality' (again Heider, 1958, p. 105). Thus the two features of 'local causality' and 'equifinality' that have been held to represent 'the essence of personal causality' (Heider, 1958, p. 103) are both encompassed by the notion of directive correlation.

is independent of environmental variation. In some ways the *informational structure* of these socialized parts of the environment is likely to be more closely adapted to the information-receiving and processing capacities of the organism (thus a hammer more clearly manifests its hammering function than does a stone). A further important change takes place in the environment because things take on new functional possibilities. Relationships can be established that would not be possible in the absence of an organism capable of forming directive correlations. These are objective possibilities in quite the same way that there is, for example, an increased possibility of grass changing into beef if there is a cow in the paddock. A description of the paddock which omitted the cow and did not allow for this possibility would be a poor basis for prediction and understanding of grass growth. In like manner, a geographical or physical description of a human environment would not encompass the objective possibilities for change. Consequently, in the next sections we will be concerned with the range of directive correlations that a human being can and does set up, particularly insofar as they determine a framework for interpersonal communication and persuasion.

Before leaving the points raised above we should note for future reference that directive correlations establish a manifold of relations between things that go beyond the readily observable causal interactions that occur in their absence – 'for example, one can cut string with scissors but not with a rubber tube, and a coat can be cleaned better with a brush than with a knife.' (Heider, 1926, p. 13). The involvement of the organism with deeper layers of causality is likely to increase the ambiguity and uncertainty of the 'off-shoots' that it receives.

3. Assumptions relating an individual to the informational structure of his environment

Human beings have a number of assumptions that reflect the structure of the physical world that we have been discussing. *These assumptions are normally tacit, deeply rooted, universal and compelling.* Their operation can be detected particularly in illusions. Thus there is the universal assumption that the sky at the horizon is further away than the sky above. This leads to the moon looking larger on the horizon. Even when one knows that the moon on the horizon is actually no further away than the moon at its zenith, the illusion persists (Kaufman and Rock, 1962). In the perception of depth as determined by shadows (as in relief photographs) there is the equally universal and compelling assumption that the light source is above the surface. Thus for example a human face lighted from below produces a sense of strangeness and unnaturalness (Hess, 1961). Assumptions of this kind appear to prevail in all the ways in which the human organism handles information from the environment. Typically, the existence of these assumptions would make no biological sense if it were not for the fact that they *represent adaptation to the persistent and pervasive characteristics of the external environment.* Thus, as Ptolemy correctly observed about the moon illusion, the space between us and the horizon is typically filled with things and places for things; the space above us is generally empty. Similarly most occasions are illuminated by the sun, the moon or starlight, all of these enter our world from outside, from above. The adaptive nature of many of these assumptions has been positively established by experiments.

Perhaps the most strikingly relevant experiments are those of Kohler and his colleagues. Using various kinds of grossly distorting goggles they were able to show that after continuously wearing these for weeks the distortions disappeared. They could safely ride a bike in traffic. Although the correlation of stimuli – sensation had been drastically altered by the goggles, the organism adapted to the changes so as to re-establish the correspondence of distal objects and the central neural representation. The process was not conscious.

There is thus a solid body of evidence that:
1. persons are oriented to their environment by a set of assumptions that are universal, tacit and compelling;
2. these assumptions are adaptive with respect to the physical world;
3. the adaptive processes involving these assumptions have as their focal condition the definition for the organism of the main structural features of the physical world that concern behaviour. As we saw with the moon illusion these features, *e.g.* the extent to which space is filled with things, are not necessarily those that the physical sciences select as important.

It is important for our subsequent considerations that persons can establish directive correlations with parts of their environment only when they have evolved assumptions about the environment whereby:

1. they can relate themselves to the *spatio-temporal framework* of the environment. If as in the experimental 'Ganzfeld' (Dember, 1960), the environment offers no such framework, then the ordinary processes of perception break down. The adaptiveness of these particular assumptions affirms that there is a single physical environment with a definite arrangement and they mean that 'the world as we perceive it has certain systematic features; its parts imply each other to a certain degree. It is not a manifold where just anything can happen but one with restrictions ... The requirement of fitting together in a consistent world puts limits on the possible effects of stimulus pattern. It is in a certain sense an internal limitation of the cognitive system.' (Heider, 1958, p. 51).

2. they can 'see' beyond the offshoots to the ever-further-removed source events and structures. 'First, man is usually not content simply to register the observables that surround him; he needs to refer them as far as possible to the invariances of his environment. Second, the underlying causes of events, especially the motives of other persons, are the invariances of the environment that are relevant to him, they give meaning to what he experiences and it is these meanings that are recorded in his life space, and are precipitated as the reality of the environment to which he then reacts.' (Heider, 1958, p. 81). This process of attribution is not to be confused with conscious inference. As the Kohler experiments show, there are unconscious adaptive processes whereby what reaches the retina is transformed in such a way as to 'undo' the transformation in the media from object to the spurious stimulus unit. Because of these adaptive processes the person sees meanings

that refer to the distal underlying causes. This *attribution of meanings is an essential part of the perceptual process.*

3. their perceptions refer as far as possible to bounded *unit formations* in the environment. It is easy to see how this is essential for directed activity; it is not so obvious that 'the presence of well articulated figures is itself essential to the maintenance of the ground from which figures emerge' (Dember, 1960, p. 146) and that the presence of a bounding contour is essential for the perception of a figure (Dember, 1960, p. 153). 'The object as we perceive it is not coupled with such properties as shape, colour and size, properties that are relatively invariant features of the object, and show consistent relations with other events.' (Heider, 1958, p. 30).

4. Basic characteristics of interpersonal situations

4.1. A question of notation

For convenience we will speak of *ABX* systems when we are referring to the basic interpersonal situation of two people, *A* and *B*, who are in relation with each other with respect to some thing, event or situation *X*, as these are observed by an external observer. When we are referring to these relations as they exist in the mind of one of the participants we shall use the notation of pox systems.

The pox notation was introduced by Heider in the first formal treatment of the way in which the attitudes and beliefs of an individual constitute an interdependent system (1946). The *ABX* notation was introduced by Newcomb (1953) when he sought to show that a parallel system existed between real people in real situations. Rather than absorb pox systems into the broader *ABX* systems we have preferred to keep them separate and thus highlight the key problem of communication, persuasion and influence – how what goes on in the real world of *ABX* systems gets into and issues forth from the intrapersonal pox systems. Rather than be landed with the misleading assumptions of equilibrium processes that tend to go with handling pox systems in isolation we have preferred to postulate that they are open systems – open with respect to the corresponding ABX systems.

Our choice of notation thus reflects our own assumptions; assumptions which in effect say that the aim of persuasion is to produce systematic changes in individuals' beliefs and attitudes (*i.e.* in pox systems), that this can be achieved by producing suitable changes in the *ABX* systems in which the individual is involved and that the effect of the psychological change is to be seen in the ways in which the individual subsequently seeks to restructure those *ABX* systems.

Taking this approach one has the task of identifying the properties of *ABX* systems and the way in which these are co-ordinated to the individual's experience of them and of identifying the properties of pox systems and the way these are co-ordinated to the individual's actions in the *ABX* system.

It is not to be expected that these tasks can be taken very far toward completion nor that, if they were, all problems of communication and persuasion would be settled. However, it does seem that one can go far enough with these tasks to indicate where further work will be fruitful and that any advance in this respect will make it easier to focus on the special problems that arise when the *ABX* relations are attenuated as they are in the mass media.

4.2. General properties of the ABX model

Proceeding from the above steps one may examine the properties of a situation in which two persons (*A* and *B*) enter into relations to each other with respect to some object or behaviour (*X*) in which they are both interested. This human situation has several basic properties. Some of these properties derive from the individual properties we have discussed in preceding sections and others only arise within interpersonal situations. The gist of our argument is that *these properties have the same universal, tacit and compelling characteristics as have the individual assumptions*. Because of this they are forces which will constantly tend to shape the interactions between people and the processes within people. At least four such basic properties can be distinguished.

I. It presents an objectively ordered field open to both of the participants.

The openness of the field is manifested in the fact that both *A* and *B* can become aware of each other and of their respective intentions, attitudes and beliefs. Both can become aware of *X*, of its spatial, temporal and causal relations, and of its relevance for both of them. Phenomenally *X* and the other person are 'out there' and are experienced by the observers as being directly presented to them. That is, the ruling attitude of persons is a sort of naive realism that 'sees no problem in the fact of perception or knowledge of the surroundings. *Things are what they appear to be*; they have just the qualities that they reveal to sight and touch.' (Asch, 1952, p. 46).

One important consequence of this is that disagreement about the outside world appears to be public disagreement about matters that are capable of communication and resolution.

Both persons will tend to assume that anyone else built as they are could observe the same thing if they were similarly placed. Correspondingly, they will tend to assume that special efforts are needed to preserve privacy of actions, intentions and emotions but, in the absence of these defences, observation and communication are simply a matter of being interested and able. They will not tend to assume that each has a different and private inner representation of the situation unless some special reason for such difference is presented (differences in interest or standpoint are examples of special reasons). Conversely, the existence of difference in viewpoint suggests that there is some underlying difference in standpoints, needs, etc. If these latter 'explanations' are kept private or if, more than that, even the differences in viewpoint are being concealed the belief will be that the hidden need, standpoint or relation is unnatural and shameful. Consequently, the *fundamental operation in the event of apparent differences is to point or demonstrate, it is not to verbalize* one's inner representation as if this were the peculiar cause of the difference. This open objective character of the situation has special significance for the effort and manner with which people attempt to communicate with and persuade each other. It also accounts for th. : strength of the disbelief that may be aroused by a direct challenge to the evidence of our eyes and our willingness to give special weight to eyewitness reports.

When in this context there is a physical thing (letter, film etc.) which purports to communicate about X then some of our earlier observations have particular force. The physical communication will tend to be referred back to that which it appears to represent. This tends to occur in such a way that we do not notice the media but appear to be smelling the mown pasture in the painting, or watching the action in the novel. However, *the effects of the media come more to the fore when we are concerned with function or causal properties of the referent*. These aspects of objects and persons manifest themselves in much more variable ways than do shape, colour etc. and hence any sample of their offshoots will be more ambiguous. Similarly *the mediating processes will be more conspicuous the less they are copies of the perceptual offshoots of source objects and events*. Words are more likely to be seen as standing between the person and the object than is a film. Such communications can only reproduce a limited part of the offshoots of the original objects and hence ambiguity will be experienced as greater than in direct contact. In the face of such ambiguity, attribution will tend to be to the least complex integration, the one requiring fewer assumptions and less data. In the absence of such ambiguity, integration about distal causes may not even begin – attribution may simply be attributing X to Y as part of Y's particularity (peculiarity).

At the beginning of this section, it was claimed that these properties were basic in the sense of being universally shared and compelling assumptions. Experimental evidence for this interpretation is given in Asch's *Studies of Independence and Conformity* (1952, 1956). These experiments put individuals in a situation where their assumption of an objectively open environment was challenged by the fact they could see that a five-inch line was larger than a three-and-a-half inch line, but no-one else could see it. The experimental design left no way out, no explanation for the disagreement. *This challenge proved to be painful (cf.* Bion, 1961).

II. The mutual confrontation of A and B attests to their basic psychological similarity.

Both are forced to assume that the other is like themselves in ways that distinguish them both from non-humans. This basic similarity does not rest simply on the perception of the contours, shapes, colours and textures of each other, but upon the recognition that both are subject to and behave according to similar psychological laws. In practically all kinds of behaviour – in laughing, loving, working, desiring, thinking, perceiving etc. – there are basic similarities between people that are open to the observations of others and underlie our understanding of differences. *Central in this perception of others is the awareness that they too can establish directive correlations with parts of the environment, i.e. they too appear in the environment as action centers.* The focal condition of their directive correlations (their goals or intentions) is revealed by such behaviours as change of direction at obstacles, cessation of activity on reaching a point, convergence of different means-actions. Because behaviour is the key way in which these action centers manifest themselves 'it tends to engulf the total (Perceptual) field rather than be confined to its proper position as a local stimulus whose interpretation requires the additional data of a surrounding field.' (Heider, 1958, p. 54). In this perception of the activities of others it seems also that the manner of carrying out the act conveys, in a direct and open way, the experience of the acting person. His hesitancy, striving, euphoria etc. are normally manifest in his behaviour.

The perception of basic psychological similarity underlies the assumption, likely to be held by A and B, that anyone else similarly placed would see what they see, feel what they feel, and do what they do. On the same grounds A can grant the possibility that B can provide him with relevant information about aspects of X which are revealed to B in his position but not to A. Disagreements between A and B about X are likely, because of assumed basic similarity, to create a desire for deeper knowledge unless some special individual difference can be imputed (e.g. colour-blindness or difference in interest). The strength of the psychological forces that may be aroused by such disagreements is well illustrated by Asch's experimental studies. As the subjects of these experiments were forced to accept the reality of the challenge to their assumption of 'naive realism' they tended to question the assumption of psychological similarity; to suspect some defect in themselves. 'These circumstances fostered an oppressive sense of loneliness which increased in prominence as subjects contrasted their situation with the apparent assurance and solidity of the majority.' (Asch, 1956, p. 32).

III. The ABX situation leads to the emergence of a mutually shared field.

Each not only sees X and the other person as they exist for him, but also recognises that the same things exist, perhaps in different ways, for the other person. Each in acting must take into account how it may affect the other and in turn be affected by the other. The importance of this property for any form of interpersonal influence makes it necessary to spell out the way in which it emerges.

'When two people, A and B, work jointly or converse, each includes in his view, simultaneously and in their relation, the following facts:
1. A perceives the surroundings, which include B and himself;
2. A perceives that B is also oriented to the surroundings, that B includes himself and A in the surroundings;
3. A acts toward B and notes that B is responding to his action;
4. A notes that B in responding to him sets up the expectation that A will grasp the response as an action of B directed toward A. The same ordering must exist in B.

It should be noted that the field of each participant is highly objectified. The other person is not simply part of my psychological field, any more than I see myself simply as part of his field. Instead, each perceives the facts as shared by both. A conversation can proceed only when:
1. the same (or a similar) context is present in the participation, *and*
2. when the context possesses for each the property of being also the context for the other.

This reference on the part of each participant to the other in the condition of psychosocial events; action in the social field is steered via phenomenal fields which are structurally similar in these respects.' (Asch, 1952, p. 161-162).

In terms that we have used before this process may be seen as one of interlocking directive correlations. At a minimum each person must take as his independent (*i.e.* coenetic) variables both X and the other person. Unless he does this he cannot be assured of achieving his intentions (focal conditions). His adaptation to the situation improves when he takes as the coenetic variable not just the behaviour of the other but the focal condition of that behaviour *i.e.* if he starts from what he diagnoses as the intention of the other. By doing this it is possible for him to act in such a way as to encourage the other to so act as to create the conditions he needs to achieve his own end. A higher degree of interpenetration starts to appear when the fate of each becomes a focal condition for the other. The more specific actions and intentions of each will then be referred to intent to harm or to benefit.

A formal representation of the different levels and different standpoints implied by this process of mutual representation is given in the following diagram:

Levels and aspects of interpersonal systems

The objective Level
(As it appears to the
outside observer)

The phenomenal level
(As it appears to the
participants)
(a) the personal aspect   For A: For B:

(b) the other's aspect   For A;B   For B;A

In this mutual representation of one's own and of the other's orientation to the situation, we have *the primary social fact* – the point at which one can grasp the psychological nature of social relations. *Without some such mutual representation and some correspondence between the representations, so ordered, intentional interaction cannot take place with the others – not even relations of competition or slavery.* The social necessity for such ordered intentional interaction arises simply from the fact that men, in order to exist, must constantly relate themselves to each other in ways appropriate not only to their own variable natures but also in ways appropriate to the objective character of their joint environment, *i.e.* they must relate as purposeful systems. This accounts for the infrequency with which men relate to each other in the absence of some mutually relevant X or relate to an X in a social vacuum (these statistical generalizations were however advanced by Newcomb as the two arguments for *ABX systems* being 'essential to human life'). It also accounts for much of the significance attached by people to being

open to communication and to striving for correspondence with the viewpoint of the other – if only to agree to differ.

As with the previous two general characteristics it would appear that in an
ABX system there are psychological forces that are acting on persons in these
directions and they will be behaviourally manifested unless there are special
counteracting forces. One derivative class of counteracting forces is when
the other person is seen to be denying this openness and refusing to seek
correspondence. In an ABX situation, unrestrained by external role systems
such as exist in medicine and religion, the emergence of asymmetry in the
correspondence of mutual representations leads to an asymmetry in potential
power. The person who gains the confidence of the other without yielding
his own is in a much stronger position to manipulate the situation to his advantage (*e.g.* as in A seeking to seduce B). In shared psychological fields one
can thus detect the emergence of certain system characteristics – of new
possibilities for behaving, believing and feeling and of determinants that
cannot be traced back to the individual actor in isolation but must be referred to the ABX system per se.

These emergent properties suggest a fourth general characteristic of ABX
systems.

*IV. Within mutually shared psychological fields the individual psychological
systems more clearly take on the characteristics of 'open-systems'.*

The boundary conditions of the personal system are increasingly defined
by directive correlations that involve others as independent centers of action.
At the same time the control over these boundary conditions will entail the
pursuit of purposes that refer equally to the requirements he shares with
others as to his own particular requirements. Put another way, the *sufficient*
conditions for changes of attitudes, beliefs, motives and behaviour will more
frequently have their focus in events which take place outside the individual-
in-his-phenomenal-field. Thus a change in B's position which affects the
mutual relation of A and B to X may result in considerable change in the
attitude of A to B and in actions of A toward B and X.

'Desirable or undesirable states of affairs may come about by changes in the social environment independently of the individual's action. A change in the person's position, *i.e.*
locomotion, can occur not only by his entering into a new activity, but by the 'ground
moving under his feet'. Even though the person is himself inactive, he may find himself
psychologically 'carried' toward or away from a goal or toward or away from an avoidance by the action of the group.' (Horwitz, 1953, p. 362-363).

Where these changes and the possibility of these changes are seen by both

A and *B* as stemming from themselves and from the other person, one can expect their attitudes to each other, their motives and their actions to be referred to this total field, not simply as in Lewin's hodological space, to the possibilities open to them personally. Morton Deutsch (1949) has experimentally demonstrated that by fixing certain objective *AX*, *BX* and hence *AB* relations in such a way that they may be readily perceived by *A* and *B* (*i.e.* so that a mutually shared field emerges) it is possible to predict a wide range of attitudes and behaviours that could not be predicted from *A* and *B* considered separately. Under these conditions *A* may be motivated to act on behalf of *B* or may accept behaviours of *B* as psychologically equivalent to and substitutable for his own. Horwitz has similarly demonstrated how changes in the power of *B* with respect to *X* may, in such shared fields, generate new motives for *A*. Recognizing this quality as a general characteristic of *ABX* systems, it is necessary to note that it is not always or even generally fully recognized. The objective relations between *A*, *B* and *X* may limit the mutual relevance of their behaviours. Thus, in a competitive situation *A* may ignore an increase in distance between *B* and *X* although remaining sensitive to any decrease. Steiner (1956) has pointed out that one of the major functions of a role system in bureaucratic organization is to delimit the area of mutual relevance so that actions of *A* and *B* remain oriented to the task of the role system and do not converge about personal goals. Mutual relevance may also be limited by immaturity, by a high level of intrapersonal tensions, or by a more general inability to enter into reciprocal relations with others, (as with psychopathic persons). These limitations do not justify the assumption that persuasion is limited to simply strengthening or weakening existing individual motives and attitudes. The above considerations provide grounds for a psychological tie-up with a sociology that conceives of 'the social structure as active in producing fresh motivations which cannot be predicted on the basis of one's knowledge of man's native drives.' (Merton, 1948, p. 115).

Given these general characteristics of *ABX* systems, it is possible to seek specific principles governing changes in the attitudes, beliefs and actions of individuals without running into the theoretical cul-de-sac of a closed system of self-regulating needs, self-balancing beliefs and attitudes.

5. Awareness, images (symbolization) and psycho-logic

In this part it is our intention to examine that part of the directive correlation that is represented by the arrow $CV_{t_0} \to R_{t_1}$ i.e. the characteristics of the human being that make it possible to generate a set of responses to match the set of environmental conditions likely to occur at t_1 because of the environmental situation at t_0. We have already outlined the chain of events from environmental information to the feedback from one's actions. We now need to return to consider that link in the chain where we previously postulated 'the formation from sensations of a central neural event corresponding to the distal event *in order that* eventual action would bear a certain relation to those distal events'. The argument of adaptation is critical to this postulate and hence we must seek for that directive correlation of which the goal state is this '*central neural event*' and which goal state, in turn, acts as the coenetic variable for the subsequent directive correlation involving the patterning of sub-actions. This statement implies a *hierarchy of directive correlations*, but such a concept involves us in no new logical problems (Sommerhoff, 1950). What is important is that the criteria for this subordinate goal state, the central neural event, are derived from the goal state of the hierarchy, and are not determinable from this subordinate directive correlation considered in isolation. That is, the goal state is not any central neural event which unifies the incoming information, but that central neural event which issues forth in the set of responses required at t to match the corresponding set R_{t_1}. Thus this central neural event must represent not just the coenetic variable-in-itself, but also the coenetic variable for the respondent. If the coenetic variable requires some locomotive response and the respondent is one-legged, then the central neural event must represent what arises from the coenetic variable for a one-legged man.

What are the terms in this directive correlation? We believe that the equivalent to the coenetic variable and the environmental variable is the current inflow of information to the CNS regardless of whether this comes from the body or the environment, (*i.e.* regardless of the sensory channels along which the information flows). The equivalent to the Response variable is the information already available to the organism whether in short term, medium or long term memory. For these two sets of variables to be directively correlated it is necessary that sensory inputs trigger off a process for retrieval of appropriate memories and also that the sensory input be preserved until some relevant memories have been retrieved. Symbolization, and of course objectification of symbols, as for instance in writing, are major ways of extending this time. Symbols do this, at least in part, by reducing the proportion of the sensory input that has to be recirculated (thus reducing the demand on short term memory capacity without simply indiscriminately 'discarding' upon the time criteria of 'first in – first out'). However, we are jumping ahead of ourselves, because symbolisation already implies the process of directive correlation which we have not yet fully outlined.

If the two sets of variables are those we suggest, it still remains to identify the goal state at t_2 and the focal condition which must relate these variables at some time t_1 (where t_1 occurs later than t_0), so that the goal state is produced. *Our suggestion is that the focal condition is the matching of each sensory input by a memory input so that a goal state is achieved in which the matched pairs and only the matched pairs are retained and only one representative of each pair is retained.* Recalling that this goal state is also the coenetic variable of the next directive correlation in the hierarchy it will be seen that we are implying that the coenetic variable for the 'patterning of sub-actions' is not the original coenetic variable as apprehended by the senses: it is some transmutation of it. The transmutation which is the 'central neural event' may differ from the original coenetic variable in that some of the sensory offshoots are not matched from memory and hence do not enter into the final event or image. Similarly some of the memories that are recalled are not matched and are therefore 'discarded', although they may have been among the recalled items because together they represented the offshoots of some previous experience of similar core events.

The central neural event which enters as a coenetic variable to pattern sub-actions may therefore differ from the original presenting stimulus pattern in a way which is effectively 'time binding' of past remembered events and the present. As we mentioned before, this central neural event is a spurious event, as it unifies offshoots from core events, some of which no longer exist.

To put it more graphically, the patterning of our sub-actions with respect to a loved one is governed not by the stimulus pattern we are currently receiving, but by a central neural event, *an image*, which represents something of the present stimulus inflow and the retrieved memories. We may well act as though oblivious to his current blemishes.

At this point we need to return to the definition we gave of the focal condition. Although there are no logical grounds for this, it might be read as implying the old notion of particulate sensations being matched to equally particulate memories. We are, however, implying no more than that there are discriminable aspects that are perceived, or have been remembered, and may be matched. The aspects may, in fact, be as minute and indivisible as a point of light in an auto-kinetic experiment, or as expansive as a sense of weightlessness or claustrophobia. Our guess is that *matching takes place at a stage when sensory input has more than particulate qualities*. The minimum degree of matching that is likely to be adaptive in the next stage, and hence in the overall hierarchy, is such that the central neural event includes those features of the coenetic variable which best represent it in its stage at R_{t_1}.

Since this, according to our postulates, can *only* emerge from matching, it means that what is retrieved from memory should tend to include features of the core event which have in the past been found to persist and to come to characterize the event at later times, and retrieval should tend to exclude features which have in the past proved transient: *i.e.* even if present now, are unlikely to characterize the coenetic variable at a later time.

Those central neural events that are of adaptive value will thus tend to be those that represent a structural skeleton of the dynamic properties of the core event, or at least those that pertain to it, for the temporal period relevant to the organism's actions. (Unless one imagines some organismic adaptations that take no time, one must specify some duration for the structural skeleton, Arnheim, 1956, p. 64). We suggest that symbolization is, at bottom, nothing more than this tendency of matching to create as the guide (the coenetic variable) for subsequent action the persisting structural skeleton of the core event which acts as coenetic variable for the overall adaptive act. If the key links in our argument so far are correct, then it also follows that symbolization will occur in any adaptive process (whose adaptation relies on its own memory), regardless of the evolutionary time span over which adaptation occurs. Thus arthropods, insofar as their actions are adaptive, must be presumed to be guided by some central neural event which is other than the pattern of offshoots of the environmental coenetic variable of their actions. The fact that the only memory input may be long term memory (instinctive) does not alter this situation.

The formulation we have given of image forming as a directive correlation has some apparent difficulties. If there were no existing memories, how could the process ever start in the human infant? For the reasons given we doubt whether it is conceivable that human beings start with a tabula rasa. Phylogenetic adaptation almost certainly indicates that man starts with what Jung has termed 'archetypes' although until these have been matched with incoming experiential data they obviously can play no part in the patterning of sub-actions. However, for the tremendous variation of conditions to which human beings must adapt this could hardly suffice. The answer seems to be that the mechanism of short term memory which makes possible matching with memory also makes it possible to match inputs at time t_1 with those received at time t_0 and still circulating (where $t_1 - t_0$ is within the temporal limits of this process). Naturally the time taken to break out of this narrow matching would be lengthy, and probably would not occur unless infants developed mechanisms such as repetitive noise production which allowed for a longer cycling time. During this phase most of the behaviour would be unadaptive.

The second problem we see with our formulation is concerned with precision of matching. *The criterion can hardly be that of exact matching*, since this would imply too much loss of information and too much redundancy of memory – generalizing and hence learning (adaptive medium-term directive correlation) could hardly emerge (Goldmeier, 1972). Whatever the mechanism controlling matching, it is almost certainly similar to the 'movie' effect; a particular cowboy picture is assumed to a generalized model of a cowboy scenario.

From this outline of a model of awareness we may proceed to elaborate along several lines:

1. consciousness
2. affects and motivations
3. psycho-logics (the two brains of men)

5.1. Consciousness of thinking

We postulate that consciousness is quite literally an elaboration of the basic adaptive process. We are conscious, *aware of our awareness*, when the goal state of symbolization becomes the coenetic variable of a similar process, *e.g.*: When the central neural event does not issue forth in the phase of patterning sub-actions, it will tend to continue the process of memory retrieval, but in this case seeking to match its own features with memories, not matching the sensory inputs. (See following diagram.)

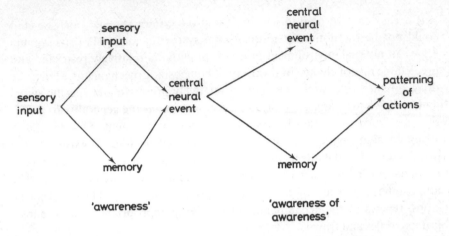

5.2. Information handling and the affect system

The perceptual system did not evolve in isolation. We think that Silvan Tomkins (1962) has successfully argued the case that it evolved in conjunction with the affect system. The perceptual system enables the organism to get information from the environmnet and itself: the affect system ensures that action is taken on that information. What is central to our concerns in this paper is that the innate (as distinct from the subsequently learnt) instigation of the affects are the most general informational properties of the inputs, not specific releasers such as have been established in some fish and birds.

'We would account for the differences in affect activation by three general variants of a single principle – *the density of neural firing or stimulation.* By density we mean the product of the intensity times the number of neural firings per unit time. Our theory points three discrete classes of activation of affect each of which further *amplifies* the sources which activate them. These are stimulation increase, stimulation level and stimulation decrease . . . there are both positive and negative affects activated by stimulation increase (interest, excitement, fear and startle, depending how rapidly density of stimulation increases), but only negative affects are activated by continuing unrelieved level of stimulation (distress, anger) and only positive affects are activated by stimulation decrease (laughter, joy) . . . such a set of mechanisms guarantees sensitivity to whatever is new, to whatever continues for any extended period of time and to what is ceasing to happen, in that order.' (p. 251-252).
'An incomplete reduction of a positive affect appears to be the most general innate activator of the shyness-shame response.' (p. 214).

The complexity of the affect system not only matches that of the perceptual system but, like it, is intimately linked to the informational flux of the environment.

It is easy enough now to see why the drive system (hunger, air, sex etc.) could not be the dominant motivational system in man. The drive system serves an internal environment that is kept within a relatively restricted and predictable rate of change by a variety of homeostatic mechanisms. Hence the drive system works well enough with relatively primitive and specific signal and feedback mechanisms. Only the affect system has the generality to match the much more uncertain fluctuating external environment. This generality ensures a high degree of error which would endanger life if it existed in the drive system, but the affects motivate learning from the errors. One has only to watch an infant mastering staircases to realise the extent to which the affects interplay to sustain the effort that produces learning. The effort starts, stops, renews to the accompaniment of highly appropriate cackles, gaps, grunts, smiles and frowns.

5.3. Psycho-logics

The affect system is so intimately related to the perceptual system that 'there is a real question whether anyone may fully grasp the nature of any object when that object has not been perceived, wished for, missed, and thought about in love and in hate, in excitement and in apathy, in distress and in joy.' (Tomkins, 1962, vol. 1, p. 134).

It is this deep-rooted linkage that assures us that there is some psycho-logic guiding how people actually think about things. A logic quite different from that which tells us how we ought to think.

Not surprisingly it was Heider who, having first applied information theory to environmental analysis and the adaptation of the perceptual system (1926-1930) first essayed a systematic statement of this psycho-logic (1946).

Shand in the 1910's was able to describe the affect system (sentiments he called them) in almost the same way as Tomkins. But it was only by applying the concepts of information theory to organism – environment relations that the *function* of the affect system could be identified.

We would expect that the affect system is as deeply rooted in man's biological adaptation as his perceptual system. Sperry's study of the different roles of the two brains of man suggests that the left dominant cortex is the main source of straight logical analysis; the right cortex providing much of the 'psycho' in the psycho-logic.

6. The extended social field and its informational structure

6.1. The assumption of an extended social field

The increased openness[1] of the personal systems which arises in a mutually shared field permits the emergence of a spatially and temporally extended field that seems to have genuine system properties. This not only implies the *temporal and spatial* extension of the ABX situation for A and B jointly, but also their involvement with distant others.

Given the multitude of ways in which the individual system establishes short, medium and long term directive correlations with its physical environment in order to meet its physiological requirements, then it requires only the development of this openness, this special sensitivity to others as similarly oriented action centres, for the individual to be involved and to feel that he is involved in a field of directive correlations that extends beyond his perception and beyond his control. Donne: 'No man is unto himself an island'.

The network or mesh of interlocking directive correlations implicates the individual's behaviour, as well as his fate, in events taking place outside his immediate psychological life space. A husband, even while at work or travelling in distant places, is in some ways still implicated in the daily home setting of his wife and the school setting of the children. He is also implicated in conditions existing well back in the past (the past of others as well as himself) as these have created or failed to create present opportunities. Similarly the future becomes immediately relevant as one acts to set in motion chains of joint action that may or may not converge or diverge in the future. If we reflect for a moment on the earlier comparison of the rolling stone and

1. It should be clear by now that by greater openness we mean a greater range of coenetic variables to which the system is responsive. We feel that the range (repertoire) of responses is better treated as a measure of sensitivity than of openness, and the range of goals and sub-goals as a measure of system complexity. Thus a system might be very open but relatively insensitive and 'single-minded or relatively closed but highly sensitive', and complex because of the range of goals being served.

the man running for a bus, it seems obvious that the spatio-temporal extension is of an order of magnitude greater when the coenetic variables of one's
directive correlations are enduring human action centres (with the characteristics of local causality and equifinality) rather than stones, tables etc. This
is nowhere more strikingly illustrated than in Heider's discussion of hatred.

'If a person is in danger from a rolling stone he has some chance of escaping by changing
immediate conditions – the stone will not make corresponding moves to cancel out the
effects of his movements. However, if he is in danger for his life because of the hatred of
another person, there is no such ready solution. No matter what moves he makes for his
self-protection, there is still the possibility that the would-be assassin will find the means
to get at him. Just so long as the other retains his life and his hatred then the victim will
go in some fear for his life. In the hatred there persists, over a wide environment, conditions that are convergent on the end-state, and if the assassin has the power that end-state
will eventually occur no matter what the victim does.' (Heider, 1958, p. 101).

We should not dismiss this with the thought that 'of course, if such a person
had a great deal of social power then . . .'. The older author had occasion to
document a case where a prison official, sound in mind and powerfully built,
went in great terror of a 'life' prisoner whom he felt would one day get him, no
matter how often he transferred to other prisons, unless he resigned from the
service and emigrated. The incredible way the prisoner had managed to get transferred after him within the national prison system gave him grounds for terror.

Thus the extended social field is not something that, for the individual,
simply extends relatively further out than his own perceivable field of action,
but something that extends to the horizon of possible human action. No
behaviour takes an individual out of this field, although it may change his
relation to it. (See Greco's critique of Sherif and the theory of individual
plus social motivation, 1950.)

In adapting to this field the individual is not simply adapting to one of the
organized groupings within the field.[2] These are co-ordinating, integrating

2. Our theory of environmental types (in *Futures We're In*) implies that environments
have system properties. The concept of fields of directive correlations has the same implication. However, in common useage the term system has for its reference the notion of an
integrated set of entities. We suggest that several levels of system organization need to be
distinguished. *Organized system* (or organization) – that which (1) has identifiable parts,
and (2) the state of no part can be determined without knowledge of the state of the
whole (at least two other parts), and the relation of the part to the whole. *Environmental
system* – that which (1) has identifiable parts, and (2) the state of no part can be determined
without knowledge of the state of at least *one* other part and their interrelation. We think
this difference between organizations and their environments is a real one. It precludes the
theoretical sleight-of-hand whereby an organization and its environment are first recognized then the lot subsumed as one big system with the assumption that it will be governed
by the system principles that hold for organized systems.

arrangements of only parts of the field with respect to limited focal conditions (cultural practices) and goals. The goals served by the extended field seem to be nothing less than the survival of the population of that kind of individual system of which it is composed within the range of conditions that confront them.

For our purposes it is not relevant to consider the factors that influence the size and degree of interdependence of human communities. What is relevant is that the field of directive correlations is at least coextensive with these communities and reaches back into the history of these communities. The individual's involvement in this field has no class boundaries nor limits short of the spatio-temporal limits of the community. The limits of the community, whether tribe of nation or something more, is a question that would need to considered elsewhere, as would also the question of how far this involvement spreads across such boundaries.

Nor is the field of directive correlations to be equated with a spatio-temporal distribution of objects and persons such as we may see with our own eyes when we look about at a social gathering. In the latter case we might well think that the appropriate questions about the environment are ones like those posed by Chein (1954), e.g. 'How rich is the environment in stimuli, cues, goal objects, noxiants, supports?'; 'What ordering is there of these characteristics into goal paths?' The field of directive correlations is a field of psychological forces, not just a spatio-temporal aggregation. It arises from and is sustained by a number of independent systems which are set to monitor each other and act in ways that are jointly a function of the others' acts and their own desired ends. The field is thus intrinsically connected, not simply collected by an act of observing. In fact it requires much more than a glance to recognize a field of directive correlations. The ties between these active parts of the field are not visible physical ties (such as contribute to the mechanical unity of an organism), or simply ordered physical arrangements such as appear in a magnetised array of iron filings: the ties are mutually related predispositions. These ties tend to be masked from direct observation, as in glancing around a social gathering, by the very variety of behaviours that are brought into play by each individual to create those focal conditions required for goal attainment. The source of the observed variety tends to be located in the highly visible centres in the field (the figures) not in the visual ground formed by the systems of directive correlation between them.

This field carries within it a great many of the necessary and sufficient conditions for each system to establish its directive correlations. Being based on predispositions, i.e. on persisting system properties, this field is also persistent; but, as we have just suggested, the persistence is not simply a matter of physical distribution in time. The field does not go out of existence for the individual system, even if the latter is physically isolated; equally the field may fade away for the individual even though he is in close physical contact with others (*e.g.* the loneliness of the city for the outback visitor). The critical factors for the individual, arising from the existence of this field, are how well he is able to establish directive correlations, and whether the others are able and willing to do so. Those system changes which render an individual unable are those that correspond to death (Sommerhoff, 1950). It is unusual for an individual to be totally excluded from the social field, but where this does happen, as with the 'pointing of the bone in certain Australian tribal groups, it makes little difference to him whether he is physically in the encampment, near it or far away: he folds up and dies (Cannon on 'Voodoo Death', 1957).

For these reasons, we find many behaviours that are social in character and cannot be explained simply by reference to a concrete face-to-face group, nor by some concrete and limited manifestations of the field in a crowd or organization.

This persistent and pervasive mesh of interlocking directive correlations is as much an objective part of an individual's environment as is the gravitational field. It also exists independently of him. It is there when he arrives in the world and if he leaves it, it may be different as a result, but not cease to exist. It is there when his social formations collapse, and it is only from this matrix, and certainly not from any coming together of individually motivated humans, that new formations emerge.

We have noted so far that the concept of a 'social field of directive correlations' cannot be equated with the social formations or institutions that arise within such fields nor with aggregations of persons. It remains to consider the properties of these fields.

6.2. Other social forms

Based as they are on organisms with a capacity for directive correlations (*i.e.* purposeful), these fields have the potentiality of establishing further directive correlations between the initial connecting directive correlations and of elaborating further directive correlations on the focal conditions of others, *i.e.* they have the potentiality of self-regulation, co-ordination and integration with respect to focal conditions that relate the field itself to its environment.

As Wynne-Edwards has amply evidenced (1962), the evolutionary process has heavily favoured the survival of social fields that have developed such self-regulating processes. At this – the biological level – there can be no doubt that human social fields have always been characterized by some such self-regulation, and hence have provided some measure of freedom for the constituent members from variance in the spatio-temporal distribution of physical noxiants and rewards (starvation!). In passing, it should be noted that such a field, even if it had a high level of self-regulation, would still not correspond to an individual organism as there is no complementary framework of mechanically related parts to maintain a hierarchy of integrated directive correlations. The more such a field is based on medium term directive correlations, rather than the long term ones we find with ants and bees, the more misleading is the analogy of an organism.

A striking example of an extended field of directive correlations is that provided by Jespersen's study of the distribution of pelagic birds over the North Atlantic (Wynne-Edwards, p. 2, 11). Systematic observations over the vast area of 10-12 million square miles disclosed a correlation of 0.85 between number of birds in the air and density of plankton in the water. This degree of self-regulation over such an area and involving so many birds could not be maintained by a simple direct correlation between birds and food. The typical mechanism involves a directive correlation between bird, and food and other bird. Thus the pelagic birds' behaviour is divided between maintaining an optimal distance from other birds, which he does by flying high up in the sky to see whether the others are on the horizon, and going down to near sea level for feeding. If feeding is good the bird spends more time down low and out of sight of his neighbours. They edge in closer so that they see him. As this brings them to the good food area they spend more time flying down low. When food is scarce the opposite happens. The variation in distribution produced by the self-regulatory process is very great. From just one bird-sighting a day in south-central Atlantic where plankton concentration was very low to over 100 bird sightings per day in the very rich plankton area of the Barents Sea.

A human social field has not and cannot have the properties of either an organism, or an insect society. Despite this, the field not only allows some general self-regulation of the form similar to sub-human groups, but more characteristically allows for the formation of integrated groups with limited purposes (to be distinguished from geographical populations).

The formation of these groups adds further to the adaptability of the field, or at least to parts of it. Tasks that extend beyond the scope of the individual can be carried out by these organized groups, and the physical environment can itself be transformed to increase the scope of the individual.

6.3. Extended social field as dilemma of man

However, while the social field is in these crucial ways adaptive, or is a condition for adaptive organized groups, it is at the same time maladaptive for the individual organism. While the chances of survival of this kind of organism are increased by the emergence and elaboration of the social field, the adaptation of the individual organism becomes by the same process more difficult. The crux of this contention is that the predictability of the individual's environment becomes less as his own directive correlations become increasingly correlated to lines of action beyond his immediate settings. *This unpredictability of the social network for the individual grows as the predictability and control over the physical environment increases.* This unpredictability would not have grown if, over the same long period of time, there had been a corresponding growth in ability to communicate and to comprehend the finer texture of the social field as it extended beyond the here and now.

From the point of view of the organism this response to the growing unpredictability would not be without dangers. Quite simply, as one moves out in all directions from one point in a net, the number of lines increases at an alarming rate. A similarly alarming rate of increase occurs in the number of potential ties as the number of persons in a group increases. If the perceptual system has only a finite capacity to handle information, then it is likely that it would quickly be overloaded by the information input required to cope with such complexity. Thus at this level of generality we are postulating a fundamental dilemma for man – *living in a social field requires continuous adaptation to the finer texture of this field but this requirement threatens to overload his perceptual system and negative adaptation.*

The critical features of this dilemma are:

1. Both horns of the dilemma arise from the nature of man – his perceptual system makes a field of directive correlations inevitable and yet, as a material system, it is itself finite.
2. Both horns of the dilemma are constantly sustained by the need to adapt – man seeks to extend and enrich the field of directive correlations, and at the same time, to increase his comprehension of the field.

3. There is, in the individual's drive to adapt to the finer texture of the field, no built-in self-regulatory features which would balance input load with information handling capacity.

Theoretically there are several ways in which load and capacity can be balanced. Information input can be controlled by referring this information back to parts of the environment, some of which are noted as relevant if they changed, some as irrelevant; some as probably likely to change, some as not probable but possible, some as impossible. At most the organism would accept only information which is relevant and at least possible. It might restrict itself to information which is relevant and probable, and be most unlikely to accept that which is irrelevant or impossible. Information can alternatively be controlled at point of receipt, *e.g.* 'colour blindness'. If input is thus controlled by some internal state, then overload might be rendered unlikely, but adaptation would be at risk. This probably cannot be a sufficient solution. Neither does the first alternative offer a solution. Although the individual can learn that some things are relevant, others irrelevant, questions of local relevance can be established only by exploring further in the social field. The field is composed of relatively independent (although correlated) action sources, and hence is unlikely to show a simple convergent structure – converging on a few sources of relevant information. Hence control of input by the criteria of relevance may lead to an increase in required input. These are not exclusive alternatives, so in fact we will end to find:

1. restriction to what is relevant and probable;
2. positive motivation against knowing too much or accepting the new. (See Schachtel on socialization to curb curiosity, and Plato on the functions of myth.)

We are thus suggesting that the dilemma facing the individual in a social field is not soluble by the individual acting on his own resources, and *yet some solution needs to be found if he is to survive.* From the point of view of the social field, its own adaptation is threatened by this dilemma, since it is dependent upon some minimum level of adaptability in some minimum proportion ('elite') of its constituent individuals. These conditions could be undermined by a high rate of breakdown or instability in individuals, particularly in the 'elite', or if too many were absorbed in a constant search of the neighbouring social field to the exclusion of acting with respect to their physical environment.

One would expect that the survival of human communities in their physical environment has been critically dependent upon how they have acted to resolve this human dilemma. The theoretical solutions discussed above are not mutually exclusive, although the determination of relevance and possibility would seem to be the least unsatisfactory solution. More important than the relative emphasis on these solutions is the fact that one side of the dilemma stands out as the side that has been most easy to handle historically – the fine texture of interlocking directive correlations extending beyond the individual's immediate setting (knowledge of the CNS). The facts of this texture are more immediately relevant to the individual than to the survival of the field. Hence the most important single constraint that can be effected to preserve the social fields and protect the individual from his own condition is to deny as far as possible the criterion of personal relevance of these facts, and to establish as the dominant criterion of relevance that which is relevant to the survival of the social field or some part thereof.

We are inclined to hypothesize that this is what has been done in the evolution of human society.

However, as we have discussed earlier, the social field is a physical reality for any individual – one can turn away from it but cannot act in complete disregard of it. What seems to operate in practice is a marked taboo on consciously discriminating the field. The field is discriminated, but people do not discriminate (become conscious of) the fact that they so discriminate. The function of discriminating the field is met by the social innovation of 'leadership'.

We do not wish in any way to discourage search for some explanatory facts closer to home, as it were. Nevertheless, it does seem that the perceptual system of man was evolved, in most of its key characteristics, prior to close settlement; prior to agriculture. The environment for which man's perceptual system was adaptively evolved would have been basically a type II environment. Elements of a type III[3] environment would have been sporadic and infrequent; quite capable of being handled by the long term directive correlations that serve the territorial behaviour of other species. In that environmental context the affect system would, and apparently did, evolve to maximise the positive affect of novelty, of new knowledge. It was no burden for Arctic Indians to differentiate 20-30 different kinds of snow; no burden for Australian Aboriginals to read the miniscule signs of an animal's passage through the bush. They were adapting to a territory long known and sign-

3. See Emery et al. 1974.

posted by their ancestors. They were living, in small doses, with agents for change (other people) who were either strangers or closely defined kinsfolk. Nothing appears to have evolved that would warn and protect the individual human being from information overload. Information overload would have been sufficiently rare to be accepted as psychotic *e.g.* amok with the Malaysians or shamanism in the Arctic regions.

As people moved into close settlement, 'culture' or, much more recently, 'civilization' has been the answer to this potentially fatal incapacity of the individual representative of the species. Our cultural and social groupings have evolved to protect man from himself, evolved to ensure that men would not fall into the traps that took away their forebears. How they did this is suggested by the folk saying 'curiosity killed the cat, information brought her back'. This gives 'information' a curiously twisted form. Puss is back if she stops being curious and accepts that what she is informed about is all she needs to know – 'what you don't know will not hurt you'. Schachtel has spent a lot of effort on trying to ferret out why curiosity disappears in the older human when it is so prominent in the young child. We suggest that Plato had already confronted and resolved this question in his discussion of the social role of mythology. More crudely, but very much to the point, we can pose and answer the riddle – 'If the function of schools is to poke out the eyes of children what is the function of universities?' 'To teach Braille!' We are suggesting that the biblical tale of the Tower of Babel refers to the emergence of settled communities, not to the first skyscraper. Cultural diversity was mankind's answer to a shared incapacity. An answer that was evoked by the emergence of Type II environments regardless of whether the particular community went agricultural. We are suggesting further that the frenetic concern for organization and ideology in the twentieth century is a reaction of people to even further demands on their capacity to cope with information overload.

PART II

The modern media and man

7. Differences between the communication functions of the mass media, for individuals

7.1. The functions of the different mass media

The basic model of all the mass media that reach into the home, press, magazines, radio and television may be represented as follows:

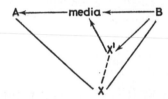

X¹ is the symbolization of which
X is the referent

This model differs from our *ABX* model of face-to-face communication in that:

1. communication is *asymmetrical*, from *B* to *A* and not from *A* to *B* and hence lacks the ordinary forces toward creating a mutually shared context;
2. communication is a two-step process in which *B*'s communication is to some degree distorted by the media (all these media being unable to provide what is given by face-to-face contact);
3. *A* is under none of the usual restrictions of politeness and respect to attend to *B*'s mediated message. *B* on the other hand is projecting his message into the home of *A* and tends to carry some of the responsibilities of a guest;
4. the referent *X* is more commonly outside *A*'s personal world.

Within this model certain differences may be noted between the typical distortion of each medium.

Table 7.1.1.

		Richness of image		
		Visual static	Auditory non-static	Audio-visual non-static
Time lag between X' and X	short medium (week +)	Newspapers Magazines	Radio —	T.V. —

The time lag in the case of magazines naturally renders them unsuitable for communication about things on which quick information is required. The other dimension is probably the most important source of distortion.

The printed word, picture and diagram have at least two advantages not easily realized on radio or television:

1. being static this message can be pored over, returned to or ignored, as the individual recipient feels fit;
2. as a result of (1), a higher level of conceptualization can be attained in print without 'losing' the recipient and it is also possible to present concurrently more of the many aspects of an event, and its determining context.

It is the setting par excellence for transmission of *knowledge about* an absent event or object. In principle it permits a recipient to choose his own distance from the communication and to inspect the object from whatever or how many viewpoints he wishes. In fact of course the range of economically available newspapers and magazines will be seen to limit this choice and the individual will have to limit his own interest to some small part of the multitude of events and objects referred to.

These latter restrictions and the static conceptual nature of this medium both contribute to it being so noticeably an imperfect mediator of something '*out there*'.

Radio is neither static nor two-way and hence is not particularly suited to conceptual representation (BBC Third Programme not withstanding). Its messages can neither be held steady nor recalled for inspection. At the same time, sound rather than sight has always been the favoured form for interspecies communication. As shown in song, poetry, humour, seduction, sarcasm and anger, speech is particularly fitted to convey a depth of personal meanings not so readily conveyed or evoked in written language. Side by side with this power there is an equally significant lack, relative to visual images or prints, in conveying the richness and complexity of the world 'out there'. 'The auditory world, available to the listener, is poor in documentary qualities. Hearing excels in transmitting speech and music, that is, products of the spirit; it renders little of physical reality. Without the services of a commentator or reporter, the event that radio purports to send over the air waves remains fragmentary to the point of being incomprehensible.' (Arnheim 1958, p. 159-160). A marvelous shortcoming when it comes forth as a 'Goon Show'.

It is however difficult for radio to transmit to human recipients the complex interrelations of qualities and processes that are essential to knowing about reality. It is easier for radio to signal that somewhere X has occurred or that somewhere Y exists. If the recipient feels that he knows about or is familiar with X and Y he may attach significance to knowledge of what is happening to them, where they are to be found and so on.

Beyond this, radio offers a communication advantage not to be found with newspapers or magazines. This is that it more readily allows a depth of personal feeling to be conveyed – it enables the communicator to convey some feeling of what X feels like as distinct from what it is or where it is. This is particularly relevant for objects and events that are not only of interest in themselves or for us (as means) but also because they are potentially part of us, because they are feelings we could have.

When radio is used in this latter way it creates for the listener a feeling of psychological closeness to the communicator and he is less conscious of the intervening medium. There is a marked contradiction between this, and the psychological distance and prominence of radio as a medium, which characterizes radio when used to communicate 'knowledge of'. In fact, it seems likely that the effectiveness of the Goon Show lay in the exploitation of this contradiction – the crazy juxtaposition of apparently real things to convey something of what they are as part of our inner, personal worlds.

Television does not share the contradictory nature of radio. At first sight it appears to resolve this contradiction and overcome the limitations of all the other media. 'For the first time in the history of man's striving for understanding, simultaneity can be experienced as such, not merely as translated into a succession of time.' (Arnheim, p. 161).

Of course all the mass media have a range of capabilities that cannot be reflected adequately at the level of the present analysis. However, at its extreme, television appears to provide the viewer with a direct vision of what is happening in the world outside. Whereas the favourite radio personality may be experienced as being at one's elbow in an etherial disembodied fashion the televised event is experienced as directly and concretely present. The closeness in television is, however, in the first place, the closeness of one's point of observation: if one were physically present at the scene of the event one would not expect to see anything other than what is on the screen (except, until recently, the colours) although one might expect to capture from the crowd noises something more of the feelings of those present. The very perfection or transparency of television as a communication medium creates the illusion during viewing that is a one-step process of communication, that the referent is now inside one's personal world and that the asymmetry is the natural one of the observer at the zoo or the 'bug-eyed' tourist (*cf.* the model above). This profound redefinition of the media carries its own dilemma:

1. 'The more perfect our means of direct experience the more easily we are caught by the dangerous illusion that perceiving is tantamount to knowing and understanding.' (Arnheim, p. 161). The viewer becomes impatient of conceptual analysis when by a movement of the camera he can be shown the object, and feeling that '*seeing is believing*' he will tend to resist efforts to convey adequate knowledge about it.
2. The reality of the television communication conceals the arbitrary character of its viewpoint. Objects, persons and events that are actually within the viewer's personal world are open to be explored from many viewpoints; these viewpoints tend not to be arbitrary but ones that are relevant to the viewer's own interests and knowledge, and their determining contents can be separated from arbitrary associations. By contrast television gives to things the reality of being immediately present *but denies their openness to inspection and scrutiny.*

This aspect of television has been analyzed in a case study by the Langs (Kurt and Gladys E. Lang, The Unique Perspective of Television and its Effect: a pilot study, *Amer. Sociol. Rev.*, 1953, 18, 3-12). They point to three sources of distortion that are characteristic of television as a medium:

'1. technological bias, *i.e.* the necessarily arbitrary sequence of the telecasting events and their structure in terms of foreground and background, which at the same time contains the choices on the part of the television personnel as to what is important;
2. structuring of an event by an announcer, where commentary is needed to tie together

the shifts from camera to camera, from vista to close-up, helping the spectator to gain the stable orientation from one particular perspective;
3. reciprocal effects, which modify the event itself by staging it in a way to make it more suitable for telecasting and creating among the actors the consciousness of acting for a large audience.' (p. 10).

Acting to realize on each of these sources of distortion are constant pressures by televisers and actors to hold their audience by making the telecast approximate to what they think are the expectations and interests of the audience. This *pressure to retain interest* also directs attention to the highlights of the event to the relative exclusion of the contextual determinants which, as with conceptual analysis, is critical to understanding the object or event on its own terms. 'A general characteristic of the television presentation was that the field of vision of the viewer was enlarged while, at the same time, the context in which these events could be interpreted was less clear.' (Langs', p. 11).

The absence in the televised object of this openness to inspection and manipulation acts, together with the restraint on conceptual analysis, to limit the effectiveness of television in communicating convincing *knowledge about* the outside world. Thus in reaction to a television demonstration of two piles of clothes washed in different detergents the housewife may feel a desire to turn the clothes over with her own hands and look more closely. This limitation does not extend to communication of '*knowledge of*'. One can see with one's own eyes that there is an X or a Y and this fact is independent of how it might look if seen from a different angle or put to a different test. Similarly, this restriction does not hold for communicating *knowledge of how something might look or feel as part of us or as belonging to us*. The impressions conveyed by direct visual experience of another are strong and are likely to be stronger than those conveyed by print or by voice alone. When confronted by an image of a person with an object or a person doing something, there will be a strong tendency for this object or action to be coloured by the impression given by the person. These observations by Arnheim and the Langs take us back to the very general theoretical points we made earlier:

'the mediating processes will be less conspicuous the more they are copies of the perceptual offshoots of source subjects and events.' (p. 28).
   'as the media becomes more apparently transparent we are less concerned that that which is presented requires reference to any deeper level of meaning or causality.' (p. 28, 22).

We react naturally to ambiguity and to incompleteness by searching deeper for meaning, for the universal in the particular. When, as in TV, it seems to be all there before our eyes we do not feel the need to search deeper. The views and the expressions of the person viewed are obviously part of him and explained by just that.

TV, in presenting things as they are, is dealing in iconic signs (Defn. 10-5: 'Iconic sign: a sign that has some of the same *structural* properties as the thing it signifies.' Ackoff and Emery, 1972).

'Structural properties include geometric, kinematic, physical and morphological properties. Hence iconic signs look, taste, feel, sound or smell like what they signify; but they need not and usually do not function in the same way as the thing they signify. Therefore, iconic signs not only signify but also *represent* what they signify and hence may be a substitute in some circumstances. A photograph, which is a common type of iconic sign, can frequently substitute for the person it represents.'

'*Iconic signs individuate*; that is, they represent things or events taken as individuals, differentiated from other things. It is for this reason that we can have an image of a horse but not an image of an animal. There is no set of structural properties to individuate animals; functional properties are necessary . . . note that concepts are not iconic; they do not look like, sound like, and so on, (like) what they signify. Second, whereas images help us *describe*, concepts help us *explain*. Herein lies the critical difference. *Iconic images connote structural properties, but concepts connote functional properties.*' (Ackoff and Emery, 1972, p. 166-167).

For practical purposes the above analysis suggests that the different media are of different value in communicating different levels of knowledge:

Table 7.1.2.

	'Knowledge about' (conceptual)	'Knowledge of'	'Knowledge of X and part-of-me, or my possessions, or my beliefs'
Newspapers	× ×	×	—
Radio	—	×	×
Television		×	× ×

Magazines are less appropriate than newspapers for conveying knowledge of what is occurring in the immediate here and now and, for technical printing and economic reasons, offer a much greater scope for elaborate, although static, imagery, pictures, etc. that convey the personal aspect of objects and events. The distinctions made here are at best a first approximation indicating the relative ease with which different kinds of information may generally be expected to pass through different media. It is not always convenient or economic to provide for the easiest path in communicating to a mass audience if only because they may have other communication needs than listening or looking at the others wishing to communicate with them, en masse.

7.2. Evidence of general differences between mass media

In line with the preceding discussion one would expect to find evidence that the audiences accept some kinds of communication from one medium and not from another. The problems of measurement are not, unfortunately, so simple. The content of the media itself tends to vary because the communication producers have their own ideas about what is appropriate for the different media. Insofar as their ideas are correct their actions will tend to reinforce audience tendencies, but where they are incorrect the sheer volume or the technical proficiency of the communication may counteract the audience tendency. Conversely, the failure to use a medium in a certain appropriate way may mean that the audience has no chance of evaluating it. In addition to this the audience reaction to a given medium may be influenced by what the audience wants. If, for instance, at one stage there is little desire for knowledge about scientific developments, certain attributes of a given medium remain unnoticed. Lastly, it would be helpful to be able to distinguish those attributes of a medium that are intrinsically related to it and those attributes that are externally determined (*e.g.* whether certain effects are simply due to the national scale of the medium to Government control, or its lack of technical development).

A detailed study of this problem was made by Leon Arons (with a quota sample of only 300 U.S. citizens but an unusually large sample of data from each individual). Seventy percent of his sample used all four of the media regularly and ninety-four percent used at least three. A further relevant characteristic of this sample was that only 10 percent could be classified as primarily interested in the mass media as a source of knowledge while, at the other extreme, thirty-four percent were primarily interested in their emotional involvement, with only incidental interest in gaining knowledge. One could, therefore, expect a certain difficulty in detecting those media differences that concern communication of knowledge in general, let alone differences between 'knowledge of' and 'knowledge about'. There were, however, significant differences in the use made of the different media, and in general these differences correspond to those we theoretically expect to find.

The Arons study was produced back in 1960 but has not been superceded. TV was by then firmly established in the U.S.A. and subsequent studies have been more bitty, although confirmatory when comparable.

A complex value analysis was made of the direct references each respondent made to the different media. The validity of the results was probably high because it was based on a case-by-case analysis and on a considerable body of varied material. The main results are given in the following table.

Table 7.2.1. Values associated with use of different mass media.
(Percent of those using each media)

Percent Mentioning	Newspapers	Magazines	Radio	Television
Knowledge (general or specific)	100	86	68	30
Curiosity (about people)	55	35	13	48
Aesthetic	4	15	26	14
Friendliness	4	4	14	8
Self-rating appeal	9	4	2	16
Human contact	2	—	6	16
Vicarious experience	6	39	13	85

(From L. Arons , *ibid* p. 29, p. 46; N = 300).

The subjects were free to bring in any or all of these values in their discussion of the media but there are significant differences in the values they do invoke:

1. knowledge, although used in the broadest sense, is associated infrequently with television;
2. both television and radio seem more frequently to create a feeling of psychological closeness, although in different ways. For radio it is the sense of being close in a friendly way; for television it is the sense of being immediately present;
3. television, and to a lesser extent magazines, more frequently give the experience of living the experiences of others.

These aspects can be explored further within Arons' data, and in part supplemented by other studies.

At least for Arons' subjects there appear to be needs for both knowledge and emotional gratifications that cannot be equally well met out of their own resources as they can be gained from the mass media. Thus, despite the fact that a knowledge orientation is foremost in only one third of his sample, there is little difference in the need for newspapers and television, in the respect attributed to them, or in the contribution they are felt to make to interpersonal discourse (*i.e.* in providing a common world of discourse within which people can relate to each other).

Table 7.2.2. Need of and respect for the mass media.

	Newspapers	Magazines	Radio	Television	
1. *'Need of' for self*					
'Most want to keep'	30	8	21	41	
'Most willing to give up'	7	46	35	19	
Net difference	+23	—38	—14	+22	
Conflict*	0.4	0.3	0.8	0.6	
2. *'Need of' as coinage of social discourse*					
Mention as source of items discussed with others	80	24	44	76	
3. *'Respect for'*					No choice
'Carries most weight'	38	22	8	30	3
'Most respect for'	38	22	9	28	9

* As an index of conflict within sample (not necessarily within individual) we may take $2.n_1 (n_1 + n_2)$ where $n_1 < n_2$.

(From L. Arons *ibid* p. 56, p. 88; N = 208).

One difference is that both radio and television show more conflict in choice than newspapers or magazines. This might suggest that whilst, these are desirable they cannot easily be accepted at the expense of the reality depicted in the printed word. The contradiction appears most clearly in the reasons given for regarding a medium as the most needed (reasons that support the earlier value analysis in Table 7.2.1.).

Table 7.2.3. Reasons for regarding media as 'Most Wanted'.

	Newspapers	Magazines	Radio	Television
Emotional involvement	1%	0%	2%	12%
'All encompassing'	6%	3%	10%	27%
Knowledge	19%	4%	1%	1%

(From L. Arons, *ibid*, p. 57).

When the media are judged solely as source of news the preference is for newspapers.

Table 7.2.4. Media preferred if 'Sole Available Source of News'.

Newspapers	Magazines	Radio	Television
54%	5%	15%	26%

(From L. Arons, *ibid*, p. 31).

Arons does not, in his analysis, raise the question about kinds of knowledge that are a central feature of the theory presented here. This data do however, give some empirical leads. Thus, one can postulate a dimension running from general knowledge, to specific events, to knowing particular persons of importance. Relative to this dimension considerable changes are found in the roles of newspapers and television.

Table 7.2.5. Media preference for different levels of information.

	Newspapers	Magazines	Radio	Television
General knowledge	94%	36%	66%	25%
Specific knowledge	78%	83%	5%	8%
Knowledge of 'newsworthy events'	76%	11%	43%	60%
Knowledge of important people	16%	10%	2%	66%

(From L. Arons, *ibid*, p. 29, 33, 35).

It will be noticed that television seems to come into its own when the item of information to be communicated is specific, isolated from its context without grievous loss of meaning and visible (*e.g.* a wedding, a football match or a plane crash). In the presentation of persons it has no peers although before the advent of television it is likely that radio performances of Roosevelt, Churchill, Hitler and the like, conveyed more of the personal touch than did the newspaper reports of the same events.

A natural experiment on these media differences is provided by Kimball's study of the reactions of a sample of 164 regular New York newspaper readers to a newspaper strike. In the absence of papers there was an increase in the felt need for a newspaper verifying the supposition that the newspapers met a real need. The feel of being out of touch with the outside world was much stronger with the better educated of both sexes; which is what would be expected if higher education leads to a greater concern with the outside world (the great body of survey evidence shows this correlation). Similarly, women who missed the paper mostly for its specific shopping information (nearly half changed their shopping habits) felt the loss of the paper as a source of news less than the men. These are indicative, but the key findings relate to the use of other media.

Table 7.2.6. Shift to other media in absence of newspapers.

Time spent	Radio		Television	
(percent)	Before	During	Before	During
under 1 hour	55	33	20	20
1-3 hours	23	30	38	30
3+	22	37	42	50

(From Kimball, 1959, per cent of 164 subjects).

The major reason for shifting appears to have been for news and the major observed shift appears to have been to radio. Television appears to have been fairly saturated before the change but the subjects acted as though by having the radio on for a longer period they would be more likely to get the news they normally got from the papers.

Other studies enable the above findings to be further extended. Most major 'newsworthy events' must first be 'known of' before than can be 'known about' *i.e.* one would expect these phases to be separated in time and to take place in one and the same exposure to information about the event. This being so one would expect from the preceding findings that television would play a much more prominent part in initial knowledge than is revealed in Arons' data on knowledge of newsworthy events. Several studies on this matter are quoted by Arons and reproduced here.

Table 7.2.7. Medium acting as first source of 'Knowledge of' newsworthy event.

News event	Location size sample;	Newspapers	Radio	Television	(Personal)
Satellite Launching (Explorer I)	Lansing 167	17%	20%	40%	(23)%
	Madison 125	22%	29%	36%	(13)%
President's illness	Palo Alto 38	10%	18%	61%	(10)%
	Lansing 205	12%	32%	38%	(18)%

The same argument about the ordering in time of media effectiveness does not of course hold for extended public campaigns. Television would be the most appropriate medium for communicating that a campaign has started but the evidence is that often, after a campaign has worn on in the press for a period the arguments about policy and concepts wear stale and the demand is once again for those things that television can best convey – 'knowledge of' interesting candidates and specific events.

Arons' findings about general knowledge can be further extended by considering where people seek scientific knowledge. This sort of knowledge is relatively heavily-laden with concepts and should show significant differences between media. Furthermore (if data are available on the educational level of the audience) one would expect to find that the media differences would increase with the level of education because the more educated persons would seek a more profound conceptual treatment of scientific matters. Both of these expectations are met by the following set of data.

Table 7.2.8. Primary source of science news.

Education	Magazines	Newspapers	Radio	Television
Grade School (N = 447)	13%	42%	6%	34%
Some High School (N = 352)	19%	43%	6%	30%
Completed High School (N = 458)	28%	40%	2%	26%
College (N = 333)	44%	39%	1%	15%

(From Swinehart and McLeod).

(The order of magazines and newspapers is reversed for presentation in this table because U.S. magazines presenting scientific news can be assumed to be more serious than the general run of U.S. newspapers. This is not true of all magazines.)

This study was carried out in early 1957 in the U.S.A. Twelve months later, and six months after the first Sputnik launching, another probability sample of similar size was asked comparable questions. The major relations depicted above were confirmed. In addition, the Sputnik had made science newsworthy with a capital 'N'. For the sample as a whole, television and radio seem to have discovered new capabilities to convey 'knowledge about' scientific findings. There might be such capabilities but, when one looks at the change for different levels of education, there is a strong suggestion that those who want serious knowledge about science still turn to the printed word; and hence there is the implication that radio and television have increased their share of mentions mainly by catering for newfound interest in *knowledge of* exciting scientific events or persons, not by taking on new communicating functions.

Table 7.2.9. Effects on media preference of a major shift in popular interest in science. (Percent mentioning radio or television as primary source of scientific information)

	$N_1 = N_2 =$	1957 Pre Sputnik (N_1)	1958 Post Sputnik N_2)
Grade School	(447; 309)	40	54
Some High Schl.	(352; 217)	36	47
Compl. High Schl.	(458; 353)	28	32
College	(333; 263)	16	19

(Adapted from Swinehart and McLeod).

Arons reported of his sample that they found television the easiest medium to understand, followed by radio, newspapers and magazines in that order. One would expect the television producers to have so shaped this scientific communication that the grade school people of Swinehart and McLeods' sample would have said that they found it easier to understand 'science' on television than 'science' in print. They would not be talking about the same 'science' as the high school college graduates who find it easier to understand science in print. Unfortunately no direct data on this were published but Swinehart and McLeod do note that those of higher education (*i.e.* those using the printed word) had a deeper knowledge of what satellites were about.

Thus there does appear to be a consistent picture of differences between media in the kinds of knowledge they can most successfully convey and hence in the major parts they play in building up knowledge about objects or people, inanimate processes or social processes.

The other major feature of Arons' findings that needs to be considered is THE PSYCHOLOGICAL DISTANCE BETWEEN THE AUDIENCE AND THE MEDIA. His data enable the problem to be looked at from a number of viewpoints.

1. The amount of time voluntarily spent with the different media can be taken as a crude index of 'degree of interaction'. Such measures frequently correlate with psychological nearness, although in this case there are marked differences in cost and availability.

Table 7.2.10. Time spent per average day with the media (in minutes).

Newspapers	Magazines	Radio	Television	Total
43'	20'	68'	144'	275'

(From Arons, p. 3).

2. Direct psychological measures are rather more convincing.

On each of these dimensions newspapers stand near one extreme and television at the other. (Ref. Table 7.2.11.) Whereas the newspapers emerge from these figures as formal and impersonal, television appears to tie people to the viewing situation, makes them feel that they are connected with what they are viewing and helps them to escape from the depressing and boring aspects of their real world. There seems little doubt but that for this sample television as a medium is very much closer to its audience than are newspapers. The rela-

Table 7.2.11. Measures of personal relation to the media.

	Newspapers	Magazines	Radio	Television
a. *Involvement in situation*				
Interruption would most disturb	2%	8%	8%	74%
Interruption would least disturb	42%	17%	15%	7%
b. *Identification with content*				
Makes me feel as though experienced myself	11%	21%	5%	54%
'Lose myself in' (Scale +3 to −3)	0.27	0.74	0.42	1.14
c. *Emotional reaction to content*				
'Gets me out of the dumps'	7%	18%	20%	52%
'Stimulates my imagination'	11%	24%	14%	47%
d. Friendly (Scale +3 to −3)	0.71	0.88	1.93	1.99

(Adapted from Arons, p. 52, 79, 48, 50).

tion of the other two is a little more complex. Radio is seen as if it created a warm psychological background with little involvement or identification, but blotted out some of the negative aspects of the everyday world. Magazines appear to be judged as if they were largely impersonal conveyors of stories. The magazines *per se* are not seen as friendly and the stories can be readily put down to be finished at a later date, but while reading them the reader tends to identify with the actors and forget his depression and bordeom. This interpretation is supported by the fact that 36 per cent selected magazines as the 'preferred sole source of stories' (55 per cent for television, five for radio and one for newspapers).

Given the pattern of media differences outlined so far, one would expect that those who turn most strongly to the vicarious element of television are those most anxious to seek relief from their own psychological circumstances, to seek friendliness in a secure impersonal setting and least concerned with understanding the outside world. These tendencies are shown in a stratified random sample of 736 drawn from a Southern U.S. city by Pearlin (1959).

Table 7.2.12. Correlates of seeking vicarious experience on television.
(Liking for 'programs that help us forget our personal problems and troubles')

		Like very much	Like less or disregard	N =
Life goals	frustrated	37	63	142
	not frustrated	28	72	525
Fear of exploitation by 'friends'		40	27	192
No fear		27	73	527
Apathy to world's problems		47	53	64
No expressed apathy		29	71	666

(From Pearlin, 1959).

This study only touches upon the connections between what a medium does and how different people relate themselves to it. It is fair warning, however, that a majority of the audience of television are restrained, by factors deeply rooted in their adjustment to their personal lives, from coming too close to the media – from accepting too much of that which the media can most readily offer. This contradiction was noted above, theoretically examined in connection with Western films on television (Emery, 1958-1959) and demonstrated with respect to an abstract film (Emery, 1958).

7.3. Media and persuasion

Future scenarios based on forecasts of communication technology have typically made much of their persuasive power. Arons' study covered only advertising but seems to closely parallel the lessons being learnt from political election campagins.

Data from the Arons' study strongly suggest that people retain the same general psychological orientation toward advertising content in a medium as they have toward the medium itself.

Table 7.3.1. Psychological orientation toward advertising in different media.

Orientation	Newspapers	Magazines	Radio	Television
Largely emotional, knowledge incidental	3%	29%	26%	50%
Largely knowledge	62%	14%	17%	15%
Total (percent with definite orientation)	65%	43%	43%	65%
Mentioning in relation to product purchase	71%	39%	20%	62%

(From Arons; p. 92, 96. N = 300).

The differences in orientation are significant, except between magazines and radio, and the existence of some definite orientation appears to be related to the importance of the media in product purchasing.

Although there is no difference between television and newspapers in the proportion having a definite orientation there is a significant difference in the felt need to take a personal attitude toward the advertisements appearing in them.

Table 7.3.2. Proportions taking a personal attitude to advertisements in the different media.

Attitudes to specific ads.	News-papers	Maga-zines	Radio	Tele-vision	None	
Especially liked	9%	11%	8%	66%	6%	100
Especially disliked	3%	4%	9%	61%	23%	100
Neutral or no response	22%	28%	45%	15%		

(From Arons; p. 97, 107. N = 300).

This difference supports the previous evidence of greater emotional involvement in the televised advertisements.

On the other side, the knowledge orientation, there are further data with which to elaborate the main finding in Table 7.3.1. Analysis of the way in which people spoke about the things they learnt from the media showed that they tended to learn from newspapers about the characteristics of general product groups; and from television about specific branded products.

Table 7.3.3. Generality of product knowledge conveyed by different media. (Percent of those mentioning – see Table 7.2.3.)

	Newspapers	Magazines	Radio	Television
Mentioning general product group	40	15	5	3
Specific product – no brand	40	29	31	13
Specific product – branded	20	56	54	84

(From Arons; p. 92, 93. N = 290).

As with the preceding data there is no sure way of separating out those effects due to what the medium does and what the audience want. We assume that by 1960 (the time of the Arons' study) the media people in TV had become fairly skilled in giving people what they wanted so that they, the media people, could maximize their advertising appeal.

Summary

Differences in the media were found at the general level of the kind of communication situation created, in the observed differences in audience reaction to, and use of, the media and to some extent in their reactions to and use of advertising messages in these media. It was suggested that these differences are potentially of such significance that they ought to be further explored.
     The main differences appeared to be:

1. the printed word provides a better medium for conveying objective knowledge about objects and events although television may be able to more effectively communicate knowledge of the identity of a thing and of how it fits with certain images of a person;
2. television creates for its audiences a greater feeling of psychological close-

ness to and emotional involvement with its communications than does the printed word;

3. while television communications are experienced as a slice of immediate sensuous reality the printed word has an aura of greater factualness and objectivity.[1]

1. It is an interesting comment on this paradox that it was only for radio and television that Arons' subjects found it necessary to justify acceptance of the communications as a basis for purchase:

Percent mentioning as 'Reasons for Purchase' (N = 300)

	Newspapers	Magazines	Radio	Television
Convincing; convincing demonstration	1	8	6	28
Believed person delivering message	–	–	18	5
	1	8	24	33

8. Television and maladaption

8.1. Introduction

There is no doubt in our minds that dissociation is the most probable negative scenario to arise from the 'telecommunications revolution'.

1. The nature of the dissociative mode within individuals and societies is the parallel of processes peculiar to a type IV, turbulent environment. Dissociation occurs 'when individuals seek to reduce the complexity of choice in their daily lives by denying the relevance or utility of others as co-producers of the ends they seek to attain,' and feeds upon the vicious circle of creating distance between self and others. So that 'even seemingly trivial involvements with others' (Emery *et al.*, 1974, p. 52-53) leads to increasingly unpredictable consequences when contact occurs – which then makes less probable the initiation of further contact. The dimensions and nature of human communication are, as is the nature of type IV environments 'so complex, so richly textured' that changes arising from increasing interdependence create uncertainty. Denial of some of the individual functions which contribute to human communication, *e.g.* use of deodorants, must necessarily increase the degree of relevant uncertainty in personal contact.
2. The evidence below that television may have unavoidably dissociative effects – the creation of myths, 'the illusion of semi-reality', the splitting off of whole brain processing from reception of information – all point to a conclusion that forms of telecommunication only accentuate and confirm the necessity for dissociative response to turbulence.

A change in the external environment, from type III to type IV will, as does a change in the internal milieu, leave 'the organism hungry for information from its environment to explain itself.' (Gazzaniga, 1970, p. 109). Television, by creating the illusion of information reception, satisfies this need created by the situation of decreasing knowledge about the external environment. It cuts through one paradox (Emery *et al.*, 1974) by creating another; the parallel within the individual.

It is only to be expected that the internal and external environments of man will mutually reinforce each other. Television as the leading part of the telecomm technology is the unique technology appropriate to a type IV environment. It is therefore primarily maladaptive and intensifies the crisis of type IV life.

8.2. The most probable of the negative scenarios – a continuation of the present

While dissociation as a personal mode does not have the high visibility of either segmentation or superficiality, trends towards the dissociative mode can be discerned as a crisis of responsibility in Western societies. Dissociation occurs:

1. when a man loses touch with a part of his nature or function such that he becomes incapacitated as a purposeful being and
2. when withdrawal into 'privatization' destroys the network of mutual obligations that characterize a meaningful social life (Emery *et al.*, 1974, p. 53).

The most powerfully documented overview of dissociation has been provided by Martin Pawley in *The Private Future*; a picture of a society 'of products and services whose social effects are demonstrably *fragmenting*' creating a vacuum within which pieces are held together by 'a new kind of social adhesive that works by dreams instead of realities.' (Pawley, 1973, p. 36). The decline of public life is both a result and a cause of privatization as the 'social form whose nature derives from the mechanisms and structures it employs to maintain the isolation of its citizens', feeds on itself and its inbuilt and pervasive technologies.

'Within the breast of the private citizen today lurks not a yearning for an older, simpler pattern of community obligations, but a desperate desire for a commodity-induced nirvana to obliterate fears of a future seemingly blocked by insoluble crises in the form of over-population, resource exhaustion, pollution or nuclear war. *If the goal system of Western affluence breaks down, what lies beneath it is not a renewed sense of community through scarcity, but an absolute social collapse without the security of inter-personal and inter-family support*. Affluence is *vital* to the social organization of the Western world because it has supplanted all the old systems of *mutual obligation*.' (*Ibid*. p. 179).

'To face a futureless future (the individual) relies on self-deception . . . fed and developed by recording and simulating technologies which have formalized it and given it the appearance of truth . . .' 'The triumph of mass media as the purveyors of secondary reality reflects the refusal of the people of the West to accept the implications of the collapse of community. The fragmentation of society is a reality, but the priceless distraction of erotic and sensory fantasy products and services conceals it.' (*Ibid*. p. 180).

Pawley argues that this process of privatization is irreversible (p. 203). We will come back to this question in a later section.

Broadcast information as one of a group of consumer products has an ostensible function which in reality is subordinated to its overwhelming function as another social isolator (*Ibid*, p. 49). It provides as does the automobile, an isolating personal environment (p. 56).

'With television it is not the programme that is important, certainly not the substance of the news. It is the *sound*, the background blur of voices that like the ticking of a clock or the cyclic 'ping' of a sonar is only significant when it changes, or when it stops.' (p. 72).

'A survey carried out in San Francisco in 1971, which involved telephoning viewers directly after the evening news bulletin, revealed that more than half of those who had heard or watched could not remember a single item in it. If news were a product pure and simple, its manufacturers would be bankrupt.' (*Ibid*. p. 174). 'The comfortable people want only wax moon faces, poreless, hairless, expressionless' – (Bradbury, 1953, p. 83) – non-threatening.

To confront the news would be to confront primary reality. Television is 'much more magical' than any other consumer product because it *makes things normal*; 'it packages and homogenizes fragmentary aspects of reality. It constructs an acceptable reality (the myth) out of largely unacceptable ingredients.' (Pawley, p. 160). To confront the myth would be to admit that one was ineffective, isolated and incapable of recreating community and human communication. Ray Bradbury explored the phenomenon in *Fahrenheit 451* and came to the same conclusion that the 'televisor' is an environment as real as the world. It *becomes* and *is* the truth. 'Books can be beaten down with reason.' (Bradbury, p. 84). His concept of a world where consumers demand increasingly high volumes of information until information and familiarity become the environment itself parallels precisely the hard data and conclusions that Pawley has collected about current Western society.

The basic assumption that all that people need is information, without the control and responsibility for processing and producing that information, seems to lie in a misunderstanding of the nature of information and of the purposeful nature of people themselves. To design systems that admit of only one part of the individual – his capacity for receipt of information – is to design-in, quite inevitably, either the Private Future or the sabotage function, by virtue of the individual's other needs. Industrial sabotage arising through denial of responsibility to human cogs for product quality is not an unknown phenomenon. Centrally controlled broadcast or storage systems, by definition, regard consumers as replaceable receptors.

As the links between telecommunications and computers grow and consolidate, more and more of the processing, editing, sifting, storing and retrieval of information will be handled in computerized form. 'Mini computers' like the Wang system now offer a processing capability exceeding that of the million dollar computer of a decade ago. Computers linked to the ERTS (Earth Resources Technology Satellite) are now analyzing and producing summary reports of the data as part of the normal programming. While telecommunications may provide 'flexibility' the further removal of processing, programming etc. from the receiver or even from a small group of programmers, editors etc. means another further decrease in the knowledge of these essential functions that is available to the receiver. The receiver will have less chance to learn from the processes involved in such functions as editing the news and the documentaries, which means that the essential question of what is the most useful or effective knowledge leading to a course of action, for any individual, will become progressively more difficult.

'There is now nothing but a vacant terrorized space between the government – which controls and maintains production – and the isolated consumer who increases his consumption in proportion to his isolation.' (Pawley, p. 8).

Compare *Fahrenheit 451*. The running together of bureaucracy, personal withdrawal and crime, by adults and teenagers alike is documented in both scenarios. The responsibility vacuum created by the withdrawal to home and 'the families' on your private telecomm system (your own Box) renders immediately vulnerable the linear, monolithic structure of supply. Dissociation and impartial violence become the same phenomenon (Emery *et al.*, 1974, Pawley, 1973).

Whilst 'self identification can now only come from personal modes of action and not the things with which you surround yourself' (Pawley, p. 38), it becomes clear that television as the leading part of telecommunication, is destructive of self identification. Through its inability to instruct as distinct from its ability to inform, it cannot increase the degree of control any individual has over particular outcomes, particularly those pertaining to his own efficiency in pursuing his own choice of action.

The inability of television to provide *knowledge* in this sense leads to the systematic pathology of existentialism and phenomenology. The demand to 'see it as it is now,' 'reality is only temporary' (p. 38) – 'Don't adjust your mind,' 'Never has the future been more NOW' (p. 38) only echoes the 'experience and express' philosophy of the Esalen school of group therapy – feel it, hear it, say it like it is – but never, note, think about its consequences for others tomorrow. 'Here and Now' experience and expression are not necessarily even purposefully linked – both appear to be unrelated goal seeking activities.

'Privatization means a media-fed life of autonomous – drive slavery *wherein every wish is gratified* and every fear calmed.' 'No manufacturer (of information) dares to stress the ineffable release from interpersonal obligation that his product represents.' (*Ibid.* p. 49). 'This interlocking process of consumer goods pull and news media push has the character of a syndrome in that it gains power with each successive cycle. The privatized individual vacates the public realm which thus falls progressively into the hands of a bureaucracy laced with speculative corruption. Such administration in turn leads to more news of families evicted and old ladies living in their bathrooms and thus confirms the wisdom of the initial withdrawal itself. Because the public realm is less and less often *experienced* and more and more *reported* it becomes an image consisting of rapes, hijackings, riots, speeches, murders and rackets. Standards of public life fall – or so it appears – and the apparent fall acts as an additional confirmation of its dangers. What else can you expect from public life? *Better by far to keep out of it,* or vicariously endure its cycles of violence and duplicity on TV.' (*Ibid.* p. 99). Rape or pack rape of the viewers?

We agree that the television children of today, released from responsibility as they have been by parental acceptance of the underlying social logic of Spock's philosophy, (*Ibid.* p. 80) and probably more released by TV viewing, certainly accept things more freely than their elders. They see them! They are! They don't analyze things. But we suspect that this does not mean they are more 'tolerant', only that they are more indifferent. They are the real victims of The Private Future. More like 'sheep' than 'people'.

The whole question of the analysis and processing of raw information as foreshadowed by those who design large telecomm systems ultimately has, on a societal scale, the same effects as a single medium such as TV has on the ability of an individual to analyse or process within himself (see below). The crisis of responsibility lies in the relation of the individual to the total process of generation of information through to its subsequent reception in a form which can enlighten and thus provide understanding. The increasingly sophisticated use of large scale information broadcast technologies regardless of their form of interface with the receiver will accelerate the process of dissociation, as the steps between generation and receipt of message lengthen and become more remote from the source of the message and the individual receiver.

Seeking to remedy this state of affairs by 'arbitrary prohibitions and the expansion of a bureaucracy of social engineers' (Pawley, p. 179) can only serve to reinforce the myth of community that remains.

'Once the syndrome has begun, draconian legislation to restrict the exercise of public rights of action inevitably follows. Implementation of this legislation generates protest, protest leads to more televised and reported acts of violence and the violence in turn confirms the necessity of the legislation as well as the need for more. The fear of the privatized citizen is continually reinforced, and with it his desire to strengthen the wall of his own privacy by *dissociating* himself from any remaining strands of obligation that still reach out into the public arena from his home or his job.' (*Ibid.* p. 99).

It is the same form of question as, 'who will take responsibility for choosing which pieces and what category of data will go into data banks?' Obviously the assumption underlying the large scale network of computerized telecomm information systems is that it will not be the responsibility of the individual whose data is under review. The breakdown is responsibility engendered by the splitting off of these functions from the information distribution function results in the mass of individuals denying responsibility for the use to which this data is put. 'Community has always meant responsibility, surveillance, concern for others' (*Ibid.* p. 47). New social forms such as extensions of present telecomm facilities can only further destroy the essential nature of community.

Such fragmentation of responsibility will have effects particularly in regard to how certain types of content will interface with a public course of action. Suspicion created by the remote control of documentation of the individual by welfare agencies, town planning bodies and law enforcement officers will only accentuate the distance between the individual and these bodies when they meet. The probability of shared responsibility for the outcome of the meeting will have been lowered by media pre-contact. While the externalities of such bodies will be familiar on contact, knowledge of effective courses of action to particular ends will have been short circuited by denial of the need to assume responsibility for shared purposes. As Pawley documents in the area of politics, 'the party is no longer important, the issues are no longer important, the rhetoric is no longer important.' (p. 132). The public has lost the means and the motivation that would enable them to speak with a purposeful vote. Such end products as remote student lecturing by audio and visual means, with or without response capability will deepen the responsibility-for-learning crisis that is facing educational institutions across the world. Individual or collective access to centrally held library material, graphs, films, or videotapes, will result in the further spread of vandalism, looking for kicks, that other centrally provided services like telephone and public transport are experiencing today.

The notion of 'response capability' as a form of participation and a safeguard against misuse and distortion of information has been put into its proper perspective by both Pawley and Norman Spinrad (1972). Jack Barron, the self-styled 'evangelistic seeker' (Emery *et al.*, 1974, p. 54) of participation and social justice runs a television talk-back show – 'This is *Bug Jack Barron*, and you're on the air, friend. *It's all yours until I say stop* ... This is your moment in the old spotlight – your turn to bug whoever's bugging you. You're plugged into me, and I'm plugged into the whole goofy country.' (Spinrad, p. 15).

Another way 'to bring about an era of clean politics and make possible the true, instantaneous democracy of the electronic plebiscite.' (Pawley, p. 75). *Bug Jack Barron* exemplifies the intrinsic logic of the medium.

'*Every question must become an open question and every decision be immediately reversible the following night. Because it has no memory television is always right but always changing its mind.* It displays the final proof of the utility of that technique of suspended judgment which Bertrand Russell called the greatest achievement of the twentieth century. *The necessity for the television commentator to always provide himself with a future entrance, a last word, then a final last word, then (in response to changing circumstances) further last words, reflects the impossibility of challenging television in real time.* The only thing you can do is to turn it off – which is like stopping a game of tennis by running away with the ball.

In political terms this is important because it partially explains the power of television as well as the curious *indirectness* of its effect. *Television politics reduces the right of spontaneous dissent to the equivalent of a self-applied blindfold and gag. Poor performances or ill-considered words can be erased from consciousness overnight; in every way the medium seems to be the perfect vehicle for mass necromancy, and yet even those who claim to use its techniques for limited and specific ends seem unable to get exactly what they want from it.*

The doubt is important and not an afterthought because with television, as with the automobile, the private house, the newspaper, the advertisement, all the shibboleths of Western living, there is more at work and at stake than the manipulative power of politicians and big business. *What they rule also rules them in the sense that they must continue to supply what the majority demand, even if that is only more of the same. In deferring its final judgement for commercial reasons, television, more than any other medium of communication, suspends judgement.* The apparent struggle between monsters with great power and humane men with great influence is somehow transmuted into something more acceptable by television, something *endless. Because the medium cannot afford to deliver a final judgment.*' (*Ibid*, p. 159).

Television inhibits action.

Jack Barron makes no secret of the fact that within the continuing framework of the show he and his crew are in perfect command of the content – *the responses.*

Building in a capability to respond is a treatment for a symptom within the inappropriate analogy of a 'diseased society' (*Ibid*. p. 40). Because it does not touch upon the inherent properties of to technology and its inherent personal effects it adds a further illusion to the illusions already present. The conclusion must be that rather than a major physical vehicle for achieving community involvement such systems with a built in response capability will, through the denial of themselves as co-producers of the product be another vehicle for further fractionation of the community.

And, while it *may* appear extremely unlikely that the majority of society could or would want to, divert from its present course of increasing productivity and living standards it is by no means clear that an analysis of the hidden costs behind mass media services will allow of an inevitable conclusion that they should be developed and applied as fast as technology and economics permit. Pawley's data on dissociative trends make it obvious that a Telecommunications Authority has a greater responsibility than to merely incorporate safeguards into developing systems or 'inform' the public – there are significant hidden costs and social consequences. If they are to design and implement systems in such a way as to reverse dissociative trends they must relocate responsibility with the whole man in the whole community.

9. Television is a dissociative medium OR tele turns you off

The trends towards the dissociation of public and private life embodied in the psycho-technical construct called secondary reality – the reality of the media – have been laid at the door of its primary technology.

'*Television, queen of the consumer durables, is also the principal assassin of public life and community politics.* It absorbs the deceptions and evasions of the real world, mixes them with its own inherent deceptions, and thereby creates a new reality of its own, a reality more acceptable by far because of its *modulation* than the fragmentary glimpses of the real thing that occasionally prompt outraged citizens to write to the newspapers. The crisis of television begins when you stop watching it. Until then it exudes *secondary reality*, the synthetic social glue of consumer society.' (Pawley, 1973, p. 160).

'For the Children of Change time has collapsed and the horizon disappeared. It was, more than anything else, TV that did it.' (Fabun, 1969).

'Alone in a centrally heated, air-conditioned capsule, drugged, fed with music and erotic imagery, *the parts of his consciousness separated into components that reach everywhere and nowhere,* the private citizen of the future will have become one with the end of effort and the triumph of sensation divorced from action.' (Pawley, p. 203, emphasis is ours).

'Because the medium cannot afford to deliver a final judgement . . . its political influence consists largely in its ability to *distract* rather than to analyse.' (*Ibid.* p. 159).

'The mind drinks less and less.' (Bradbury, p. 60).

'The television personality can be admitted to a cage of snarling radicals without waking the suburbanite.' (Pawley, p. 72).

'It is in this way, watching while not really watching, listening while not really listening, that the individual citizen uses television.' (Pawley, p. 73).

'I saw 10,000 talkers whose tongues were all broken . . . I heard 10,000 whispers and nobody listening'. (Bob Dylan, A Hard Rain's a-Gonna Fall, 1962.[1])

The following data tend to confirm the above: the nature of the medium itself works in the first instance to dissociate the holistic nature of the human brain, thereby creating the conditions under which an illusion of reality, a mythical world can be developed and appreciated. These data illustrate the 'inherent deceptions' of the medium and its prolonged and systematic after-

---

1. We consider that A Hard Rain is in fact one of the earliest television scenarios and that Dylan unconsciously put his finger on the emerging private future long before the data started to pour in (*cf.* p. 50 *Futures We're In*).

effects. In a later chapter we will consider McLuhan's conclusions in the light of these data.

Television, as a media, consists of a constant visual signal of fifty half-frames per second. Our hypotheses regarding this essential nature of the medium itself are:

1. The constant visual stimulus fixates the viewer and causes habituation of response. The prefrontal and association areas of the cortex are effectively dominated by the signal, the screen.
2. The left cortical hemisphere – the centre of visual *and* analytical, calculating processes – is effectively reduced in its functioning to tracking changes on the TV screen.
3. Therefore, provided the viewer keeps looking, he is unlikely to reflect on what he is doing, what he is viewing. That is, he will be aware but *not* aware of his awareness. The TV producer, on the other hand, is very much concerned about what the viewer is doing, particularly with whether he is continuing to view. The producer might be said to be striving to be 'the conscious ego of the viewer', as Margaret Ribble described the mother as 'the ego of the infant'. Put another way, *TV viewing is goal-seeking but purposeless.* Its end is in its immediate consumption. '*The Children of Change* want miracles. And they want them *now*.' Switching from one TV programme to another is not a choice between means but a conditioning to one consummatory behaviour rather than another, to old films or modern domestic dramas.
4. The immediate consumption of TV is inherently rewarding. TV producers have to constantly strive to sustain viewing and conform more closely to the viewer's self conception. But the intrinsic rewarding effects of viewing, the ratings, are the only end points for them, not sales or votes.
5. The power and control exerted by the television signal have far reaching and cyclic effects on the total system of the individual.

9.1. Vigilance and attention

Both vigilance and attention are *necessary* conditions for purposive behaviour, but neither is sufficient in itself (Head, 1920). The evidence is TV not only impairs the ability of the viewer to attend, it also, by taking over a complex of direct and indirect neural pathways, decreases vigilance – the general state of arousal which prepares the organism for action should its attention be drawn to a specific stimulus.

The individual therefore may be *looking at* the unexpected or interesting but cannot act upon it in such a way as to complete the purposeful, processing gestalt.

William James (1890) said that 'everyone knows what attention is . . . Focalisation, concentration of consciousness are of its essence.' It 'is a condition which has a real opposite in the confused, dazed, scatterbrained state which in French is called *distraction*.' (p. 403-404). Voluntary attention is purposeful and involves effort, it cannot be 'sustained for more than a few seconds at a time.' (p. 420). 'No one can possibly attend continuously to an object that does not change.' (p. 421). 'Discriminative attention' is necessary even for simple sensations (p. 224). The continuous trance-like fixation of the TV viewer is then not attention but distraction – a form akin to daydreaming or time out. 'The passive experience of something visually impinging, as contrasted with the active focal perception of an object, occurs not only in the perception of colour and light but also in the *impingement of the total visual field* . . . The total visual field impresses itself on the eye; it seems to come toward one and to lose the qualities of distance and spatial structure if one gazes at it without trying to see any particular object. At the same time, light and colour and indistinct multitude become the outstanding qualities seen.' (Schachtel, 1959, p. 113).

The fact that the nature of the visual stimulus is such as to decrease vigilance and reduce the ability to process and integrate, results in the apparently paradoxical conclusion that the high volume of *sensory* output from TV results in a set of phenomena that are most closely approximated by so-called 'sensory deprivation.' This does not contradict the fact that TV output gives poor representation of the supposed sources of its message.

Our argument is complicated by the fact that the human nervous system is patterned on the principle of redundant functions (*not* a redundant parts design). Safeguards, against malfunction of any one of most parts of the nervous system, are built in by way of multiple and interdependent channel flows and multi-functional parts. Television exerts the effects that it does in reducing the functioning of human beings to the level of goal seeking by virtue of its homing in on one of the few flaws in the design of man. Our thesis is that despite the variety of content and the high volume of information which is fed into television its effects are not enriching but resemble those of experience within an impoverished environment (Rosenzweig, *et al.*, 1972).

People usually try to achieve visual efficiency. The 'line of sight (of the eyes) must be appropriately directed so that the proportion of the image that is to be seen acutely will fall exactly on the fovea. In addition to this, the lens system of the eye must be focussed for the distance of the object.' (Guyton, 1964, p. 3). A child carefully places itself at the optimum distance for maximum ease of fixation of objects on the TV screen (usually faces). Adults intuitively buy the size of screen that fits their household viewing space and then similarly position themselves at the optimum distance from the screen.

Thus people strive to get from the low definition image of TV the highest achievable information/clarity ratio to movement of the eyes, or effort, (*i.e.* efficiency). This search for information without effort and yet with maximum acuity, usually happens in about one fifth of a second. Given a single small, low definition focus – a TV screen – with the person placed at the appropriate focal distance for him, there may be little need at all for searching or accommodating eye movement. This is the first level at which TV accommodates to, or encourages immobility, or inactivity. The very fact that both children and adults do observe this pre-viewing ritual gives rise to the suspicion that there are rewards to be gained.

9.2. Visual stimuli and the left cortex

Man has a 'unique perceptual system (which) allows consideration of what the brain may be taking note of in a particular stimulus display.' (Gazzaniga, 1970, p. 29). Let us look at just a few of the most critical functions and relationships that exist within the human brain.

We start with a visual stimulus. The message from the eyes is relayed to the primary visual cortex (present in both hemispheres of the brain) which interprets a few meanings of the visual sensation but primarily relays the rest to the visual association areas. Here further processing is carried out and the signal is then relayed to the *angular gyrus – the common integrative area* for 3 major association areas. It is here that all types of sensation are integrated to determine a COMMON meaning – '*deeper conclusions*' (Guyton, p. 255) than can be attained by any one of the association areas above . . . Any damage to this area is likely to leave the person mentally inept; (including 'marked speech disturbances', Grossman, 1967) even though the different association areas might still be able to interpret their respective sensations, *this information is almost valueless* to the brain *unless its final meaning can be interpreted.*' (Guyton, p. 255, emphases are ours).

'This common integrative area is located in the angular gyrus of the *left* cerebral hemisphere in at least nine tenths of all people.' (*Ibid.* p. 255). It is one of the most marked areas in terms of specific uni-function and the consequences of it alone being reduced in effective function are felt throughout the whole organism. '*The left angular gyrus becomes the most important portion of the entire cerebral cortex.*' (*Ibid.* p. 255). The whole complex of disturbances and malfunction that result from damage to, or deterioration in left cortical function as a whole, together with the maladaptions and incompetencies that occur when right and left cortexes are separated have been thoroughly documented by the 'Split Brain' experimenters.

The position and function of area 39 of the brain is also significant in its relation to the ideo-motor area, immediately anterior to it. The function of the ideo-motor centre 'is to decide on *a course of action* in response to the co-ordinated information from the common integrative area.' (*i.e.* area 39) (*Ibid.* p. 260). ('Activities are very rapid and initiated almost automatically on the part of the ideo-motor area', *ibid.* p. 260).

But the prefrontal areas generally have two functions in relation to the ideo-motor area.

'*Suppression of the ideomotor area.* The prefrontal area keeps the ideomotor area suppressed most of the time. As a result, regardless of the incoming sensory signals, the ideomotor area, though capable of responding rapidly and violently, is inhibited in its response until the prefrontal and other thought areas of the brain *can have time to think over the type of response that will be most advantageous.* The common integrative region transmits its sensory information to the prefrontal lobes, to the temporal lobes, and to the memory circuits of the different association areas. In these areas, thought processes are initiated, and memories are immediately called forth of similar situations in the past. Then, these memories seem to funnel their information into the prefrontal lobes, where it is all coordinated into one master thought process.

Excitation of the ideomotor area. Once the prefrontal region has considered all the evidence both from the incoming sensory impulses and from previous experience, it then functions in unison with the other areas of the brain to determine the action most likely to lead to a satisfactory outcome. This constitutes the excitatory function of the prefrontal lobes. It is likely that the person will run when he is hit in the face by a large adversary but will strike back if the adversary shows all the evidence of being conquerable.' (*Ibid.* p. 260).

'*Other functions of the prefrontal area.* The prefrontal lobes are also the loci of most of the abstract thoughts of the mind. It is principally the prefrontal area that is responsible for a person's ambition, his conscience, *his planning of his future,* and *his worrying about details in order to achieve better efficiency in activities.* In other words, the prefrontal lobes seem to be continually concerned with *the welfare of the individual,* and they are always calling forth information from every part of the brain, sorting this information, *attempting to find the secrets of better ways of living.* It is also the prefrontal area that is capable of performing rigorous mental gymnastics such as solving difficult mathematical problems, and this area is the *depository of the considered judgment* necessary to a legal authority or a good medical diagnostician.

The difference between the function of the prefrontal lobes and other areas of the brain is their ability to store and utilise hundreds of small 'bits' of information all at the same time. The storage of these bits is usually temporary, for only a few minutes at a time, but so long as the bits are present in the frontal lobes they can be combined together to form complex thoughts. For instance, an animal without prefrontal lobes that is exposed to a series of sequential experiences loses rapidly the information gained from moment to moment. He might forget the presence of a plate of food on the opposite side of the cage if he is not looking at it.

Similarly, a human being without prefrontal lobes, on dismantling a watch, loses all concept of the positions of the parts, or *on attempting to solve a complicated problem in logic he loses most of the information that is required for solving the problem before he is anywhere near the solution.' (Ibid.* p. 261, emphases are ours).

Please note the results from the 1971 San Francisco survey of retention of television viewers! (p. 65).

Our concern in this section is with the inhibitory function of the cortex over the angular gyrus and particularly the ideomotor area. We explore below the special conditions under which the prefrontal area suppresses the function of the ideomotor area to such an extent that it cannot implement: cannot act, there is only a 'suspended judgment' (see p. 70).

'*Effect of loss of the prefrontal lobes.* Occasionally the prefrontal lobes are completely destroyed by a disease or trauma, and sometimes they are destroyed purposefully (as a medical practice) because harmful patterns of thought develop that cannot be stopped in any other way. *When the prefrontal areas are gone, the ideomotor and common integrative regions are left mainly in charge of the thought patterns and motor responses of the brain.* The person without prefrontal lobes is likely to exhibit extreme reactions to sensory impulses, some of which are very happy in nature while others have the characteristics of extreme temper. In all instances the responses are rapid and are likely to lead to disastrous results.' (Guyton, p. 261). 'The crisis of television only starts when you turn it off.' (Pawley). '*As long as the person is unprovoked, he has very much the same personality as a giddy teenager responding with feeling to everything but without much thought. When provoked he is likely to fall into a state of rage which cannot be easily quelled at the moment, but which will be totally forgotten a few moments later.'* (Guyton, p. 262).

'The frontal lobes . . . control the active state of the cortex, . . . and play an important role also in the execution of intentions that determine the direction of human activity and impart to the latter an elective and purposive character.' (Luria, 1973, p. 22). A pronounced effect of reduction of frontal lobe functioning 'is a disturbance of the independent choice of programs of action.' (*Ibid.* p. 14).

There can also be reduction of emotionality, general affective reactions to sensory input, and also of intellectual abilities, depending on the particular area which is damaged (Grossman, p. 123). *Limbo 90* has explored the use of prefrontal lobotomy as a deliberate mechanism of societal control and pacification. But there are other ways of rendering this cortex non-functioning than by extirpating it.

There is within the organization of the human brain a close and fundamental relation between vision, verbalization, consciousness and the purposeful nature of man. A greater area of the cortex is given over to vision than any other sensory mode and vision carries the most information.

While split brain experiments have shown that there is a measure of redundancy in most cortical functions and for short periods the minor, the right hemisphere, can take control, there are really 'two separate visual inner worlds, one serving the right half of the field of vision, and the other the left half.' (Sperry, 1968, p. 725). When the corpus callosum, the physical link between the two hemispheres, is severed 'no evidence exists that what is perceived in the right half-field has any influence on the perception or comprehension of what is seen in the left half-field.' (Gazzaniga, 1970, p. 101). 'All cases failed to achieve even the simplest sort of integration between the two visual half-fields.' (*Ibid.* p. 104). While both can emote, and the right can precipitate a vague gross response, the left is 'unable to get at the cognitive aspects of whatever produced . . . emotional change.' (*Ibid.* p. 107). 'Ipsilateral deficits can be elicited and are quite striking in more complex tasks that require 'gnostic sophistication.' (*Ibid.* p. 37). That is in tasks and activities which require the good functioning of brain area 39.

'The left hemisphere is equipped . . . with the main centers for the comprehension and organization of language . . . and also communicates . . . about all of the more generalized, less lateralized cerebral activity that is bilaterally represented and common to both sides.' (Sperry, 1968, p. 728). It is thus the key to making conscious all the activities of the right brain. 'Month after month of testing the right hemisphere alone revealed it to be mute.' (Gazzaniga, p. 117).

'No subjects were able to give accurate spoken reports for even the simplest kind of sensory information projected to the right hemisphere.' (*Ibid.* p. 117). 'The right hemisphere, like a deaf mute or like some aphasics, cannot talk about the perceived object and, worse still, cannot write about it either.' (Sperry, p. 725). While it can use some *non verbal responses* to show it is still partially gnostic it is incapable of being aware of itself or of bringing to awareness the function of any other structure. Its inability to communicate through speech or writing means that *with only right brain processing operating there is no mature purposeful course of action open to the individual.*

It should be noted here that severing of the corpus callosum has organizational motor effects of a more general nature than speech and writing (*Ibid.* p. 727). Similarly when the left hemisphere has lost contact with incoming sensory information, or is inactive, 'all patients have marked *short-term memory deficits* . . . and it is open to question whether this memory impairment ever clears completely.' (*Ibid.* p. 727).

The left neo-cortex then is the critical locus of data from old brain, new brain and subcortical centres. The nature of the processes carried out in the left cortex and particularly area 39 are those unique to human as opposed to other mammalian life. It is the centre of logic, logical human communication based on analysis, integration of sensory components and memory: (Gazzaniga, p. 259) the basis of man's conscious, purposeful, and timefree, abilities and actions. It is the critical function of man that makes him distinctively human – it is his distinctive competence.

These data tell us what is to be expected when either the left cortex is injured, or the corpus callosum directly linking the two hemispheres, is severed.

But there are other ways of reducing left cortical function and separating the hemispheres than by causing gross anatomical damage.

Let us now look at ways in which left cortical functions including those of the prefrontal areas, the angular gyrus, and the ideomotor centre are effectively reduced.

Our concern is with the *habituation* of response to a stimulus rather than adaptation (The distinction follows Grossman, 1967, p. 641). 'Habit diminishes the conscious attention with which our acts are performed.' (James, 1890, p. 114). Habituation is the process whereby 'The desynchronization of the cortical EEG produced by the initial presentation of a novel stimulus tends to shorten and gradually disappear completely with repeated non-reinforced stimulus presentations . . .' (Gastaut *et al.*, 1957). Rusinov and Smirnov (1957b) have reported complete habituation of the EEG response to light, although many more trials were needed than with stimuli of other modalities (Grossman, p. 642).

Habituation does not represent a breakdown of receptor or transmitter function . . . but rather the sensory mechanisms seem to be actively inhibited by some central process which is itself subject to extinction or 'disinhibition'. The organism appears to learn not to respond or not to transmit sensory in-

formation which has been without significance or consequence in the past
. . . habituation may represent a simple learning process'. (Grossman, p. 641).
The history of clinical work has shown that man is capable of learning self
destructive patterns as well as adaptive. Similarly the mentors of *The Terminal
Man* made their fatal mistake in forgetting that man can learn to control *any*
process. Peper (1972) has demonstrated that subjects may be trained for very
specific control. Learning to control autonomic function is now becoming an
established method within medical treatment for high blood pressure, etc.
There is also evidence 'that a conditioned response of the alpha rhythm may
occur to a *subliminal* level of stimulation.' (Barratt and Herd, 1964, p. 18).

'The effects of habituation generalize to the extent that fewer trials are
required to habituate the orienting response to the second stimulus.' (Grossman, p. 642). 'And an injured hemisphere may . . . produce a generalized
diminution of attention in its contralateral field.' If one substitutes 'impaired'
normal response for 'injured' it becomes clearer that there can be a spread
of effect from left brain to right. The rapidity and completeness of habituation appear to be, at least in part, a function of stimulus complexity, (Grossman, p. 642), rhythm, and rapid repetition (Grey Walter, 1973, p. 116). In
other words *the less complex and more rhythmic the stimulus, the more rapid
and complete the habituation.*

'The effects of habituation are prolonged, although apparently not permanent. Depending
on the number of non-reinforced stimulus presentations, some localized desynchronization
usually returns within hours of the habituation experience. Complete, generalized alpha
blocking reappears typically within *days* of the last trial.' (Grossman, p. 644).

We make it quite specific here that we are not suggesting that habituation
occurs in the primary visual cortex but in the more non-specific parietal and
frontal areas (Grey Walter, p. 116), those whose functions we have listed on
p. 76. That is, stimuli are still received, reacted to as stimuli and some minimum processing is done. But the communication from outside stops there.
It does not proceed further except perhaps in severely attenuated form to the
more rigorous processing areas, because of the blocking of these pathways
by structures which are subject to habituation.

'John and Killam (1959) report that photic driving of the EEG in response
to the presentation of intermittent light stimuli disappears gradually form the
mid brain reticular formation and hippocampal formation with repeated
stimulus presentation.' (p. 645). This loss of photic-driving response seems
to occur more rapidly in man than in other species (Jus and Jus, 1959), in
spite of the fact that desynchronization responses to light are more difficult
to habituate (Grossman, p. 645).

There are 'fibres coming by way of the lingual gyrus from the part of the visual cortex where the periphery of the retina is represented.' (Maclean, 1964, p. 195). Hippocampal structures may receive the direct effect of the repetitive visual stimulus. It is useful to try a small experiment for yourself. Sit in front of a television screen and read a book. Look at the TV out of the corner of your eye while looking at the book.

While it is easier for people to concentrate on a figure rather than the ground or context in which it is embedded, the ground is a determining factor in the appearance or meaning of the figure. Our television signal is the ground, and it is determining the effects of the figure (the content of the screen). Just because in a normal viewing situation the viewer is unaware of the ground and its effects does not mean that these effects do not exist. This experiment shows quite clearly that there is a ground and that its effects are feeding into that part of the brain which provides the contextural affective properties of all human action.

9.3. Diencephalic and mesencephalic functions

'The progressive diminution and eventual disappearance of the response of the primary sensory mechanisms to environmental stimulation . . . suggest that central mechanisms can in some way control the sensory input to the brain.' (Grossman, p. 646). There is 'an active suppression of the sensory pathways.' (*Ibid.* p. 654). 'The fact that the reticular formation affects sensory input is beyond doubt.' (*Ibid.* p. 647).

Composed of two separate parts, the mesencephalic and the thalamic, the reticular activating system, when stimulated, causes very diffuse flows of impulses upward through widespread areas of the thalamus and hence to widespread areas of the cortex, causes generalized increase in cerebral activity; and activates localized regions of the cortex. The recticular activating system apart from its direct and diffuse ascending projection relays whereby it controls the sleep/wakefulness cycle, together with the thalamus and hypothalamus generally, is richly supplied with both direct and indirect sensory afferents from all parts of the body, and all levels of the nervous system. (Guyton, Grossman, Isaacson). *This complex below the cortex could be as subject to repetitive stimulation as is the cortex itself.*

Therefore as a part of this interlocking system we have the two halves of the neo-cortex communicating with each other through the thalamus and mesencephalon (Guyton, p. 263) as well as through the corpus callosum.

In fact many movements such as of the eyes and rotation of the head, can be controlled directly by lower centres in the mesencephalon, pons and medulla *without participation of the cortex at all* (*Ibid.* p. 263).

If the reticular activating system is gradually shut down, the organism drops off to sleep and ceases to show further signs of motor, emotional or strictly 'intellectual' activity. If the thalamus and the hypothalamus gradually shut down, there is a generalized diminution of all physical, sensorimotor and proprioceptive, and nervous acitivity, including autonomic.

Because visual reception in man is the dominent sensory mode and source of information and because both neo-cortical and subcortical centres are direct receivers and hence habituators of constant visual stimuli, we are proposing that *television as a simple, constant, repetitive and ambiguous visual stimulus gradually closes down the nervous system of man.*

9.4. The characteristic mode of response to television

What does habituation of a visual stimulus mean in terms of the observable response of the human nervous system? If we measure the activity of the brain it means that fast (beta) waves are replaced by slow synchronous waves: the production of a phasic state (Luria, 1973). Beta wave form or 'alpha block' has a frequency of greater than 13 cycles per second while the alpha rhythm tied more closely to the visual system in man than any other sensory mode is a slow form with a frequency range of 8-13 c.p.s. 'Alpha waves have no function . . . as electroencephalographers know, in nearly all persons alpha waves are only present when the eyes are closed and *no information of a visual nature is being processed.*' (Lippold, 1973, p. 21). '*Cells, when idle, tend to synchronise.*' (*Ibid.* p. 20). We know now that periods of alpha are possible when the eyes are open (Mulholland 1969, p. 100) which only tends to confirm that it is idleness *per se*, not the absence of stimulation that produces alpha rhythm. They are a sign not of a simple uni-determinant function but of a complex pattern of micro- and macro-behaviours which centre about the lack of *intention* or *directed attention*. We will come back to intention.

In the setting of the conditions under which significantly continuous alpha occurs we can include lack of eye movement, fixation, lack of definition ('for most individuals a slightly defocussed picture . . . is compatible with the presence of alpha', Lippold, p. 7), general conditions of macro or bodily relaxation. That is, *a syndrome of idleness*, inactivity. Alpha represents a blank visual field.

'Those subjects who can lose fixation and achieve a blurred, indistinct visual image can voluntarily produce more or less occipital alpha.' (Mulholland, 1969, p. 105). 'On the other hand, it may be noted, that occipital alpha was always reduced at the time the subject *read* the instructions.' (Creutzfeldt, *et al.*, 1969, p. 161).

'No organized thought is possible in these (phasic) states and . . . selective associations are replaced by non selective associations deprived of their purposeful character. It is possible that much of the peculiar logic of dreams can be explained by these physiological facts.' (Luria, 1973, p. 5).

Data on habituation make it clear that a visual stimulus can turn off the orienting, arousal, attention response, distract rather than analyze, evoke old brain mythical rather than evoke time oriented logical thinking. That is, it turns you off reality (primary reality – Pawley) and off time – the essential ingredient for purposeful or ideal seeking behaviour. If there is any evidence that television evokes a pattern of activity that anywhere near approximates what we would expect from habituation then the results from split brain studies must be taken seriously. One thesis of ours is that *television produces a quality and quantity of habituation that approximates destruction of critical anatomical structures*. The only cheerful part of this data is that the results of habituation only take days to clear – not the years which regeneration and redundancy of function takes to recomplete the nervous system after extirpation or serious damage.

Herbert E. Krugman has supplied, with an experiment on just one woman[2], the critical link in this detective story of who has been doing what to whom. A full record was made of the EEG spectrum for the last 56 seconds of a magazine reading period and the subsequent duration of a TV viewing. He 'had expected that the TV might be more relaxing (than reading print) but not that it would instantly produce elements of drowsiness and a *characteristic mode of response*.' (Krugman, 1970, p. 12). This 'characteristic mode of response took about 30 seconds to fully develop' and there was no significant deviation from it through three repetitions of three quite different contents, ranging from 'classic and very gentle' to 'very explosive' (See Table 9.4.1.).

The response to the print added up to 'a picture of relaxed attention, interest and mental activity' (p. 11). The 'pattern' response to TV – 'the wave patterns throughout were at any one moment mixtures of the overlapping wave actions. It was not some seconds of one frequency followed by some seconds of another but an overall state, mode or style of reception with elements of different wave types.' (p. 11) – may be described as 'a relaxed condi-

2. It would appear that there has been no replication of this experiment. (Personal communication between Krugman and M.E.) We must really ask why not. (See p. 105).

tion with elements of both drowsiness and alertness.' (p. 12). Over the course of the viewing the slow waves gradually increased and the fast waves decreased – 'a fair indication of boredom.' (p. 13).

The three contents evoked 'a very little difference on the first trial and *none* by the third.' (p. 14).

Table 9.4.1. Krugman's Data: Comparison of effects of print and TV. (Number of seconds spent in each of three ranges of wave frequencies)

A	Print	TV			TV			TV		
		1st viewing			2nd viewing			3rd viewing		
		Content			Content			Content		
		1	2	3	1	2	3	1	2	3
Delta *slow*	5	21	24	24	22	24	28	24	25	26
Alpha	16	18	15	16	20	16	15	16	16	16
Beta *fast*	28	15	14	13	13	14	12	13	12	12

B	Average no. of seconds for contents of TV			Average no. of seconds for repetitions		
	1	2	3	1	2	3
slow	22.3 ⎫	24.3 ⎫	26.0 ⎫	23.0 ⎫	24.7 ⎫	25.0 ⎫
	⎬ 40.3	⎬ 40.0	⎬ 41.7	⎬ 39.3	⎬ 41.7	⎬ 41.0
alpha	18.0 ⎭	15.7 ⎭	15.7 ⎭	16.3 ⎭	17.0 ⎭	16.0 ⎭
fast	13.7	13.3	12.3	14.0	13.0	12.67

'It appears . . . then that the mode or response to television is more or less constant and very different from the response to print. That is, *the basic electrical response of the brain is clearly to the media and not to content difference.*' (p. 14). 'It seems also clear, as suggested by the earlier studies of involvement or of eye-movement, that the response to print may be fairly described as active . . . while the response to television may be fairly described as passive.' (p. 15).

Krugman's data led him to conclude that McLuhan was ahead of the transportation type of theory with his emphasis on passive participation in an *experience.* 'Television as experience is deficient in that reality is presented minus the feelings. This is McLuhan's 'cool' medium, in consequence said to be breeding a generation yearning for feelings and meanings behind the superficial happenings.' (p. 17). 'Our EEG data confirm McLuhan in the sense that television is not communication as we have known it. Our subject was *trying* to learn something from a print ad., but was passive about television.' (p. 17). That left-processing mechanisms are centrally involved is confirmed by a subject of Peper (1972) who stated that to keep on his left central-temporal alpha 'he relaxed his tongue and felt like a zombie'. In order to 'learn' this sort of control the subjects had to 'learn to forget about trying' and just let it occur (*Ibid.* p. 168).

'Television is . . . a communication medium that effortlessly transmits huge quantities of information *not thought about at the time of exposure.*' (Krugman, p. 17).

'The TV viewer is well equipped to *recognize* many things in life seen beforehand on television,' (*Ibid.* p. 18), that he becomes *familiar* with them, but because there has been no processing of information at the time of receipt, the response to real life contact emerges 'unformed' and shapeless, 'an awkward spontaneity . . . *where purpose or intent* has not yet crystallized.' (*Ibid.* p. 18, emphasis is ours).

Krugman's data confirm the process of deduction leading to the consequences of habituation of a visual stimulus, and his conclusions as to the uniqueness of the nature of the television response accord with the impressionistic data of others and our own theory of purposeful systems. It becomes quite clear then that while there is a learning potential within the medium it is not that which involves the content or the information volume *per se.* We will come back to this point when we compare the characteristic mode of response to television with other patterns – an exploration that has consequences for weighing up the probabilities of scenarios for superficiality and segmentation.

We will just pick up two additional points from Krugman. The first is that his subject had a television set at home and was therefore habituated already. We do not know how long it takes for the extinction of alpha block to occur. But the fact that the subject took only 30 seconds to establish the patterned response confirms conclusions from the literature that *days* must elapse before habituation response disappears, and secondly that on re-presentation of the conditioned stimulus (TV) there is an almost instantaneous renewal of the habituation effect.

Secondly, Krugman's data that we have presented here build on previous studies which have shown that TV is a *low involvement* medium. 'The same kinds of advertising in TV and print evoked in the TV form many fewer personal connections between the advertisement content and something in the life content of the viewer.' (*Ibid.* p. 1). While adding to our conclusion that television de-activates, these data confirm that not only does television not instruct or produce further control over potential courses of action, but that it further erodes the choice situation in that it decreases the contact between externality and the unique personality of the viewer himself. That is, while it informs in creating *a sense of familiarity* this does not touch the irrational, old brain-based configuration that is essentially involved in a personal choice, a personal judgement. Therefore even in this sense TV, the function of *informing*, is incomplete – as Krugman points out this kind of familiarity leads to an *unformed* and shapeless response – a dissociated or anonymous depersonalized response.

Starting with habituation and Krugman's data it is possible to see a relationship between the blank-visual-field and sensory deprivation. If the ascending reticular relays have actively blocked incoming visual information, regular viewing is going to amount to visual sensory deprivation or more seriously perceptual deprivation (Vernon 1970, p. 109 and 111).

Table 9.4.2. makes the relationship between television and deprivation quite unambiguous in terms of nature and degree of effect. Deprivation data are drawn from Heron's 1957 presentation and have been translated back into percentages to give a common base to both sources. Both Krugman and Heron used electrodes in the occipital region.

Reading across and down Table 9.4.2.A. establishes quite clearly that Krugman's subject was responding to everyday conditions in exactly the same manner as Heron's 'normal' subjects. Her pattern of response falls centrally within the normal range, closer to the pattern of A than those of B or C. All four subjects show more fast wave activity than alpha and more alpha than slow wave activity, under these conditions.

In Table 9.4.2.B. we have a direct comparison of the effects of watching television and perceptual deprivation. Each of the four subjects show a reversal to the predominance of slow plus alpha waves. Ninety six hours of deprivation is a fairly lengthy experimental period and yet Krugman's subject was as seriously affected by a few minutes television as subject C was by his 96 hour experience. The change in B's pattern of response from a very high percentage of fast wave activity under normal conditions to the low percentage after deprivation suggests that people with a normally low per-

Table 9.4.2. Comparison of effects of both television and sensory deprivation with normal waking state.
(Percentage of time spent in 3 ranges of wave frequences)

A	Krugman's subject under active (print) condition	Heron's subjects under normal active (0 hours of deprivation) condition		
		A	B	C
slow	10 ⎫	12 ⎫	4 ⎫	4 ⎫
	⎬ 43	⎬ 44	⎬ 14	⎬ 42
alpha	33 ⎭	32 ⎭	10 ⎭	38 ⎭
fast	57	56	86	58
Total	100	100	100	100

B	Krugman's subject during TV viewing	Heron's subjects after 96 hours of deprivation		
		A	B	C
slow	45 ⎫	30 ⎫	57 ⎫	17 ⎫
	⎬ 75	⎬ 91	⎬ 95	⎬ 74
alpha	30 ⎭	61 ⎭	38 ⎭	57 ⎭
fast	25	9	5	26
Total	100	100	100	100

centage of alpha frequency might be more susceptible to the effects of television than others.

Fortunately Krugman has provided photos of the EEG tracing for the last two seconds of reading and the first two seconds of TV viewing. Figure 9.4. compares Krugman's record with those of Heron's deprived subjects and a normal drowsiness tracing from Gibbs and Gibbs. The difference between the pattern for print and viewing is immediately obvious.

After a search of EEG records in general the Gibbs' pattern is the closest we can find to Krugman's viewing record. But it is obvious that it is *not* the same pattern. It would appear that the tracing recorded during viewing is so far unique.

Having established that there are empirical grounds for linking viewing and deprivation we would expect parallel perceptual and behavioural effects. These together with the implications of the following data are discussed in 10.1.

Figure 9.4. Krugman's records.

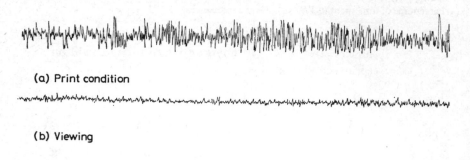

(a) Print condition

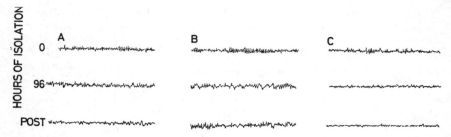

(b) Viewing

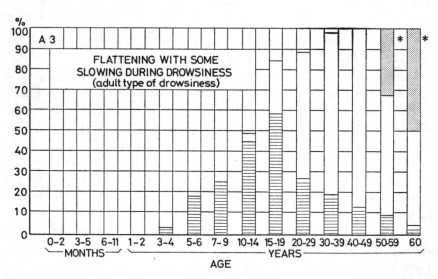

Heron's records. Normal and deprivation conditions.

(Gibbs and Gibbs. *Atlas of electroencephalography*, 1950.)

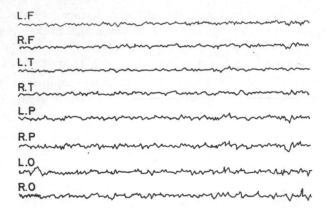

(Gibbs and Gibbs. *Atlas of electroencephalography*, 1950.)

9.5. Old brain function

Let us now go back and look at what the old brain, the rhinencephalon is doing while the functioning of the neo-cortex is impaired by the television signal.

The thesis is that while some parts of the old brain come directly and indirectly, through the reticular formation, under the control of sensory afferents, there is in general an 'inverse relation between hippocampal and cortical activity . . . maintained during rest or sleep' (Grossman, p. 631). This has significant consequences for television viewers; while the neocortex rests or sleeps the old brain comes out to play.

Nearly all particular structures within the old brain have been identified at some time as originating impulses *e.g.* area 24, the anterior part of the cingulate gyrus, which through connections with the reticular substance blocks spontaneous thalamocortical activity, suppresses electrical activity of the cortex, and paralyses thought and action (Maclean, 1964, p. 190). The inverse activity relation between old brain and new is a two-way confirming and reinforcing system. 'It is possible that the limbic system mediates arousal to internal drive stimulation . . . whereas the reticular formation mediates an arousal response to external stimulation.' (Grossman, p. 638). But, as the reticular formation also assists in deactivating other internal drive mechanisms the old brain will be active in its own right without necessarily arousing cortical awareness.

'If the old brain were the kind of brain that could tie up symbolically a number of unrelated phenomena, and at the same time lack the analyzing ability of the word brain to make a nice discrimination of their differences; it is possible to conceive how it might become foolishly involved in a variety of ridiculous correlations. Lacking the help and control of the neo-cortex, its impressions would be discharged without modification into the hypo-thalamus and lower centres.' (Maclean, 1964, p. 200). It 'eludes the grasp of the intellect because its animalistic and primitive structure makes it im-possible to communicate in verbal terms.' (p. 201). The hippocampal forma-tion and associated structures are implicated in the 'dreamy state' (Hughlings Jackson), 'a kind of 'double consciousness' . . . (where) the individual has the sense of being in contact with reality, but at the same time has the *feeling* he was experiencing a dream or something that had happened before.' (*Ibid.* p. 185).

A sense of familiarity? 'Maybe I've seen it on TV.'

In addition to mediating the sense of smell, the old brain serves as a non specific activator for all cortical activities influencing appropriately such functions as memory, learning and *affective behaviour* (*Ibid.* p. 184, emphasis is ours). But the old brain will be reviewing and creating affective associa-tions – a dream function – in isolation from the structures that are critical for the awareness and integration of this material, *i.e.* while these structures have been deactivated and are under the control of the external stimulus. The old brain becomes even more dissociated from the total function of man than usual.

9.6. Black and white versus colour

Altogether then we have a picture of a structure which is split three ways; an old brain and two new brains. The old brain is most active when the new brains are resting or shut down and relies on the function of dreaming to make known or accessible to consciousness and analysis the results of its work. The two new brains also rely heavily on each other for the execution of each distinctive function and in order again to make a conscious, workable and integrated picture of the function of the whole system.

One of the right hemisphere's most important functions is to allow for 'echo time' in the processing of incoming information (Gazzaniga, p. 142). This reverberation time allows 'the system to check and cross-check the proposition and subsequently possibly to initiate qualifying remarks.' (*Ibid.*

p. 143). The fact that a large number of subjects show alpha rhythms of higher mean voltage and of somewhat wider distribution over the right hemisphere than the left may demonstrate this echo time (Peper, 1972).

As we shall see the nature of these 'qualifying remarks' is heavily tied to the emotional and affective systems and serves in itself to integrate man's logical and cognitive processes with his own unique self and the primitive and collective unconsciousness of man. 'Separating or destroying the processing system usually active in assisting the propositional system, namely the right hemisphere, would indeed have the effects observed' in split brain experiments (Gazzaniga, p. 143).

On top of this we have the fact that the old brain and the right neo-cortex are more closely linked in nature and function than are the old brain and the left neo-cortex. Certain sorts of incoming data go straight to the right cortex. These include colour and music, not words, but tone of voice, tactile recognition, the perception of certain kinds of spatial relations particularly, we suspect, the perception of similarity, and the recognition of faces (Gazzaniga, p. 104, Zurif *et al.*, 1972, Milner *et al.*, 1972, Rosenzweig, 1972).

Compared with the active and objectifying allocentric perception of form and structure, the perception of *colour* and *light* does not require an active and selective attitude. They *impinge* upon the eye, which does not have to seek them out attentively but *reacts* to their impact. Goethe speaks of their sensual-moral effect, and describes how one is . . . carried away by various feelings.

'Goldstein has shown how *the impact of color affects the entire organism and is especially marked in patients in whom the objectifying attitude is impaired.*' (Schachtel, 1959, p. 107-108, emphasis is ours).

These, particularly colour and the *recognition of faces*, form the basic stimuli from which human affects develop and consolidate. As we shall see below, interference with the development of right hemispherical function in children could result in permanent retardation of affective functioning and thus fully human functioning.

It seems very likely that the effects of colour TV, arising from its interference with right brain functioning, will be multiplicative of, not just additive, to the effects of black-and-white TV.

Thus, viewing black-and-white TV causes:

1. massive reduction in the function of the left cortex;
2. some reduction of function in the right and also lower structures;
3. a breakdown in communication between right and left such that old brain and right hemisphere functions will be pretty well rendered inaccessible

to logical, conscious processing, the right hemisphere will still be able to do some processing of information received directly, apart from the simple visual signal.

Whilst viewing black-and-white TV the right hemisphere is likely to be actively engaged in some level of review process. This review is not the analytical thinking cngagcd in by thc left-hemisphere when for instance reading print (an active reflection on what is being read, awareness of awareness), it is the 'primary process' thinking of the right hemisphere – the lazy, easy, daydreaming of free association.

But the signal from a coloured television, while maintaining its habituation effect, is simultaneously flooding and tying up the processing capability of the right. The spare capacity of the right to provide 'processing space', the 'echo time', will be used in the effort to process the further dimension of colour. Communication between right and left and integration of logical-verbal and irrational-affective will be even further reduced. Thus the feelies and smellies of the Brave New World were only extending this process of capture and subversion from within to a full range of old brain functions.

As the co-ordination of the separate and specialized right and left functions breaks down, the greater the dissociation and the chance of resulting superficiality of response, if any. Given the prolonged effects of habituation, the response after television is turned off, is likely to be more superficial or without depth (reaction rather than a response) to colour TV than to black-and-white. Because of the accumulation of old brain processes and material that has been denied channels during the habituation experience, the ideo-motor centre is more likely to trigger impulsive, aggressive acts when its function is restored.

9.7. TV is inherently rewarding

Most of the reward and punishment centres that have been isolated have been in the complexes containing the thalamus and hypothalamus. As most of the centres isolated so far have been rewarding rather than punishing (Grossman, p. 591) there is a pretty good chance that stimulation of the thalamus and hypothalamus is going to be rewarding. The thalamus in particular determines whether or not the sensation is pleasant or unpleasant, i.e. it is the critical structure in terms of the affective nature of a sensation (Guyton, p. 239). 'If the sensations are pleasant the person becomes quite tranquil; if unpleasant, he usually becomes excited and takes steps to remedy the situation.' (*Ibid.* p. 249).

Television does provide a simple constant repetitive stimulus and it has no inbuilt stop signals. Purposeful behaviour ceases when the object is obtained but television is 'endless' (*cf.* Pawley). Even consummatory behaviour like eating and sex have built in limits (except in cases of extreme damage of pathology) but viewers, like James Old's rats with electrodes implanted in the pleasure centres, or the hypnotized person, seem to require the interruption of some external duty or command. We are dealing here with a reward system that is *irrational*.

The role of the old brain contributes somewhat to this rewarding function in the same fashion as it does during conventional 'day dreaming'. It is pleasant, given comfortable relaxed surroundings, to bask in the flow of id-like associations – another form of massage.

Dember (1960) has concluded that stimulus complexity can serve as a rewarding operation in the establishment of instrumental learning (Dember, p. 365). Similarly that 'perceptual variety is basic to the motivational and emotional states of the individual.' (*Ibid.* p. 369). That this is the essence of the paradox and confirms the irrationality of the response to television leaves us in no doubt that we have to agree with Krugman that it is the medium itself, and its starkness, that elicits the characteristic response; and that this forms the basis of the rewarding function, not the everchanging content. This is the obverse conclusion to what would have been reached by a study of the high variety of content, but did not question television in relation to the structure and function of the human nervous system. It shows that man is as perverse in choosing this way to spend his time as were Old's rats in preferring electrical stimulation of pleasure centres in their brains to food, sex, novelty or complexity, or other conventional rewards. Man can be seduced from purposeful functioning in such a way that he is unable to become aware of his deficit. That man's pleasurable vices can be used to degrade him (Huxley, 1932) does suggest a failing in an otherwise extremely well designed system.

9.8. Effects on the motor system

Personal observation by the authors and their friends lead to a unanimous conclusion that television tends to put you to sleep. In fact once you have set yourself up in front of it, together with all the necessities, you feel quite loathe to move at all.

We will not go into detail to substantiate these observations except to mention:

1. 'Sensory-motor integration commences its long sequencing of events in the visual system itself.' (Gazzaniga, p. 58).
2. The reticular activating system is involved in a feedback loop which sends impulses down the spinal cord to increase the tone in all the muscles of the body.
3. The sympathetic nervous system functions amongst other things to prepare the organism for activity.
4. The ideo-motor centre is a key point in the control of all motor and pre-motor activity.

9.9. A note on motivation

'A communication that produces a change in any of the relative values the receiver places on possible outcomes of his choice motivates him, and hence transmits motivation.' (Ackoff and Emery, 1972, p. 144).

In the theoretical analysis of *purposeful systems* considerable attention is paid to the motivations that enter into choice behaviour as 'relative intentions'. When the question is raised as to what produced the intentions we are primarily asking how a person is *affected* by the situation he observes.

It is clear from our data that *while television rewards it cannot motivate*; that the affects aroused by television modify only the relative intention of viewing itself.

10. The long term consequences of regular viewing

10.1. Dream deprivation and its effects

We suggest that when control of the prefrontal areas is removed by habituation to the TV stimulus the ideo-motor and common integrative areas are left in control, and hence free to act on impulse to sensory data. They are however effectively controlled by the recticular activating system during the viewing period. The reticular activating system, because of its more direct access to other internal data, will wake or throw off the habituated response before the prefrontal lobes and there will be a phase in which the ideo-motor centre is acting without control from the prefrontal areas. We would thus expect that one of the long term consequences of regular television viewing will be an increase in impulsive, and most probably aggressive, response (*cf.* p. 91, herein and *The Private Future* and *Clockwork Orange*). In 9.4. we presented data on the similarity of the effects of sleep deprivation and TV. Given this striking similarity at this level of similar function we suggest that the psychological and behavioural effects of the two may not be so different. Work has been done on impoverished environments where the critical variable is that the animal lives alone, or the child has been institutionalized. In Pawley's terms, they have both been 'privatized'. This research confirms, as far as one can generalize, Pawley's hypothesis of the far reaching and systematic effects of privatization as deprivation. It is of particular importance that impoverished (privatized) environments reduce synaptic contact (Rosenzweig *et al.*, 1972). The greater the interrelations in terms of synaptic contact the richer, the more intelligent, the mental life.

Let us consider the coincidences between deprivation, hyperactivity, psychoses of various types, dream deprivation – and television. We are not going to expound yet another uni-dimensional theory of mental illness; but, whatever the primacy of the chicken or the egg there is a commonly acknowledged thread. Some of the data which we present below acknowledges the development of various forms of childhood behaviour disorders into adult forms

Table 10.1. Matrix of correspondencies in theory and evidence.

	Hyperactive children*	Sensory deprivation** Slow waves (cortical) (1)	Psychoses*** Abnormal	Dream deprivation**** Slow (cortical) Desynchronized (limbic)	Television***** Slow (cortical) (1)
EEG		Slow waves (cortical) (1)	Abnormal	Slow (cortical) Desynchronized (limbic)	Slow (cortical) (1)
BEHAVIOUR restlessness		×	×		×
distractibility		×	×		×
inattentiveness		×	Korsakoff	×	× Neophiliacs (3)
impulsiveness			×		×
irritability		×	×	×	hyperactivity and passivity (2)
			mania, manic-depression some schizophrenia		
aggressiveness			×		× (2)
violence			×		×
moody		× 'childish emotional response' (1)	×		
chip on shoulder			× paranoia		
suspicious		×	× some schizophrenia	×	× (8)
low self-esteem			×		'indifference'
low motivation		×	× depression		privatization (2)
		×	depersonalization (self-other defect)	×	'alienation'
speech difficulties			×		
poor co-ordination		×	×	×	
poor performance		×	×	×	
?			short term memory deficit	×	× (2)
		thinking impaired		×	
		perceptual disturbances		×	
		hallucinations		×	time distortion (6)

		having dreams while awake (1) (3) susceptible to super-natural superstition (1)		× (bookshops) fascination for doom (Ellis) see p. 102
SLEEP AND DREAMS	sleep disturbances	sleep disturbances	sleep disturbances REM sleep deficit Delta wave sleep deficit	sleeping tablets (4) soma (5) tranquilizers and barbiturates (incr. sales) compensatory sleep (7)

References to table 10.1

* Stewart, 1970
Mendelson *et al.*, 1971
Claghorn *et al.*, 1971

** 1. Heron, 1957
2. Solomon *et al.*, 1957
3. Hebb, 1955
4. Rosenzweig *et al.*, 1972
5. Goldberger and Holt (1958) in Vernon, 1970

*** Meissner, 1968, (a) and (b)
Fast, 1967
Sandor, 1967
Mendels *et al.*, 1971

**** Meissner, 1968, (a) and (b)

***** 1. Krugman, 1970
2. Pawley, 1973
3. Booker, 1969
4. Bradbury, 1953
5. Huxley, 1932
6. Fabun, 1969
7. SydneyTelegraph, Sun.30th March, 1975
8. Pearlin, see Table 7.2.12 (p. 60)

which go under different labels. It occurs to us that 'dissociation' is a social science equivalent for 'schizophrenia' and the data on both a descriptive symptom level and on a neurophysiological level tends to bear out this synonymity.

Therefore, the first question we ask is what is television doing to dreaming? We ask this question because dreaming is a biological necessity for man. Reduction or simplification of directed conscious thought seems to be more tolerable to human beings. We expect that reduction would reduce the need for and hence the amount of dreaming. The waking experience of watching TV has already been reduced by TV producers to predigested common iconic forms – the better to hold the attention of as many as possible. Thus the TV presentation of an hour in a 'Coronation Street' pub is less likely to create material for working over in dreams than an hour spent in one's own local where one is much more directly implicated in what is said, or not said. In the latter, life and its implications do not stop at the switch of a knob. The reduction in dream work should be a simple function of time spent before TV. Its effects should be cumulative.

Table 10.1. presents a series of correspondencies in various pathologies. It is our contention that the critical link between the five columns is sleep, but more particularly dream deprivation. While actual hard data on the effects of television is almost non-existent there is also much confusion within available data on the function of dreaming and its role in health and pathology. Our hypothesis is that television seriously distorts the dream cycle. There is always an effort on the part of the organism to compensate for this distortion and much of the waking behaviour of the Children of Change (Fabun) could be seen as a compensatory syndrome.

We consider that the obvious conformity (to each other, not to elders) of the young today, is one dimension of this phenomenon; there is a general shapeless response which does not bear in any given individual the stamp of unique personal *vitality*. In the sense of John Wyndham's *Midwich Cuckoos* the television generation have become sub-parts of a collective and anonymous entity.

This generation might have to work much harder at being groupie and establishing human contact precisely because their phylogenetically older and more uniquely defining characteristics have been lost from awareness both to themselves and others, by the technologically based process of dissociation. (Have you ever noticed how loudly a lot of young people speak? – shades of screaming in the wilderness – or how do I know its me? or that I'm real?) Familiarity breeds a short term sort of confidence, but not competence and the confidence that flows from that. Fabun sees this as the young taking over the function of TV producers. 'The tactics are excactly those of the TV sponsor. Reach enough people in a dramatic enough way and you will sell your product yourself.' (Fabun, 1969, p. 13).

The young seem to have gone out of their way to make up for some deficit. Apart from the extended periods of time they spend just talking to each other, their variation on print – the underground press – makes greater demands on the reader than does the old fashioned ordinary newspaper or magazine. 'The purpose is to induce the reader to look at things in a new way, and to be able to do so he must be prepared to toil his way through the mass of confusion and complexity set before him.' (*Ibid.* p. 28).

It would seem as if the incongruities of print and TV have been intuitively recognized and set, one against the other, to make this difference apparent. That there is a 'press' toward truly and wholly integrated human function on the part of people is not in doubt. The role of television however *is*.

Talking about what you have seen on television, particularly amongst young children, is a very popular pastime, and we suggest that this is a form of compensatory activity or 'secondary revision' (Breznitz, 1971). Secondary revision seeks to restore something in the nature of sense and coherence following dream work. Its aim is to change the material offered into something like a daydream; *readymade fantasies are preferred to new dream – thoughts (Ibid.* p. 408, emphasis is ours). If no processing is happening during the viewing period it is easy to see that there will be an extensive need for an interpretative and integrative secondary revision during waking hours.

That dreaming, as the third major type of function after non-dreaming sleep and wakefulness, is a cognitive process is no longer in doubt (Meissner, 1968, a and b). We will here be concerned with dreaming as a total phenomenon although the neurophysiological pattern described as NREM[1] sleep ('high amplitude, slow synchronous cortical activity along with hippocampal desynchronization', *Ibid.* p. 699), is remarkably similar to the pattern we have described as that operating while viewing.

'The dream process has a specific function in the psychic economy which is fulfilled by no other mechanism.' (*Ibid.* p. 77). Dream deprivation has profound psychological effects and 'must play a significant role in adaptation of the organism.' (*Ibid.* p. 65). 'Psychotic episodes are not infrequently preceded by periods of insomnia . . . experimental sleep and/or dream deprivation can produce pseudo psychotic symptoms.' (*Ibid.* p. 66). A small sample –

---

1. Non Rapid Eye Movement.

'Combination of central activation with peripheral blocking has prompted comparison of REM sleep and schizophrenic withdrawal.' (*Ibid*. p. 64).

'Considerable overlap in the symptoms of schizophrenia and psycho-motor epilepsy.' (*Ibid*. p. 71).

'It is established that aggressive, anti-social behaviour in a child may precede the development of schizophrenia in the adult.' (Mendelson *et al*., p. 278).

'Depression – a long standing deficiency in state REM sleep.' (Mendels and Hawkins, 1971).

'Hyperactive children have unusually high D^2-Times and high REM density within D-periods.' (Small and Feinberg, 1969, in Hartmann, 1970).

'D-deprivation may produce improvement in depressed patients.' (Vogel *et al*., 1968, in Hartmann, 1970).

One of the most commonly observed effects of psychotic and pseudo-psychotic states is that of lowered self-esteem sometimes to the point of feeling a separation from the world, being in limbo (Fast, 1967), a confused sense of identity, etc. (Lorand, 1967).

Difficulties with self-esteem regulation is a function of lack of relatively enduring *organization of qualities* constructed by the ego to identify that which it perceives and conceives as being the self (de Saussure, 1971). Irene Fast has suggested that the mechanism leading to this lack of organization in depression is the inadequate establishment of self – other boundaries in the second six months of life. The picture looks very close to the disorganized and unintegrated limbic functioning occasioned by dream deprivation and sensory deprivation. It is a near perfect description of hyper-active children. 'Some psychiatrists have suggested on clinical grounds that these children may be depressed.' (Hartmann, p. 317).

One of the most notable traits of people who suffer from self-esteem regulation difficulties 'is their readiness to attribute an unusual degree of power to visual forms' (de Saussure, 1971). It is also a striking characteristic of primitive peoples. Narcissism (another form of privatization?) as one type of self-esteem defect is characterized by magical beliefs and regressed self-images. Self-esteem difficulties are common in Korsakoff patients where *primary process kinds of organization* are demonstrated (Meissner, (b), p. 705). 'The Korsakoff patient functions in waking moments with cognitive organization which parallels in many striking aspects the cognitive organization of normal dreaming. The thought processes which subserve logical reconstruction and recall of experience are severely impaired.' (*Ibid*. p. 705). One of the most striking deficits arising from the primary process organization is in activities requiring planning or sequential organization of thought patterns or material to be learned. Korsakoff patients also have in common with regular television viewers an impairment of recent memory.

2. D stands for dream.

'Momentary forgetting is associated with an altered ('*distracted*') state of consciousness and the content of such forgotten thoughts has much in common with latent dream themes. The entire picture of momentary forgetting is consistent with a transient shift in the pattern of activation which relatively increases excitation in the septo-hippocampal circuits and produces transient states of disorganized memory function.' (*Ibid.* p. 704). 'Momentary forgetting neurophysiologically, as well as psychologically, may be a transient waking equivalent of the cognitive organization of dreaming.' (*Ibid.* p. 705).

This is the pattern of activation which we suggest is not the transient but characteristic mode of response to television. This is consistent with Atkinson and Shiffrim's 1971 proposal that short term memory mechanisms are primarily those of rehearsal. If there is no rehearsal which is the active processing response we would expect short term forgetting. 'All human information processing requires keeping track of incoming stimuli and bringing such input into contact with already stored material.' (Posner, 1969, p. 49). 'Data . . . presented from simultaneous audio-visual presentation argue strongly for the importance of verbal encoding if visual information is to survive in the presence of continued input.' (*Ibid.* p. 54). That is, short term memory failure in terms of content may be the most readily observable symptom of television as waking dreaming.

'The balance of activation of the hippocampus by these two input systems determines the state of functional integration in the ongoing behaviour of the organism' (Meissner, 1968a, p. 68), *i.e.* from subcortical and cortical structures. Thus it is easy to see how, if television can provide an interference within waking hours of this balance, functional integration can be damaged. It is entirely possible that television disturbs the built-in biological rhythm which dictates the periodicity of the oscillations between dream work stimulated from above and below (*Ibid.* p. 68).

'Sensory deprivation in the non-sleeping subject; the isolation from prestructured experience . . . produces a disorganization which affects the functioning of limbic structures and introduces a regressive movement to consciousness . . . There is a release of unbound and unmoderated unconscious energy. This release of unbound energy disorganizes limbic functioning and produces the disorganization of experience found in hallucinatory phenomena and feelings of unreality.' (*Ibid.* p. 76). 'The hyperactivity syndrome is not confined to children.' (Stewart, 1970). Much of the impulsive Clockwork Orange type of behaviour in current Western society looks very like the release of unbound and unmoderated unconscious energy. It could well be one of the by-products of the suppression of sensory afferent pathways by television with its consequent deprivation.

A similar conclusion can be drawn from the work of Van der Kolk and

Hartmann (1968) and Wood (1962) who found that sensory and social deprivation both increased amounts of REM sleep. They suggest the organism needs a certain amount of external stimulation and that if this is lacking, internal sources of stimulation (such as REM sleep) may increase (Hartmann, 1970, p. 51).

Heron's discovery that sensory or perceptually deprived subjects become obsessed by the supernatural and superstition rings a particular chord of present day revivalist fascination with astrology, mysticism, the occult and doom. Bob Ellis in his article on cinematic cataclysms (*Nation Review*, April 11-17, 1975, p. 675) asks 'why are we all thus half in love, of late, with the coming image of doom?' He suggests that we are 'trapped and struggling within *some huge and turbulent* object and can't get out.' (emphasis is ours). We need not elaborate on Jung and the nature of the collective unconscious.

Favourable results have been obtained from *sleep treatment* in non-psychotic states, anxiety neuroses, phobic states, obsessives, alcoholics, some mania depressions and particularly the phobic anxiety – depersonalization syndrome (Meissner, p. 66) whose symptoms are highly reminiscent of Pawley's description of modern man:

1. spontaneous changes in consciousness;
2. distressing feelings of a change in self;
3. an oppressive sense of loss of spontaneity in movement, feeling and thought;
4. *deja vu* experiences (it is the role of the old brain to produce such double consciousness).

If this is a possibility then it becomes more obvious that the hallucinatory activity of sensory deprivation is indistinguishable from what we know about dreams (Hebb, 1955). 'The stability of man's mental state is dependent in some sense on adequate perceptual contact with the outside world.' (Meissner, p. 76). Given the prolonged effects of habituation to television it is possible that there is less than adequate contact with the outside world even after the viewing period has ceased. Zubek *et al.* (1961) exposed their subjects to homogeneous perceptual stimulation over a period of two weeks. Although there was some improvement when the situation returned to normal the resulting abnormalities in brain activity were still present a week later (see p. 80). There was a corresponding loss of motivation (Vernon, 1970, p. 113). Drabman and Thomas (1974) compared the response time of two groups of children to the demands of the same social situation; one group who had been watching television and one which had not. The television group took significantly longer to respond than the non-television group and more of them did not respond at all. The viewing period for the television group was only eight minutes.

It is worth exploring this small piece of data a little further. The two groups had been placed in a position of responsibility for looking after by closed circuit TV two smaller children whom they believed had been left to play on their own. Both groups were specifically told to go and get adult help if 'anything does happen.' The two young children began to fight which appeared to end in the destruction of the closed circuit TV equipment. The meaningfulness of this situation makes this data very powerful. That most of a group of primary age children did not attempt to get help to prevent damage to younger children or expensive equipment when they had explicitly been given the responsibility to do this, is some confirmation of the habituation hypothesis and Pawley's contention that television has far reaching social consequences. While Drabman and Thomas explain that the differences in response that they found were due to the violence portrayed in the initial film we are led to suspect that it was the eight minute exposure to the medium itself which produced their results. If Krugman's subject took only 30 seconds to assume the characteristic television response pattern this would have been almost certainly well established in a group of middle class American children after eight minutes. 'What is needed to maintain the integrity of normal functioning is not quantity of sensation, but a continuous meaningful contact with the outside world.' (*Ibid*. p. 76). This is exactly what Pawley and our own data would lead us to believe is not being maintained.

'Is it possible that the disturbances of psychic functioning produced by sleep and dream deprivation are reflections of disorganization in limbic functionings and that the beneficial effects of sleep treatment are due to a reorganization of disordered limbic functioning?' (Meissner, p. 66). Our attempt to put into perspective the effects of television would suggest an affirmative answer. In both *Brave New World* and *Fahrenheit 451* the effects of television were controlled on one level by consumption of 'soma' and sleeping tablets. We wonder then if the increasing use of tranquillizers and barbiturates today has a relation to disorganized old brain function and increasing consumption of television, particularly colour television.

10.2. Television and the young

'The importance to the organism of maintaining contact with the external world has long been recognized. Animals raised in isolation showed disturbances in behaviour and in learning capacity.' (Meissner, p. 75).

Vernon (1970) has concluded from a survey of the literature that 'indefinite prolongation of exposure to perceptual deprivation might result in *long-term impairment* of cognitive ability and emotional stability. Furthermore, the effects might be even more severe with young children' (p. 116). 'The neonate is . . . an extremely exploratory creature, with a split, or partially split, brain.' (Gazzaniga, p. 132). In his normal process of development both right and left systems develop some over-lapping as well as some specialized functions. But during the process of development 'dominance is waxing, and information duplication is waning,' (*Ibid*. p. 133) at the same time 'as the brains become more communicative with each other.' (p. 133).

'The lead hemisphere, the dominant left, would be attending to external information and, while receiving and processing it, would be holding the other disengaged.' (*Ibid*. p. 134). Also, as an auto-centric sense, colour perception is predominant in infancy and early childhood (Schachtel, 1959, p. 112).

Similarly research data indicate that REM sleep in particular may have an ontogenetic function. Whereas the adult level of REM activity is in the vicinity of 20% that of the mature neonate is around 50% and there is a plateau at the age of 5 years (Meissner, 1968).

Our questions are simply, what happens to the process of development of:

1. specialized lateralized functions.
2. the communication between right and left brains.
3. ontogenetic organization and integration of emotional and cognitive process.
4. self – other boundaries.

when children are subject from an early age to the dissociative effects of television?

The most common form of treatment for hyperactive children is some form of amphetamine (Stewart, 1970, see also Claghorn *et al.*, 1971). 'Amphetamines act on the reticular formation . . . and produce specific effects on the metabolism of norepinephrine, or noradrenalin in the brain cells. Norepinephrine is highly concentrated in such areas as the hypothalamus and the brain stem, and injection of minute amounts of norepinephrine in the reticular formation of the rat lowers the animal's activity level and responsiveness. Amphetamines have been shown markedly to reduce D-time in man. Their effects are dramatic but short lasting. The similar decrease in D-time produced by anti-depressants has a much longer term effect.' (Hartmann, p. 311). Amphetamine 'may therefore repair a deficit in the activity of norepinephrine or in some way restore the normal balance of activity between norepinephrine and acetylcholine.' (Stewart, p. 198). When the thalamus and reticular formation in particular go into a state of paralysis during a viewing period it becomes clear that the norepinephrine and acetylcholine balance is bound to be disturbed and that the effects will reverberate throughout the total autonomic nervous system.

While the data on the relations of depression, hyperactivity and deprivation are full of contradictions and inconsistencies there is clearly an underlying biochemical syndrome. This is affected by levels of sensory and perceptual stimulation and also by disturbances more generally to sleep-wakefulness cycles. Television viewing's interference with these normal systems and cycles probably produces similarly abnormal effects.

As watching television is such an ubiquitous phenomenon it is almost inevitable that some individuals will be more sensitive to its effects than others (cf. subject B in Table 9.4.2.).

There is generally a positive correlation between beta, theta and motor activity and a negative correlation between alpha and motor activity. But for example, there are a proportion of individuals who never show alpha rhythm and there are some individuals classified as 'motor passive'. These people have a less than average level of asymmetry of EEG in the frontal lobes with a higher level of asymmetry in the occipital lobes. There are sufficient variations within the range of normal function to account more than adequately for the 6-10% of children who are currently classified (U.S.A.) as hyperactive, and the increasing number of adults who are classified under different labels but display the same constellation of symptoms.

We have no proof but our suggestion is that given all the above, there is a very good chance that the recent and continuing epidemic of hyperactive children could have as much to do with television as in 1918 that epidemic had to do with encephalitis. We think there are grounds for predicting that as colour television spreads across Australian society our figures for hyperactive children will move closer to current American figures.

10.3. Some speculations back into reality

Putting together all the available evidence our opinion is that television acts in such a way as to dampen down the sympathetic system, thereby precluding a *vigilance* (Hernandez-Peon, 1969, p. 418) or *flight-fight* response and inhibits the response capability of the parasympathetic system – thereby precluding the possibility of a 'creative' pairing response (Bion, 1961). The comparison of the known and hypothesized effects of television and the same order of effects of transcendental meditation makes quite clear that while transcendental meditation may provide the internal neurophysiological and bio-chemical environment for a creative response, television does not (Wallace *et al.*, 1972, Orme *et al.*, 1972, Seeman *et al.*, 1972). While slow wave forms are elicited by meditation they are under the control of the individual and are therefore a purposeful choice. Transcendental meditation could be one way of bringing under conscious control the 'creative pause' (Szekely, 1967).

The characteristic mode of response to television is controlled (habituated) by the stimulus itself and cannot therefore be a purposeful response. This reduces the choice situation by handing over control – especially, note, to a piece of technology. It looks like Bion's statement that the individual has a desire for security and dependence is an answer to that (Bion, 1961, p. 91). Television may well be the ultimate answer to 'the hatred of learning by experience.' (*Ibid.* p. 86). The individual 'wishes, even with the impulses that are not satisfied in the dependent group, for a state in which, without undergoing the pains of growth, he could be fully equipped for group life.' (*Ibid.* p. 91).

We are suggesting that television evokes the basic assumption of *dependency*. It must evoke a basic assumption because it is essentially an emotional and irrational activity (compare Old's rats). Television is the non-stop leader who provides nourishment and protection.

The fact that the literature is almost completely devoid of research studies of the effects of television is enough to alert us to the very real possibility that questioning and confrontation of television has been put aside in order to maintain its role as leader in the dependent mode. The dissociation that television provokes on all levels confirms Bion in that the leader should be 'mad' or a 'genius' yet at the same time people feel 'compelled' to believe he is a dependable leader. It other words, television can be seen partly as a technological analogue of the hypnotist. Hypnotism seems to involve a willingness on the part of the subject and we have noted television's 'lever pressing' effect. Our hypnotist in this case is not concerned to demonstrate his power and control in more directions than one-continued viewing. The 'plan' (Miller *et al.*, 1960) of television as it structures behaviour is simple and unchanging.

But this is where the analogy ends. The subjects of television do not appear to change themselves in the direction of the hypnotist's commands; they do not respond to the content. They only, as Bion documents, make use ... of such parts ... as they can conveniently weld into what appears to be an already well-established *corpus* of belief (Bion, p. 83). The bit they appear to have chosen is the opportunity to stimulate a 'pleasure centre', the collective unconscious, and the re-activation of myths. The rest of the pattern into which television fits will be explored below.

This is another dimension of the rewards that television offers. The painfulness of having to take responsibility for one's own learning is automatically handed over to the hypnotic, high-volume, information machine. The fact that no real learning may occur, no increase in personal understandings, is of little consequence to a society which is prepared to accept the illusion that it does – as long as it establishes 'a sense that the situation is familiar and unchanging' (Bion, p. 78) – as long as the escape from responsibility and control continues to be rewarding.

10.4. Television and education

In so far as television cannot instruct nor therefore enlighten, its role in the learning process is a strictly limited one. It can simply inform, or in William James' words provide 'knowledge of'. As a means of creating some familiarity with exotic places, peoples and events, television will be more effective than other media. But familiarity is not understanding. A degree of familiarity may be a good introduction to a new or difficult problem. A high degree of familiarity without the other necessary components of the learning process often deceives, giving a feeling of understanding and precluding the desire to learn more. 'Familiarity breeds contempt.' There must also be present in a learning situation some 'knowledge about' and this cannot be provided by television; it can only come through an active and personal involvement with the subject (Ackoff and Emery, 1972, p. 42-53).

If one of the purposes of education is to produce active responsible citizens with a real understanding of their world and their affairs, it becomes obvious that the informing function of television cannot provide a major part of education. While it may play a small but useful role in providing 'knowledge of' it must be enmeshed in a total process and system which is creative, dynamic and purposeful. The risk is that it will always, insistently and insidiously, subvert the learning process (see Bion, above).

For those who are already highly motivated to learn, television may be more of a nuisance than a help. These people will be forced to spend part of their time and energy avoiding its dissociating effects and will eventually find more active and satisfying ways of becoming 'familiar with'.

It is doubtful if children or adults who are actively pursuing their educational purposes will care to spend much time in front of their television, unless they have run themselves into a cognitive overload situation. In this case a little television can be a therapeutic massage but this is hardly an educational function.

11. Further notes on maladaptive strategies

11.1. Organizational consequences of dissociation: laissez-faire

Let us look briefly at some implications of the above for social and organizational life. Krugman's data confirm the mass of indirect evidence that an habituation process is the primary response to television. Firstly this means that the characteristic slow wave response will not have completely disappeared for some days after the habituation experience. After a night of watching television it is entirely possible that the variety of stimuli you make contact with the next morning will be received and treated by your nervous system as was the information coming through the set. You go to work *distracted* and you do not perform in a purposeful, analytic manner. There is a spread of effect from leisure into work, school, family life, community, business etc.

Our picture is one of television as a 'malignant tool'; one that has been 'used to contract, eliminate, or replace human functions', 'reducing the range of choice and motivation.' (Illich, 1973, p. 85). We must ask then, for what or for whom it has been a tool, and our answer to this question has been elaborated in 9.1. But a tool can grow out of man's control and while television is *the* telecommunications tool for a mature bureaucratized society its effects may well produce the mirror image of bureaucratic organizations: *laissez-faire*.

'Finally, the whole system came crashing down in one last paroxysm of dolls and guns. *Reality* was left in ruins and *Possible*, stripped of all its dolls, reverted to a barren wilderness where chaotic improbabilities reigned supreme.' (Herbert, 1973, p. 3).

We have looked at various ways in which control and co-ordination have been attenuated or destroyed.

1. Internal to the individual, by the neurophysiological effects of television,

the individual's own conscious functioning is impaired; and the integration of sub-structural, affective and cognitive functions has been disorganized. Purposeful activity has been reduced.
2. Man has been cut off from man by the rewarding pleasure centre stimulation which effectively puts each individual into his own box.
3. The escape to secondary reality is breaking down the controlling and coordinating role that the private (public) citizen used to perform in his own community affairs. The era of the 'so what' response has effectively cut communications between traditional customs and mores, the official sources of law and order, and the man in the street.

Therefore, in the laissez-faire situation, control is located entirely within the individual and the here-and-now. Television has contributed to and reinforced this by its deteriorative effects on intra-individual control and its interpolation of a secondary reality. It has further shortened the *range of vision* (Emery *et al.*, 1974, p. 22).

These three points make clear the structural nature of laissez-faire. While the structural relations between individuals are tenuous at best within a bureaucratic society (Emery and Emery, 1974) the dissociative superficiality-increasing effects of the telecomm revolution have weakened the strong structural ties between the individual and the higher levels of societal management. In laissez-faire it is *each man for himself*. 'Our era is distinguished by much public discussion of patriotism, security, prosperity, parenthood, social welfare, community values, law and order, to singularly little real effect. So much so that it is clear that all such talk is only camouflage to obscure a guilty, but relished, private indifference, a massive withdrawal from public life and from *de facto* responsibility for any of these matters.' (Pawley, p. 114).

This further break in relations means ultimately that there can exist no longer an organized goal. All goals and purposes become individual. Laissez-faire is the organizational form of individualism without responsibility. Pawley quotes (p. 65) a saying: 'It is a shocking thing to have happened and eventually someone must take responsibility for it.' This is the language of guilt and failure mixed with the hope of a *personal* evasion of responsibility, the classic Western pattern of scapegoatism.'

Laissez-faire is an absence of persisting organization and represents *random* process, the 'collapse of community' (*cf.* Pawley, p. 103).

To say that laissez-faire approximates random process, both within the individual and his normal forms, is to say that within the process there are hidden some assumptions about the environment in which one is operating.

Laissez-faire is an interesting form in that it evokes the perception of both type I and type V environments.

For the reasons that 'we cannot conceive of adaptation occurring in such a field' as a type V (Emery *et al.*, 1974, p. 21), it is obvious that laissez-faire is not an adaptive form, even though it is the adaptive form of response to type I fields. The laissez-faire society will evoke two responses, an active and a passive. The active is an appropriate adaptive strategy within the narrow confines of randomized areas of society, like Harlem, and maladaptive within type V. The converse applies similarly. To do your own thing in a vortical situation is to self-destruct. 'Vortices develop at system boundaries when one system is moving or evolving very fast relative to the other '(*Ibid.* p. 21) and laissez-faire can only be a very transitional form of organization.

Given that there will always be a few active participants within the short laissez-faire period, it will come more than close to 'an old fashioned mad house' (Bedlam) or a Nazi concentration camp. Within a type I environment 'there is no distinction between tactics and strategy' and the only concern is with maximum advantage to oneself. At the moment one tends to think particularly here of groups of adolescents who, having been deprived of a meaning for their particular stage of life (Aries, 1960), very easily fall into a laissez-faire form. Parents, friends, strangers, all can be used, exploited without significant loss to the self, because the self is cut off from the sort of contact that would otherwise render such behaviour painful and unthinkable. There is no consumer (other) and therefore there is no necessity to consider such detail as consumer (other) satisfaction.

Scenarios based on so-called 'individual freedom' and the institutionalization of such into organizational form, founder inevitably on the conflict between individual rights. Laissez-faire is as conducive to conflict, competition and the deterioration of human relationships as is bureaucracy. We do not want to breed Marya Mannes' 'spiritual illiterates' – people without self-control and with only one goal in life – to get what they want regardless of anyone else, and to get it now. People who think freedom means the instant gratification of desire – *their* desire – and are forgiven everything because they are young.' (Pawley, p. 86).

Work and productive processes would have little future within a laissez-faire society. As laissez-faire cannot provide conditions for meeting psychological job satisfaction criteria and external control and co-ordination have disappeared, there is little chance of a society meeting its productive needs.

Let us briefly explore how laissez-faire is incapable of meeting some of the basic needs of man in an industrialized and productive society.

1. Insofar as it provides so much elbow room for the individual that he just doesn't know what to do next, *i.e.* he is always at a loose end, it cannot provide variable and optimal freedom. It is easy to see how the continuous necessity to make decisions can approximate the fatigue and pathology of overstimulation.

2. Chances of learning are severely reduced by the randomized processes of laissez-faire life. Transience and the superficiality of individual goal setting make it difficult to correlate feedback with goal. Low motivation for purposeful pursuits will reduce attempts at collecting feedback and ultimately also there is no goal setting. Because there is no goal setting there is, strictly speaking, no behaviour. The circumstances under which *conditioning* occurs are those of a *blank, unvarying environment* (Emery *et al.*, 1974, p. 23) which are exactly those we have specified as the habituated effects of the viewing situation. It is as difficult to *learn* from your experiences in a laissez-faire situation as it is to learn from your television set.

3. Over-optimal variety in a setting of casual relationships, lack of organization and total individual freedom to make personal decisions would rapidly produce boredom and its consequent pathologies (see above, *e.g.* Heron, 1957). Continually 'looking for kicks' is self-defeating.

4. By reason of the breakdown in significant human relationships there is no chance of mutual support and respect within a laissez-faire society. While informal and spasmodic relationships may occur, the quality of these is that of in-group relations, and in furthering the goal of the instantaneous in-group it is not likely to be the individual that is valued for himself.

5. There is not in laissez-faire a mechanism or criteria for deciding what is in society's interests as there is basically no longer a concept of society. Hence, it is not possible for an individual to get a sense of his unique place or contribution. All the concepts subsumed under meaningfullness are irrelevant in the laissez-faire setting. If there is no sense of a meaningful contribution there can be no sense of the quality of that contribution.

6. Neither for the individual, nor for the society, can laissez-faire provide a desirable future. Laissez-faire is such an extreme phenomenon and does so little for the individuals within it that it can only ever provide a point of transition from one form of organization to another, from one scenario to

another. That the nature of its disintegrative potential is so great may lead us to a more stable solution – that of segmentation. Segmentation could occur if an individual or a group gained sufficient means of control and co-ordination to foist a 1984 type society onto that of laissez-faire. But there are good reasons, both in terms of the means available and the nature of the environment, why there is small chance of this event.

Let us examine further what a laissez-faire society would look like. Magoroh Maruyama (1974) has provided a framework within which the paradigm of The Individualists reminds us of Pawley's 'choices in favour of privacy, in favour of individual freedom, in favour of anonymity.' (Pawley, p. 61).

The philosophical basis of laissez-faire is described (Maruyama) as nominalism: only the individual elements are real and society becomes an aggregate. Add to this the fact that as each individual serves his time alone without significant or purposeful ties with others, his motivation to build these relationships decreases – reinforcing the motivational deficit incurred by his television viewing and his bureaucratic life style. Laissez-faire is a self-feeding schedule.

The planning procedure for a community viewed as egocentric is one where everybody makes his own plans. While in terms of social policy this may be seen as 'decentralization' the combination of each planner doing his own thing without consideration for others, or a holistic appreciation, approximates to a distortion of the aesthetic principle – haphazard, hotchpotch. 'The aesthetic dimension can serve as a sort of guage for a free society.' (Marcuse, 1969, p. 35). 'The beautiful would be an essential quality of their freedom.' (*Ibid.* p. 52). 'Beauty has the power to check aggression.' (*Ibid.* p. 34). It can be only through the ideals of man that freedom is truly obtained, and that laissez-faire provides the most unfree of all possible organizational forms should become obvious (Emery *et al.*, 1974, p. 58).

In terms of the scientific paradigm, causality virtually disappears as each event is seen as independent and with its own probability. Information decays and gets lost and a blueprint must contain more information than the finished product. Perception is viewed as isolating and knowledge as selfserving – 'why bother to learn beyond one's own interests?'

Although there can be no stable power or communication patterns within laissez-faire there will be *manifestations* of power and communication. Power will be exercised by short-lived groups or mobs which by the random process within a random placid (type I) environment have discovered a temporary common interest. For the period during which they sustain this interest their aggregative power and force will be greater than that of an individual. Their behaviour under these conditions could never rise above the basic assumptions. Therefore, the nature of their communications will follow those described by Bion and Carter as being characteristic of basic assumption groups.

While functioning under a basic assumption the individual has always a feeling of incompleteness, insecurity – and therefore makes a one-dimensional response. Laissez-faire because of its inherent instability and transience of behaviour is incongruent with a segmentation scenariol. Similarly, there was no sense within any of the above data that television could brainwash, produce a given 'persuasion' or in a way pre-determine or direct on a social scale. As a mass media it is obviously serving different ends – those of dissociation, laissez-faire and superficiality.

Laissez-faire is the appropriate organizational form for a society characterized primarily by superficiality or dissociation. As an organization form of processes which are individualistic, exploitative of resources, and lead to an outcome of inhumanity which is inherently ugly, it is that form which is most removed from, and indeed completely opposed to, the conditions under which ideal-seeking behaviour can occur. It is the form which fits least well with the *nature* of man.

11.2. Two other negative scenarios

These scenarios present current thoughts on the alternatives to dissociation. We include them for the sake of completeness. Neither has the power or the relevance that dissociation has in the present context – except to lead to laissez-faire.

11.2.1. Segmentation

Both Illich (1973) and Marien (1974) have painted pictures of a segmented society where the basis of segmentation was information and knowledge. We shall briefly compare their reports although we agree with them both that this is not the future for Western society.

Illich calls his construction *managerial fascism*. Marien writes of the *Discovery and Decline of the Ignorant Society*, from the vantage point of 1983.

We have already identified above that the trends and technologies which are obvious today are those which incline more to a mass sense of dependency than a truly segmented situation such as 1984 where the 'proles' were free and self-determining within their confines. Illich and Marien have spelt out why a segmented society based on knowledge or information is a possibility but cannot develop from current trends.

'The institutionalization of knowledge leads to a more general and degrading delusion. It makes people dependent on having their knowledge produced for them. It leads to a paralysis of the moral and political imagination . . .

'This cognitive disorder rests on the illusion that the knowledge of the individual citizen is of less value than the 'knowledge' of science. The former is the opinion of individuals. It is merely subjective and is excluded from policies. The latter is 'objective' – defined by science and promulgated by expert spokesmen. This objective knowledge is viewed as a commodity which can be refined, constantly improved, accumulated and fed into a process, now called 'decision-making'. *This new methology of governance by the manipulation of knowledge-stock inevitably erodes reliance on government by people.*

'Overconfidence in 'better knowledge' becomes a self-fulfilling prophecy. People first cease to trust their own judgment and then want to be told the truth about what they know.' (Illich).

'. . . because the schools did not recognise the value of lifelong learning, most of the population of post-industrial nations discredited their own experience.' (Marien).

'No longer can each person make his or her own contribution to the constant renewal of society. The knowledge-consumer depends on getting packaged programs funneled into him. He finds security in the expectation that his neighbour and his boss have seen the same programs and read the same columns.'

'The growing impotence of people to decide for themselves affects the structure of their expectations. People are transformed from contenders for scarce resources into competitors for abundant promises.'

'It has been obvious for a long time that Western societies have been evolving towards more complex forms and processes.' (Illich).

In the midst of these long-range trends, *there was a lag in the recognition that a complex society demands a sophisticated understanding among all of its citizens.'* (Marien).

'Faced with . . . impending disasters, society can stand in wait of survival within limits set and enforced by bureaucratic dictatorship.'

'Man would live in a plastic bubble that would protect his survival and make it increasingly worthless. Since man's tolerance would become the most serious limitation to growth, the alchemist's endeavour would be renewed in the attempt to produce a monstrous type of man fit to live among reason's dreams. A major function of engineering would become the psychogenetic tooling of man himself as a condition for further growth. People would be confined from birth to death in a world-wide schoolhouse, treated in a world-wide hospital, surrounded by television screens, and the man-made environment would be distinguishable in name only from a world-wide prison.' (Illich).

'. . . the *myths* of education and science, and a sense of pseudo-ignorance created by the knowledge explosion, kept us from an earlier discovery of the problems of real ignorance, *having to do with the entire system of communicators and audience* – problems of *social complexity* and individual capacity, of production, distribution, and obsolescence of knowledge.'

'In the USA one of the major barriers was the myth that we as a nation were well educated, simply because an unprecendented number of young people spent an unprecedented amount of time in what we then called educating institutions. The false equating of 'educational attainment' with learning when much of the attainment was little more than a puberty rite, blinded us to the more fundamental ratio of qualitative achievement relative to rising needs. Even the learning attained was often socialisation for a society of the past, and was, therefore, counterproductive.'

'An equally potent binary myth was that of *technological omnipotence* and *scientific omniscience*. Because a vast quantity of scientific knowledge was accumulating, doubling every 10-15 years, a false sense of security was engendered by images of a scientific age, an automated society, the age of moon conquest.' 'Secure in their expertise, the super-specialists ignored their ignorance of larger concerns.'

'We now recognise that many of the problems of institutional stagnation and loss of authority that occurred during the 1970s could be attributed to 'drop-outs' from the non-formal processes of continuing learning. Indeed, convinced that they were knowledgeable by virtue of their credentials, many of the elites are now viewed as among the most ignorant in our society, by virtue of what they ought to have learned added to their incapacity to learn. And to think that a decade ago we considered our national manpower problem to be unemployment!'

'The knowledge 'explosion', as previously mentioned, contained a major paradox. Despite the flood of books, monographs, reports, journals and working drafts, it was discovered that *much of this knowledge was of little value in resolving the social problems of recent decades.*'

'Even as the bulk of our knowledge production shifted to a policy and/or futures orientation during the 1970s, it was felt by many that the complexity of our problems was still outstripping our capacity to manage them, consequently compounding our condition of growing ignorance. Specialised knowledge had always been the preserve of holy men or aristocratic elites. Following in this tradition, *academic elites constructed a system of communication among themselves*. But the system of education in the schools and colleges left much to be desired, and communication with the general public was practically non-existent.' (Marien).

'The bureaucratic management of human survival is unacceptable on both ethical and political grounds. (But) People could be so frightened by the increasing evidence of growing population and dwindling resources that they would voluntarily put their destiny into the hands of Big Brother.' (Illich).

But manipulation of knowledge stock will conflict inevitably with the current understandings of the common man which will lead him to a suspicion and contempt of technocrats, academics and governments (see phone freaks). Similarly, retrieval systems will tend to encourage the contemptuous to pull out sufficient information to dispute with and organize against any incoming Big Brother. As the technical education level rises the number of technology freaks will grow; we suspect to such an extent that both the institution and maintenance of 1984 could not compete with the current openness and technical ingenuity of the young well-educated society.

In examining the probabilities of segmentation and superficiality we must explore the role of telecommunications technology as it affects:

1. location of control in society;
2. judgments about the nature of information and its value;
3. location of processing or co-ordination of information.

For a truly segmented society to arise there would have to be one central source for these 3 factors. And that it would be supported by a massive telecomm system for data collection and surveillance we have no doubt. Stopping short though of a massive catastrophe we have to agree with Illich that managerial fascism would be a futile exercise and that 'with rapid social change, growing social complexity, and knowledge fragmentation, the discovery of the 'ignorant society' (is) inevitable.' (Marien).

11.2.2. Cycles of superficiality

'The very forces which rendered society capable of pacifying the struggle for existence served to repress in the individuals the need for such a liberation.' (from Marcuse; p. 50 of Emery *et al.*, 1974). What is the nature of such forces as are operating today?

We have noted dissociative trends towards a mode of dependency where individuals or groups only choose from the mass what they need to help complete *their own pre-conceived scenarios*. As there is evidence at the moment which looks very much like the cult of individual freedom or 'I'm alright Jack, so what about you?' it is worth exploring the interrelations between some current assumptions and superficiality.

The Neophiliacs (Booker, 1969) illustrates nicely for us a psychic epidemic of superficiality, the power of fantasy to lead men away from reality and the unity and meaning that can come only from a balance of fantasy and reality. A basic collective fantasy took over English life in the fifties and sixties with the contagious psychic force of evil (Booker and the English were not alone in this). Man's controlling mechanism of his orderly instincts broke adrift and led him down the path of illusion and instability.

'One of the most insidious properties of fantasy (is) that by diverting attention solely to *outward appearances and away from the meaning* that underlies them, it strives continually to blur or erase the distinction between itself and reality.' (Booker, p. 315, emphases are ours). 'Technology has reshaped society, breaking up the organic unity in all directions . . the onetime servant, the Machine, has become the master, on whom he (man) is *dependent* for his whole life, from cradle to grave, for food, for physical health, *even for the illusion of purpose*. Having cut him off from his roots, deprived him of all that truly nourishes his being and reduces him to a state of neurosis, it even supplies, through television, films and advertising, through all the tricks and toys of his technological wilderness, the almost ubiquitous stream of unresolved imagery to keep his mind drugged in a state of acquiescence.' (*Ibid.* p. 326).

Superficiality as the evil, forced society into a distracted state of novelty seeking – a 'melange of titillating fragments and suggestive images' (*Ibid.* p. 22). *It was a dream.* In his study of this madness Booker states that he found few real villains, only VICTIMS (*Ibid.* p. 13). The constant search for novelty and sensation had finally consumed everything but itself.' (*Ibid.* p. 249). The dream had become a nightmare.

Planners also have dreams and they have also produced nightmares (Schaffer, 1970). It gradually becomes obvious that in many current planning situations planners are making assumptions and having fantasies which fit Maruyama's planning paradigm precisely. For example, the assumption that with the growing alliance between telecommunications and computers it will be possible for a vast range of visual, computer-assisted, hard copy and mobile data services *to be provided*, and that it is expected computers will be increasingly linked by telecommunications to form networks in which the collective information and processing capabilities will be available to all *users* is the classic optimizing distinction between providers (planners) and users. This distinction has in recent times led to the appearance of the *phone freak, the multi-nodal network of underground information and dissemination resources and game playing with centralized systems as an end in itself. Radical Software* and *Alternative Technology* are now regularly published journals through conventional distributors. The capability to tie up large systems is no longer regarded as irresponsible or out of bounds. These people are living out *their* scenarios not those of the planners. The lack of congruence of the optimizers approach with either the type IV or type II environments can only result in a rapid expansion of resources which need to be mobilized to retain the distinction between providers and users in the face of offensives by such as phone freaks. If the line of responsibility is broken in the socio-technical system it is inevitable within a bureaucratic society that bureaucracy has to grow to defend itself. Projections of this process show it to be maladaptive, close to crisis point. The fact of users having a 'capability to respond' to centrally broadcast material cannot be equated with the spontaneous generation of content itself which would make providers and users one and the same.

The second part of this assumption of the continuation of centralized control over and responsibility for *the network* is the ordering of priorities within the planning process; the degree to which the technology can produce a predictable response. The ultimate expression of this approach is the definition of *perfection as the programming in of an accident* (from *The End Product*, Colin Free, ABC TV, 1974). While the bureaucracy must grow to maintain its control, the only variable over which it can exercise this control is in fact the nature of the hardware; not the extent to which the hardware is functioning well or to capacity. The APO probably keeps figures for telephone boxes out of order, time and money spent checking accounts, complaints, cutting off and reconnecting telephones etc. Our point is that at the moment there are very few, if any, systems for which planners can predict a response.

The assumption that society is only an aggregate of individuals (Maruyama) leads obviously to beliefs that the essential fabric of the planning process is technical. When this belief is predominant in the minds of planners there is little chance that creative solutions appropriate to the new social environment will be sought. We can expect from this type of planning only an elaboration of what is already available and *seems accepted*.

If there is any chance that we can assume 'more of the same' in the planners' approach, we are led inevitably into an information based society; one in which an ever increasing amount of accessible information is an end and virtue in itself. It other words Neophilia. The television data have shown that we have been operating on a basic misconception between to-inform and to-learn. Marien has documented for us the paradox in *'Futures We're In'* that increasing information can lead to decreasing understanding. In this type of situation the ultimate consequences of the 'so what' response and 'the nice tame animals' of *Brave New World* do not seem so remote. But given the present (see above and below), they may not in reality be so tame.

Emphasis on increased range of services and facilities which progressively assume the role of face-to-face communication takes on another dimension as one examines the base on which this range is extended. There is firstly the implicit assumption that to increase the range of services is to increase the range of choice. To extend the range of services is not to necessarily extend the choice, because the range of services itself is not chosen, and within the bureaucratic mode – 'ninety-six identical twins working ninety-six identical machines' (Huxley, p. 18) – the conclusions that 'the gods are just. Haven't they used his (man's) pleasant vices as an instrument to degrade him' (*Ibid.* p. 185) is obvious. While the designers of the *Brave New World* had calculated that feelies and smellies would be appreciated by the captive and choiceless audiences, their 'pre-conditioned receptacles of long standing' (Marcuse, in

Emery *et al.*, 1974, p. 46) the nature of the media themselves were such as to make certain the absolute nature of the effects. While *Brave New World* inexorably moved into the ultimate expression of Marcuse's profile of the *One Dimensional Man* – 'as though death were something terrible, as though anyone mattered as much as all that' (Huxley, p. 163) – we do not consider that superficiality will become the dominant societal maladaption. It may however be that, if there is not a radical change in the nature of social planning, superficiality may again and again burst out of the main dissociative stream. Dreaming is a necessary and recurrent phenomenon and the old brain too may come out 'looking for kicks'.

The integration of computers and telecommunications into new more powerful information systems raises even more questions about the hitherto unequalled individual access to information – 'The Wired City'. Such questions as from where amongst the 'so what' respondents does the system find the necessary dedicated resources to build the new organization which is necessary to *protect* the data and hardware organizations?

The concept of a 'wired city' is itself an example of superficiality – a planners dream or fantasy. It contains the same fundamental misconception of information, understanding and human needs. To quote Illich:

Reprinted from 'The Penguin Leunig'.

'The world does not contain any information. It is as it is. *Information about it is created in the organism through its interaction with the world.* To speak about storage of information outside the human body is to fall into a semantic trap. Books or computers are part of the world. They can yield information when they are looked upon. *We move the problem of learning and of cognition nicely into the blind spot of our intellectual vision if we confuse vehicles for potential information with information itself.* We do the same when we confuse data for potential decision with decision itself.' (Illich, p. 86).

We have already noted the confusion created by Shannon's so-called Theory of Information (*Ibid.* iii). We can do no more than underline Illich's thoughts and substitute 'understanding' for 'information'. If we cannot design a system which allows man his full, responsible and purposeful reign, to generate, as well as to transform information, then our negative scenarios are worth as much as the thoughts of the alien who interviewed the last man – '*You saw (these things) yourself, but you never thought about them. That was a mistake.*' (Carr, 1973).

12. Taking stock of McLuhan

Throughout the preceding analysis we were well aware of some areas of convergence with the views expressed by Marshall McLuhan.

Since we regard McLuhan as by far and away the most insightful and challenging of thinkers about telecommunication we shall here attempt to 'take stock' – to assess what in his storehouse can be usefully handled within our mundane conceptual framework, what remains beyond our grasp to tantalize and challenge, or even to provoke where he searches, classify where he probes and postulates. These activities he castigates. But then our concern extends beyond his primary and natural concern that Finnegan Wake to what he does when he wakes.

We start this stock taking from the not negligible common ground of agreeing that the 'classical' social science research into TV, *e.g.* Schramm (1961), Himmelweit (1958) and Emery (1959)[1] showed not the slightest understanding of their subject matter (we are not suggesting that the mentioned studies were not highly professional researches). Nor is there evidence that the situation has changed in the social sciences. In 1973, the professional world received *The Early Window*, by R. M. Liebert *et al*. This reported on 'the series of investigations recently completed for the Television and Social Behavior Program of the National Institute of Mental Health (U.S.A.). One of the most systematic and purposefully co-ordinated attempts to employ the efforts of a large group of researchers with relevant expertise and diverse viewpoints.' (R. M. Liebert *et al.*, 1973, p. XV).

This was not a program of research that was limited by funds from making the most of their 'diverse expertise', and 'systematic, purposefulness'. Between 1969 and 1971, N.I.M.H. funds of about one million dollars were expended on researching TV impact on children (*Ibid.* p. 73). However, in the Liebert report we find not a single reference to McLuhan, not a single reference to any of the key concepts listed below (none to 'involvement' just

1. For my part it seems that I was too pre-occupied with the psycho-dynamics of the preceding media, the film as the content of TV. – F. Emery.

two to 'intelligence'), nor any discussion of the nature of any media. There is no discussion of what it might mean to have 'an early window', only statistics about what is now displayed through the window.

Leaving the world of the new dismal science, behavioural science, let us try to get to grips with McLuhan. He has expressed himself on everything from Roman highways to net stockings. However, there are a limited number of key metaphors that together unambiguously identify McLuhan's very special contribution. We have taken the liberty of ordering these metaphors so as to ease our task. The temporal order in which McLuhan presented these metaphors may, in any case, bear little relation to when he started thinking about and using them.

12.1. The key McLuhan metaphors

1. a. 'all technologies are extension of man'
   b. 'all technologies shape a new environment for man.'
2. a. 'communication technologies are extensions of the central nervous system of man.'
   b. 'the communication technologies create a shift in sensory balance of man.'
3. a. 'in man's relation to communication technology 'the medium is the message'.'
   b. 'in man's relation to TV 'the medium is the massage'.'
4. TV is:
   a. iconic;
   b. cool, not hot like radio;
   c. audio-tactile, not visual like print.
5. a. in the new environment of TV people become 'cool, participatory involved.'
   b. TV is re-tribalizing man, to the world village.
6. a. higher definition of the TV image would change it from a cool media to a hot one.
   b. societies as receiving-sets, to be tuned-in, tuned-out, heated-cooled, by media planners.

Consider *metaphors 1 and 2*. We have already discussed at some length the distinction between thing and medium and the fundamental role of this distinction in the emergence of man's perceptual system (including the central uervous system) and his directive correlations with his environment.

We find ourselves led to a very similar conclusion to McLuhan. *All technologies are an extension of man*: of his senses, body or mental functions. We recognize a technological innovation when some part of the physical environment is drawn into directive correlation by man and to that extent becomes relatively independent of the normal environmental processes governing its shape, character and spatio-temporal course. It is in these ways that we identify flints as tools although they are found in rubble heaps away from any current civilization. It is important to remember that unlike dung, they are not simply the product of man (from which of course much can be inferred about man-environment relations). As an extension of man they are coenetic variables in the directive correlations he forms with his environment *and with others*. Because other men have similar properties the objects that he takes into directive correlation as coenetic variables can also be taken up by them with harm or benefit to him. *The relationship between men is thus changed by these technologies.*

As any sense or function is externalized in this manner it becomes embedded in directive correlations that can exercise greater regulatory influence than the natural directive correlations between the different senses. *Thus each new technology changes the ratio between the senses and faculties*, and *each sense or faculty that is so externalized tends to be rendered a closed system with respect to the other senses.* If by commonsense we mean the natural ratio between the senses then many of our technological extensions of the senses would appear to have undermined commonsense. It is in this light that we should examine McLuhan's dicta in *The Gutenberg Galaxy* of the restoration of commonsense with TV. With TV the other is not only heard but seen and seen not just out there at some past time but out there in its real context, simultaneously with being here on the goggle box (to be goggled at).

With the printed word everyone must be, and must appear to be, ordering his affairs in a linear connected manner such that there are identifiable causes followed by identifiable effects. Unless real life can be squeezed into this form it is almost uncommunicable by the printed word and hence cannot be the basis for joint action (*Ibid.* p. 91). Hence the drive toward machine type organizations. This is an unachievable goal and hence to each written measage there is an undertone of meaning; for each formal organization an informal organization.

With the telephone this linearity is not necessary – only one person can speak at a time and that person can only be saying one thing at a time but the total tends to be organized as a temporal gestalt, i.e. many things although occurring sequentially, are experienced as occurring at the same psychological moment. The telephone user becomes 'man the time-binder.'

With video-tape the capabilities of TV are taken out of the mass media world back into the concrete face-to-face world that the telephone crudely connects. In fact video-tape probably takes us back before telephone to give us a multi-dimensional telegram. The sender and the receiver already, in most cases, have a fairly concrete relation with each other, much more so than an advertiser pushing a message through mass media to 'someone out there.'

Embedded in the context of close living relations the iconic nature of the audio-visual media becomes a strength, not a weakness. In this context the video-tape enhances the ability to communicate that 'this is what is happening', 'this is what is', and more clearly justify or demand answers to 'why'. Percept and concept have somewhat more chance of achieving the balance demanded by commonsense.

Looking at technologies and media in these ways seems to us to make a great deal of theoretical sense and to raise meaningful questions. McLuhan has aroused great hostility amongst the mandarins for throwing these things at their faces with great arrogance and appearing to play fast and loose with the evidence. Often it seems that he has only cut loose on established preconceptions about the evidence. However, we are not concerned with any specific social change that may have followed on from say, introduction of moveable type face. Our point is that he appears to be right in the scale and pervasiveness of change he associates with media change as against the messages. Further, it seems to us inevitable that a new technically based media will create new patterns of communication habits and new sensory ratios.

Metaphor 3, has aroused the greatest ire. It just seemed so obvious to people who live by the printed word and the written lecture that the message is what communication is all about, what we wait for, what we try to get across to others. To state dogmatically that the medium is the message seemed so wrongheaded that we would have to suspect the motives of the person saying such a thing. This reaction led McLuhan to emphasize the extent to which people are unconscious of their environment and suggest that fish would be about the last ones to realize that they are in water. Overstated no doubt, but not by much. It is difficult now for most people to recall the sheer incomprehension with which, in the same two years, scientists greeted Rachel Carson's (1963) claim that the environment was a system not just a catch-all word. Nor the deafening silence that greeted the environment centred theses of Tomkins and Wynne-Edwards, both 1962. A study was made by the Tavistock Institute of the public reactions in England to the Carson thesis. This was after several local ecological disasters had highlighted the environmental issue. The study found comprehension amongst the young and amongst women. Incomprehension characterized the older men, *particularly* the better educated, the ones in positions of social authority.

The evidence is that McLuhan's message suffered from similar incomprehension, whatever the media he used. Certainly print did not help in some quarters. He made it perfectly clear in 1962 that the referents for his pronouncements were the environments for man created by new media technologies. In 1964 he quite clearly wrote that:

'the 'message' of any medium or technology is the change of scale or pace or pattern that it introduces into human affairs. . . . it is the medium that shapes and controls the scale and form of human association and action. The content or uses of such media are as diverse as they are ineffectual in shaping the form of human association and action.'

Economic theory grew out of the same realization that in an open market economy it was the general forms of exchange that mattered, not who was fiddling what, who was Simple Simon, who Shylock. The forms of exchange were what mattered for the big picture; the innumerable concrete exchanges in the open market cancelled each other out.

More than a hundred years since William Petty started to do this service to economics, McLuhan tried to make a similar statement about communications. The referent of his communications had no existence in the minds of some of his most literate readers. They readdressed his communications to referents they knew. Theodore Roszack gives us a clear 'psychological' definition of McLuhan and his ideas. Of the notion that 'the medium is the message' he writes:

'Those of us who have been touched to the marrow by the power of an idea know better – and we ought not to let McLuhan tell us differently than our own living experience does.' '. . . we *know* full well that we have been shaped by other human culture and that in it lies all our hopes of achieving wisdom. Who then, is Marshall McLuhan that he should seek to talk us out of our richest experience with nothing more than a catchphrase? There is indeed a kind of ultimate barbarism about any conception of culture which allows itself to become obsessed with the physical artifacts of communication and ignores their profoundest personal meaning.' (Rosenthal (ed.), 1967, p. 264).

McLuhan clearly stated he was not referring to that kind of *ABX* situation. An Arab street trader or a 19th century Midlands manufacturer could have expressed the same feelings about Adam Smith, 'Who is Smith to tell us that the anguish of the price haggle means nothing in the big picture?' It just happens they are talking about different things. There is the added sting-in-the-tail that McLuhan and Smith help us also to understand the professors and the traders, but the opposite is not true.

What is a little sad is that the literate mandarins who feel so threatened by 'ultimate barbarism' seem to have little or no insight into the implicit assumptions that adaptation to the natural physical media has already brought into their own perception of the world or their own communication with their learned colleagues (see Part I).

There is a reality that attaches to messages, and up to a certain level we do not give a damn about the media through which the message comes. At another level we just take for granted the media we have and organize our affairs about the messages and nuances that they make possible – we become like the fish.

Our earlier theoretical discussions showed how significant the properties of media were to successful adaptation and the extent to which adaptation was based on implicit assumptions whether it be in perceiving the physical world or in the ABX situations of social intercourse. As man's technological advances create new media we think it natural that adaptation to the new world situation it creates would be as profound and as difficult as man having suddenly to cope with having two heads, or an ice age.

The previous chapter gave clear enough evidence that there are media differences regardless of the message.

The Krugman experiment, referred to earlier, showed this very much more directly. A medium like TV which switches the reflective mind into neutral is a medium with a difference. A medium like TV, which reduces cortical activity to a flux of alpha and slow waves could well be described as a 'massage'.

The further point that has been made against 'the medium is the message' is that without an appealing message TV could not hold attention. This is too simple a view. It bears relation to the facts of viewing. The most basic persistent fact of TV viewing is that people tune in to the same old channel regardless of what is on. We have already discussed the general way the affects motivate the individual to attend to the informational characteristics of the environment. Such characteristics are not only provided by structured messages. Even in conversation the communication is not just what is said. Tomkins puts it succinctly, 'Complex stimuli are extremely attractive to the human organism if they possess both sufficient novelty and sufficient familiarity so that both positive affects are reciprocally activated, interest – excitement by the novel aspects of the stimulus and enjoyment-joy by the recognition of the familiar and the reduction of interest-excitement.' (*Ibid*. p. 213).

Dember, in summarizing a large body of relevant experimental evidence puts it simply, 'perceptual activity has value (to the individual) in its own right.' (1960, p. 373).

Those who would survive as producers in the world of mass media have to show a sixth sense for getting the right blend of familiarity and novelty for their target audience.

However, the producers are only working with the media. The low, fuzzy and constantly changing information content of the TV media, within its present technical limits both demands and allows the viewer to do his own dreamwork on the material flowing in. So the producers of TV, unlike stage or film producers, coach their performers *not* to act, *not* to project themselves or their speech but to 'hang loose' like a Rorschach blot giving the viewers every chance to make what they will of their character to fit their own dreamwork. 'The human face, particularly the eyes and the muscles around them, are the most important organs of expression and communication of affect.' (Tomkins, p. 192). 'The human face innately and by learning evokes intense and enduring affect.' (*Ibid*. p. 215).

This is the stuff dreams are made of and the challenge thus to complete the image is greater with this material than any other. The face is the most complex object in the life space of the human being. 'The eyes, mouth and voice in concert are capable of emitting an extraordinary quantity of information at a bewildering rate.' (p. 215). 'We can see two objects at the same time but not two faces at the same time . . . Only the human face can milk our glance dry . . .' (de Chazal, quoted by Weiss, in Rosenthal, 1969, p. 56). All of the viewers of TV have had great direct experience of the human face as a source of information and hence are very aware (not necessarily conscious) of the gap that needs to be filled between the impoverished sample of offshoots on the TV screen and the attributed source. In watching the TV screen, viewers typically fix on a face not, as in film, on action and setting.

As McLuhan notes (1964, p. 309), children hardly take their eyes from the faces even during scenes of violence. They are fascinated, building their dreams around the character's affective reaction as incompletely written on the image of his face. So the producers fill the screen with close-ups in a way that a film maker would not dare. On the film the image is such a good definition of the source that the close-up comes like a smack in the face, with no room in ambiguity to duck. 'For what gradually rises to the surface, as the disinterested viewer can observe in soap operas, true-life re-enactments, children's programmes, game shows, interviews . . . is the *subdrama of the human face, voice and gesture . . . We could not possibly observe the 'process of human interaction fully if we were dramatically concerned ourselves.'* (Weiss, in Rosenthal, 1969, p. 55).

The final chapter of *Bug Jack Barron* gives striking illustration of how a TV audience is held captured by play on facial images – direct control over the image on the screen (*e.g.* really close-up to distant, voice off) and indirect manipulation of the affects of the interviewee. Rather like David Frost. Note what this adds up to. The nature of the TV media makes it not only easy to hold attention without stressing a message but makes it necessary. If the producer wants to hold audience attention, for whatever it is he is selling, he must play down the conceptual message, bring on the faces, the *iconic symbol* par excellence (Emery *et al.*, 1962).

Of the characteristics attributed to TV by McLuhan, *metaphor 4*, that of being iconic has already been subscribed to. Once iconic is defined it is obvious that TV is markedly iconic compared to preceding mass media. The three media characteristics are those most frequently evoked by McLuhan to explain how a media has its effects. He sometimes seems to use them interchangeably to give radically new explanations of what has happened in the past and amazing predictions about what could be done in the future.

Metaphor 4
a. Iconic   versus conceptual
b. cool (low definition) versus hot (high definition)
c. auditory/tactile   versus visual

Following McLuhan's writings (1964) we can order the main media as follows:

	Visual		Auditory/Tactile	
	Iconic	Conceptual	Iconic	Conceptual
cool	cartoon	—	TV (conversing telephone) (video-tape)	—
hot	photo	print film ('learning machines')*	radio (phonogram)	(Braille) (lecture)

* Those in brackets are simply illustrations.

Our form of presentation makes this look like a rigorous classification. McLuhan (1967) has insisted that they are simply the significant parameters, common to media systems that enable system differences to be explored; therefore an empty cell does not designate a gap in a Periodic Table that should be filled, if the theory is right. A difference does not indicate a difference such as between black and white. In a clash of media in a society it is not only the relative difference on these dimensions that matters but their relative weight in terms of history and penetration into the society.

The diagram suggests why McLuhan seems to use the characteristics interchangeably. Writing about print or the film he could use hot, visual or conceptual – they are all of these things. Writing about TV he could use any of the three opposite characteristics, cool, iconic and auditory-tactile. However, to place radio in relation to print and film he would have no choice but to use the parameters of visual / auditory/tactile and of iconic-conceptual. It might be argued that the iconic-conceptual distinction could be dropped as all that has been said about radio versus print is that it is non visual ergo non conceptual. This is not so. The lecture is a non visual (at least not necessarily or primarily so) but conceptual media. Unless the iconic characteristic of radio as a media were recognized we would still be wondering why the BBC Talks Programme failed to gain the following of the Goon Show.

To put radio in relation to TV one would have to use the parameter of hot-cool. This is the only one on which they are distinguished.

Thus we think it safe to say that McLuhan is postulating and seeing at least these three different parameters; not just switching between terms that are synonomous in his mind.

Therefore, it is not enough that we can accept the iconic-conceptual distinction. The others must be considered in their own light.

McLuhan is quite precise in his definition of 'hot' and 'cool'. ' A hot medium is one that extends one single sense (whether visual, auditory or tactile) in 'high definition'. High definition is the state of being well filled with data. . . . a cool medium . . . a meager amount of information.' We will make only one assumption, which seems to tie in with his subsequent useage, namely that by 'data' and 'information' he means data and information consciously received. The definitions can then be formulated as 'hot – a high density of conscious report to message; cool – a low density of conscious report to message.' Consciousness is awareness of awareness, reflection by the organism on what it is involved in.

Put this way then there is little difficulty in going along with the above diagram. The evidence suggests less conscious activity (more synchronous slow brain wave activity) per unit of exposure time for TV than for radio and the other media.

For all the precision that can be given to this distinction and its relevance, the choice of terms has created difficulties. When we ordinarily talk of communication as hot, heated or cool, the meanings tend to be:

Commonsense

Hot – like religion and politics in an officers' mess, is likely to arouse a 'taking of positions', arguments, tempers, prejudices, divisiveness (*i.e.* 'hot issue'). Cool – neutral, something one can sit down and consider soberly, weighing pros and cons or can discuss rationally with others and find grounds for agreement, suspension of judgment or disagreement without rancour.

The modern usage of 'keeping one's cool' retains the essential commonsense meaning. McLuhan's usage does not. By his usage a heated discussion of religion or politics in a Belfast pub could be a very cool thing – a minimum of conscious report other than awareness of mutual hatred. Similarly, a very cool discussion between Kissinger and Brezhnev could, and hopefully would, be very hot – a high density of conscious report to message (that is, we would hope that they were not waffling on or beating around the bush).

What makes TV so cool, so low a density of conscious report to message? We do not think it is a direct function of low sensory definition. Rather as explained earlier in some detail, the peculiar nature of the sensory input switches off the intervening but critical processes of reflection (as indicated by dominance of slow waves). The viewing is at the conscious level of somnambulism. The somnambulist is aware enough to negotiate the furniture, the door, the stairs, the gate – he is just not aware of his awareness.

What has to be born in mind is that in this and other matters, McLuhan is talking about a newly recognized phenomenon, the environmental systems created by media technologies, not about face-to-face communications (*A*, *B*, *X*'s). Not that that stops him punning and raising a veritable cloud of dust about his propositions.

His definitions are quite clear with respect to *his* referents. His terms, hot and cool, are used by him to put into one capsule the producer and the product; 'high definition' and a hot society or people drawn up under opposing banners; 'low definition' and the end of ideology. The only point at which his usage refers to the individual in the viewing, listening, reading situation is in his hypothesis about participation in message completion. We would like to defer consideration of that until we come to his sixth metaphor, because it is obvious that he does not mean that in cool TV the viewer is hotly participating or that in the hot cubicle the scholar is coldly standing off from what he reads. He has another and different thought in that hypothesis.

The third dimension provides the biggest shock to the uninitiated. Television, an auditory tactile medium! Surely it is perfectly obvious, which ever way one looks at it, that television is an audio visual medium and dominantly visual at that. If the sound goes you can watch it with some amusement, if the picture fades the repairman must come immediately. It is broadcast film and when we get cable television we will all get more and better films.

This, we seriously suggest, is illusion. Let us, with Rudolf Arnheim, go back to ask 'First of all, what is the fundamental problem involved in television? Eyes and ears have quite different tasks and correspondingly are made different.' (p. 156). We then get to his conclusion that it is radio and television that go together, not film and television. Arnheim, the psychologist, could work that out in 1935 in a very penetrating book on *Film as Art* (the technology of TV was fundamentally known in the mid-twenties).

What McLuhan has done is to call attention to the structure the media imposes on the messages that pass through (as did Heider in 1926). Does the message arrive in particulate or continuous form? The structural difference he postulates is that with which our culture has already been plagued – the continuity of infinitesimal calculus versus the discreteness of algebra; the continuity of Einstein's strictly deterministic, even though bent, world versus quantum theory. We use these simply as analogies. We except that mathematicians and physicists would now claim that these were really very technical matters of no general relevance, even if Einstein did not realize it. In the social sciences we cannot even pretend at denying the significance of the difference (see Ackoff and Emery for the distinction between variety decreasing and variety increasing organizations, 1972, p. 227-229).

If this difference between the particulate and the continuous is so critical in the social sciences could it then be less relevant in the extensions of man? A fine statement but a little direct evidence would help.

We may have such evidence. McLuhan has stated that when the newspaper is fragmented into the modern frontpage and when TV gives poor definition we have viewers with particulate information. The receiver carries the tension to make a picture, a gestalt of the incomplete gestalt.

The question, again delaying the question of participation, is whether the media do differ significantly in this respect. We think yes. Film and print do seem to have a continuity that is significantly greater and more constantly sought for than radio and television. The latter do not just make do with the staccato makeshift elements, they thrive on them.

'*TV is cool, participatory, involving.*'

This is McLuhan's most challenging deduction from his theory of media. By 1967 he could put it as strongly as is implied in the following:

'How shall the new environment be programmed now that we have become so involved with each other, now that *all* of us have become the unwitting workforce for change.' (1967, p. 12).

There is something wrong here. The notions hang together but seem to hang in mid air. TV can be fairly accurately described as cool, participatory and involving in a way that the older media were not. There is much in our current societies that is 'cool, participatory and involving' which was not present before the sixties. Just two catches. The cool participatory involvement of an individual in unreflectively weaving dreams around insubstantial pre-edited images does not look at all like the cool co-operation of management, workers and unions to heighten participation and involvement in work, nor like similar efforts in community and government. The former is at best goal seeking in fantasy, the latter very much purposeful, even ideal seeking in a very real world. Second catch, the descriptions do not seem to be referring to the same people. The people addicted to TV viewing are not typically those who have been on the streets seeking more involvement in the decisions that affect their lives. Nor, in our experience, those who initially provide leadership in democratizing work places. The survey facts are clear enough. The flesh and blood feeling of the difference comes out in a novel by Thomas Disch where he describes what TV is for one of his characters: –

'Once the box was on Chapel became another person . . . It was not the stories that engaged him so, it was the faces of the actors, their voices, their gestures, the smooth, wide-open, whole-bodied way they moved. So long as they themselves seemed stirred by their imaginary problems, Chapel was satisfied. What he needed was the spectacle of authetic emotion – eyes that cried, chests that heaved, lips that kissed or frowned or tightened with anxiety, voices tremulous with concern.

He would sit on the mattress, propped on cushions, four feet back from the screen, breathing quick, shallow breaths, wholly given over to the flickerings and noises of the machine, which were, more than any of his own actions, his life, the central fact of his consciousness, the single source of any happiness Chapel knew or could remember.

A teevee had taught Chapel to read. It had taught him to laugh. It had instructed the very muscles of his face how to express pain, fear, anger and joy. From it he had learned the words to use in all the confusing circumstances of his other, external life.

And though he never read, or laughed, or frowned, or spoke, or walked, or did anything as well as his avatars on the screen, yet they'd seen him through well enough, after all, or he would not have been here now, renewing himself at the source.

What he sought here, and what he found, was much more than art, which he had sampled during prime evening hours and for which he had little use. It was the experience of returning, after the exertions of the day to a face he could recognize and love, his own or someone else's. Or if not love, then some feeling as strong. To know, with certainty, that he would feel these same feelings tomorrow, and the next day. In other ages religion had performed this service, telling people the story of their lives, and after a certain lapse of time telling it to them again.' (Disch, T. M. *334*, 1974).

The 'cool, participatory' description looks like classical McLuhanese, as described by his critics. Use terms loosely so that things that are very different can be described analogically; then proceed to speculate as if they were part and parcel of the same syndrome, not just analogous.

Yet we pause.

12.2. The missing link: the face and shame

We have found with other parts of McLuhan's writings that it was much more fruitful to suspend judgment. The weight of the evidence is that Mc Luhan has 'Blake's vision'. We have not found him to be a storyteller or dishonest; a successful showman certainly, but if we recoil at that style so what? 'Where are you Christian Barnard, I need a heart transplant!' Going on our experience with trying to fathom McLuhan for thirteen years it seems worthwhile to explore the apparant paradox. It might be that we have not grasped what McLuhan is driving at, no great surprise, or that McLuhan has sensed a connection but not grasped the connecting link. We think it is in part the latter. McLuhan has clearly proposed one connecting link – the emerging TV generation. A generation of children grow up on a TV diet, and the more affluent families get sets, then multiple sets and are more likely to use it as a substitute for their presence with the children. The children grow to adolescence, spend less time viewing but already have a different world view. They challenge the world view of their parents face to face and next you have both generations out on the streets over Viet Nam and conservation matters and the kids from affluent middle class backgrounds challenge the assumptions of school, university and the corporations.

This seems to be straightforward and cogent. The explanation does not imply that TV has little or no effect on adults. In other contexts, discussing media effects on nations, McLuhan makes it quite clear that media effects compete. Someone brought up in the 'massage' of the older hot media is not so readily and quickly shaped as the toddler viewing 'Sesame Street'. (The 'preconditioned receptacles' of Marcuse.)

However, this does not solve the paradox. What is the miracle that transforms the TV c.p.i. (cool participatory involvement) into the mature c.p.i. of the adult democrat? The process of ageing seems inadequate as an answer. Ageing would most likely produce only selfish libertines, a world view of laissez-faire, do your own thing (alone).

Rosenthal, editor of the very critical set of essays on *McLuhan: Pro and Con* put his finger on just this point:

'... if television is supposed to have the revolutionary effect on us that McLuhan claims, he will have to build a bridge between sensation and consciousness ... his description is unsupported by any system of esthetic or emotional perception ...' (1969, p. 12).

We think that there is an explanation which makes McLuhan's connecting link into a producer-product relation. Let us go back to some points made earlier. In explaining why TV was even less dependent on the message than other mass media we drew attention to the use of facial images. McLuhan noted the phenomena (1964, pp. 309, 317) but went straight on past, he was obviously looking for bigger game. The quote we selected from Tom Disch to depict a TV addict (a c.p.i. viewer) ought to be re-read at this point (see p. 133).

All right, say we have looked back at these two points, what do we conclude? Interesting, a good practical guide to the TV producer; McLuhan might have said 'TV is the Face, not the Box, its the icon without walls.' (see 1964, p. 283).

No, more than that is involved. We suggest that we go back to square one – information, adaptation and survival. We are *not* going to suggest that TV is man's answer to any of these. We are going to argue that TV as a technical innovation of man to extend his directive correlations with his outer and inner worlds, has extended from givens in his own nature. The face has been with us long enough to be part of the world within which man's biological equipment evolved. For a species dependent upon co-operation it is little wonder that the human face has evolved as the most potent transmitter of information that we know and the transmitter we most readily learn to tune into. No mechanical electronic means we have yet devised have come within reach of this transmission – receiving capability, and hence not within reach of the communication capabilities of the *ABX* situation. Nor are they even likely to approach this unless chemical communication can be achieved regardless of distance. The face furthermore gives a high level of feedback which is probably isomorphic with the transmissions one is making, *e.g.* blushing, smiling, stern, stiff upper lip. We blush, the message goes through to others and in a multitude of ways we get the same message and feel humble, fooled, confused. We get a feedback the other way: he, the stranger we know of, smiles, we relax, smile back and get the message; the heart does not beat so fast or so steadily.

We have already stated or implied as much as this. The critical step over the threshold is that *there has been a long standing taboo on looking into faces particularly their eyes and this taboo is critical to the innate affect of shame and humiliation – TV breaks that taboo and negates all that men have built around that affect.*

As Tomkins points out this taboo is universal. The taboo of incest would be nigh on uncontrollable if parents and adolescents looked directly into each others eyes. In some cultures people develop the *ABX* into a close mutual smelling setting, in some into a literally tactile setting. In practically none has 'eye-balling to eye-balling' seemed a human way of relating, outside sexual seduction. Tomkins has his own theories about why this taboo has been so universal. Briefly:

1. it is, given the transmission potential of the human face, too potent a source of information overload and emotional contagion;
2. it gives more information about the 'other' than is reconcilable with any pecking order of superiors and inferiors.

TV viewing constantly breaks with the quite universal taboo on looking into the eyes of others (Tomkins II, ch. 17). The viewer like Disch's character stares straight into the eyes of the screened faces without eliciting in himself the affect of shame that would occur in real life. We suggest that *constant TV viewing erodes the sense of shame and drastically lessens the ability of others to shame, humiliate or put down.* To the school teacher, such a child seems a shameless little monster, brazenly staring straight back at you as if you were some kind of thing when you try to correct him: such a child would also appear uncontrollable because the usual control techniques of a superior, the techniques of shaming, humiliating and contempt would be like so much water off a ducks' back. To a boss it must be equally disconcerting when he when he tries 'to carpet' a young subordinate. As the TV generation emerges this erosion of shame must have great social effects because the crucial prop has been knocked out from under:

1. all social arrangements based on humiliating subordinates, all pecking orders;
2. all patterns of socialization based on shaming and suppressing the positive affects of excitement and joy.

That is, the connection McLuhan needed, does exist. However, the connection is not that they learn from television to be democratic, it is that they don't learn to be slaves.

In stressing the non-learning of shame we should not forget a very real learning that is taking place. As Disch put it about Chapel 'It (TV) had instructed the very muscles of his face how to express pain, fear, anger and joy.' As de Chazal explained it, we could not learn so much if we were dramatically involved. For a person who is not ashamed to look right into the faces and eyes of others it is valuable learning. It opens up, authenticates and gives a spontaneity to human interaction. It also teaches how to 'dead pan' when confronted by hostiles. Adults from the pre-TV era go to expensive encounter groups to develop this openness etc. by learning 'eye-balling'.

McLuhan had some feeling for the change the TV media was making on the sense of shame and guilt. By 1967 he was constantly stressing that 'ours is a brand-new world of all-at-once-ness', connoting that something had happened to the old world of shame, guilt and atonement. More pointedly, 'The new feeling that people have about guilt is not something that can be privately assigned to some individual, but is, rather, something shared by everybody, in some mysterious way.' (1967, p. 61).

We think that it may be the same vague feeling that the TV is eroding the sense of shame and guilt that drives frantic Mrs Whitelaw and the Festival of Light movement. If so, it will do no good to their cause simply to cut out scenes of violence, sex and bad taste. They would have to abolish the faces, and then there would be trouble with holding viewers – TV would become about as magic as the old magic lantern.[2]

Let us now explore the social consequences likely to flow from the erosion of shame. We have suggested that it will tend to undermine all forms of social organization and all social arrangements based on superiority – inferiority. We will now go further and suggest that its effect will be much stronger than

2. Imagine if we filled the TV programme with lectures by parsons, priests, and nuns on how 'thou must not stare into the other's eyes'. To hold the audience we would have to have lots of close-ups.

that brought about by greater education or greater affluence (with its reduction of competition for scarce resources). It will certainly have effects very
much greater than any ideological struggle under the banner of freedom and
quality or 'Maoism'.

The reasons are not hard to see. To paraphrase the Gettysburg Address;
'There is no way in which any structure of social dominance could *force* all
of the people, all of the time, to do all of the things desired of them.' Only
man's innate vulnerability to humiliation, shame and contempt and his socialization around this vulnerability provides the cement for pecking orders.
Terror, pain and gratification are like islands in the Pacific. Even in a prison
setting the use of shame, humiliation and contempt is far more pervasive
and effective than use of physical rewards and punishments (Emery, 1970,
p. 5, p. 33-37). We have already suggested what happens in the classroom
when the child is invulnerable to being humiliated because he has failed,
forgotten, been clumsy. The primary school of Cook, A.C.T., was struck
and picketed by its students in 1973. Mass thrashing or decimation were not
options but all the usual techniques to humiliate and cowe were tried and
simply failed. The headmaster, without knowing he was in the new world of
TV could simply reiterate 'In secondary schools, with adolescents, yes, I can
understand; but children, in primary school, No, No! These are *only little
children*'. TV saturation in Australia was achieved 10-12 years before.

Work of all kinds is for the most part organized in authoritarian, bureaucratic settings. The hierarchical relations of dominance are maintained by
the usual techniques of exploiting vulnerability to shame and contempt.
Friendliness and respect are bi-furcated. Friendliness proferred to a subordinate provided he clearly understands the inferiority of his position, and
hence is wide open to being painfully humiliated by contempt and put back
in his place 'if he presumed on the friendship'. Respect is demonstrated for
a subordinate, 'an up and coming young man'. But friendliness is reserved,
distance maintained. At all costs the way must be left open to humiliate him
if he shows signs of 'getting too familiar'.

Between peers in bureaucratically organized work places the overriding
psychological process is that of invidious comparison. This is not just envy,
but envy and shame. The recognition or advancement of the other shames
oneself; one's own recognition can create feelings of shame for having, without intent, shamed the other.

What happens as a new TV generation moves into the junior positions and
are not vulnerable to shame, look straight into their bosses eyes and see how
they tick? What would it gain a boss to carpet such a subordinate? From

within the Australian Public Service two types of outcomes have been reported to us. Either they are looking at you as if you are some peculiar kind of
animal, or they have this dead pan mug, you have no idea whether they are
taking the slightest bit of notice, and at the end they say 'So what?' What
happens to the mechanism of invidious comparison that splits peers off from
each other, blinds them to their common interests and sets them to lick
boots? If persons cannot be shamed just because they have done a lousy job
or because they have lost out in preferment then the whole vile traditional
notion of employment as a series of zero-sum games (my win is his loss)
becomes like the famed 'emperor's clothes'.

Such esteemed theorists of organization as Herbert Simon have realized
that there is more to organization than the play on the affects with carrot and
stick. They assumed a process of implicit sanctioning by the underlings. We
suggest that it is no such thing. We suggest that it is vulnerability to humiliation. Which is also probably why the masses have so readily betrayed their
own revolutions e.g. Hungary, 1956. As Marcuse wrote just before the Polish
and Hungarian revolts of 1956:

'From the slave revolts in the ancient world to the socialist revolution, the struggle of the
oppressed has ended in establishing a new, 'better' system of domination . . .' 'The ease
with which they have been defeated demands explanations . . .' 'In every revolution, there
seems to have been a historical moment when the struggle against domination might have
been victorious – but the moment passed.'
'An element of self-defeat (see 10.4) seems to be involved in this dynamic (regardless of
the validity of such reasons as the prematurity and inequality of forces). In this sense every
revolution has also been a betrayed revolution . . . guilt . . .' (1956, pp. 90-91).

Bred and brought up as cur dogs, people will at the snap of the master's
voice behave as cur dogs.

If television has fundamentally disturbed the programming of children
for servile adult work then work, such as has to be done, will need to be re-
programmed about interest, excitement and enjoyment. These affects are
rendered salient by TV.

Here we come face to face with the fact that the major effect of TV is un-
learning for today's adults and non-learning for the children. TV is, inadvertently, debureaucratizing work and school but there is nothing about
TV that is learning people what else to do. The media, the viewing behaviour
and the content give only one message 'do your own thing, without shame',
rather like an advert for masturbation. The widespread university revolts
through 1968-71 were against all the various forms of dominance but so
little conscious of how to do their own thing together that they settled for co-
optation of their respresentatives to staff committees.

McLuhan's assumption of a simple carryover from the cool participatory involvement of television viewing to cool participatory involving forms of education and work is very unsound. The shameless can be organized in more ways than one. In a turbulent social field more ways than one are likely to be tried.

Between social pecking orders and individual socialization stand social norms. The effects of TV on emergent generations would be expected to significantly influence the normative structure. If people cannot be shamed, humiliated or effectively treated with contempt because of their feminity, their blackness, their foreignness, their lack of years, their homosexuality, then what happens to social arrangements based on these differences? 'Black becomes beautiful!' We are quite sure that no amount of legislation could sustain the traditional social fragmentation or segmentation in the face of the new generation.

The norms of the 'Protestant Ethic' we have already touched on with respect to work.

More drastic for our existing social fabric is the probable *undermining of the normative value attached to norms*. The role of norms, guilt and conscience we have already discussed in the previous volume. We were not then aware of how far they were being undermined by TV's erosion of shame. The evidence was there but not our understanding.

Between and around work and the family as a socializing agent are a welter of 'regulative institutions', churches, associations, clubs and the like. They do not raise children nor make products. They justify themselves on the grounds that without their help these fundamental things would not be done properly.

What happens to church organizations if the new generation cannot be ashamed for themselves or their family's sake to keep up appearances. What happens to the Surf Lifesaving Association, the Football Leagues, and the rest of the organized world of sport if young people cannot be shamed into 'doing something useful' with their spare time? What happens to Rotary, the Lions and the Jay Cees if the new generation of businessmen do not feel some sense of shame about their personal good fortune?

Beyond the norms that give some sort of sanctity to churches, sports bodies, RSL, Red Cross and the like are the norms that dictate 'what is proper in public places'. What happens to these norms when people are not ashamed of their appearance, their clothes, their cleanliness, their language, their affections for each other?

Is it any wonder that the older generation in the USA have flocked into T-grouping to learn the art of shamelessly eye-balling to eye-balling. The rapid spread of encounter groups and T-groups may be no more than a stage of adjustment for the older generation that was socialized before TV. It offers them re-socialization in 'openness, authenticity, spontaneity, and sensual awareness, so that they can 'be with it' with the TV generation.' Next thing they are decked out in the gear of the young.

The rejection of ideologies by the young generation, even during the 1968 Paris rising is probably related to the weakening of shame. 'The role of shame and contempt in revolutionary political activity has yet to be fully appreciated. The threat of shame and contempt in such movements is scarcely distinguishable from the threat of shame implicit in excommunication in Middle Ages.' (Tomkins, 1962, vol. II, p. 232). We would add that this is true of most ideological movements.

Enough said. If TV acts the way McLuhan thought, and we assert that, then there are changes already in the pipeline. In *Midwich Cuckoos*, John Wyndham has already looked at this problem of what it might be like if we were confronted with a new breed of kids, and he explored the solutions open to us of the older generation. We might have to find a better solution than blowing them up.

The socialization of children is more fundamental than the question of our social organizations or our social norms. We treat it last because it appears to offer more lead time.

By far and away the most fundamental thing that we have been doing in bringing up our children which TV disturbs is negating their natural curiosity, the interplay of excitement and joy. We have consistently used shame to stop the child staring at the strange person, asking about the strange features of its world. In this book we have ourselves up till now, looked at the erosion of shame by TV in terms of adult forms of social control over the younger, the junior members of our society. In looking at the effects on socialization our concern must now be with how adult interference affects the ability of children to control the development of their capabilities.

In TV viewing shame is not elicited by inter-ocular looking. The child viewer avidly looks on. That child viewer is not likely to know any limits to curiosity. For that child the Oedipal myth is dead. For that TV child the threat of informational overload is dead – its information assumes closed iconic forms or it is out. The ever expanding, ever demanding conceptual form of knowledge is out, unaccepted.

Where can parents and surrogates get to in trying to socialize such a child? As parents we make a big thing of cleanliness and tidiness. Where does that get us if the children cannot be shamed by the dirtiness and disorder?

'As parents we make a lot of noise about appearances, noises and smells. Where does that get us if the children cannot be shamed about how they look, how their clothes look or whether they have had a bath in the past week, or how loud their music is?

The ideology of shame goes further than we can explore here. The fact that shame is the one affect that has *the self* as its object has made it particularly liable to play a central role in so called character building, particularly when it is supposed to be a mark of character not to show affects and to deny the pleasures of the flesh. It is central to the so-called Protestant ethic and to puritanism (Tomkins, 1962, vol. II, pursues this to much greater depth than we can afford here).

It is enough to note here that although McLuhan did not know the how's of the matter he clearly noted the wherefores. *For a very large part of the next thirty years we will have to cope with the dragon's teeth already sown. Our concern will not be with what new technologies might do but with what they have already done.*

In a situation like this no person or corporate body, public or private, would bring yet another technical medium into existence nor sneak in a major upgrading of the capabilities of any existing media on the grounds that it would be simply more of the same, only cheaper or better. We think we have enough problems on our hands due to the mad media technologists. 'Mad?' Well, you would have to be slightly mad, like Dr Strangelove, to design a new upset of everyone's sensibilities just to prove that a technical possibility can be actualized.

This sounds crazy? From our earlier considerations it seem quite possible. The current poor definition of TV allows some free play in the system between source – image – viewer. The nature of the free play seems highly conducive to doing dreamwork instead of thinking but it is still largely the viewer's dreamwork. Take the free play out of the system by higher image definition and we may be back with the Hollywood dream factory and with much more editing and control over the product. With higher definition the face would probably regress back into the setting and action become the focus. With the dreamwork taken out the viewer would have to accept or reject the readymade fantasy he is offered – he would have to take a viewpoint. We feel, with McLuhan, that 'Once we have surrendered our senses and nervous systems to the private manipulations of those who would try to benefit from taking a lease on our eyes and ears and nerves we don't really have any rights left.' (1964, p. 168).

A generation that has grown up with the free play of low definition TV might find as little time for high definition TV as they do for film. The other aspect of McLuhan's sixth metaphor was his notion of 'societies as receiving sets'.

'The computer could program the media to determine the given messages a people should hear in terms of their overall needs, creating a total media experience absorbed and pattern-ed by all the senses . . . By such orchestrated interplay of all media, whole cultures could now be programmed in order to improve and stabilize their emotional climate . . .' (1969, p. 72).

To ask who would program the computer would be to bring society and social organization into the picture. McLuhan has swept those questions under the carpet. His action with the broom is deft. First, he identifies the viewer with the screen, 'the viewer, in fact becomes the screen . . .' (*Ibid*, p. 61). Now we are free to discuss *either* the technical properties of the screen or the psychological properties of the viewer. With this sort of technological determinism it would be redundant to discuss both. McLuhan chooses the screen; after all the viewer is not very interesting, he is in a state of '*Narciss-istic narcosis*' (*Ibid*. p. 54, see p. 99 herein.) Second, he identifies the people with the media (apparently they are all glued to their media) and social questions become technical. Cause and effect become as one. That's total partici-pation.

12.3. Summary

We set out to take stock of McLuhan and found that we had to take stock of what we knew in order to grasp his thesis.

This certainly seems to have led us into areas of deep concern for our society, and many clues as to the kind of society that is emerging. After all most of the children now watching TV will be alive and running most of the affairs of society in year 2,000.

However, throughout McLuhan's writings there is a pervasive air of his aiming at a *cultural* theory and history of the media not a social or socio-psychological explanation. That is, that with his background in literary cul-ture he came more under the influence of his early colleague Edmund Car-penter, the anthropologist, than his idol Harold Innis, the economic his-torian. Perhaps this is why McLuhan failed to raise the following questions:

1. Why people went over so fast and thoroughly to TV and why such massive social resources were so readily allocated to it?

2. Why, when TV came in, did parents so readily acquiese in their children spending so much time viewing with so little adult supervision of programmes? (Particularly of the cartoon programmes)
3. As we have already asked, why was McLuhan so little concerned to find some link, through consciousness and purposiveness, between sensations and the changes in social life?
4. Why, on balance, the social influence of TV would favour what is represented by the hippies and the communes and not the life style of the skinheads and droogs?

We think these questions have to be answered if McLuhan's insights are to have any value in helping people to consciously shape their future. The cultural insights need to be embedded in the broader context of the bureaucratization of society that marked the last eighty to ninety years and is now so widely under challenge.

In *Futures We're In* we tried to outline this larger setting. Within it the communications revolution appeared as only one of five main strands. Whilst not going over all that ground again we will try in the next part to see how this strand is woven in with the others.

PART III

Human communication and the adaptive response

Introduction

As dissociation is the major *passive* maladaptive response little wonder that our adaptive scenario shares some of the concern with values of the corresponding *active* maladaptive response-'evangelicism'.

However, what we see as an adaptive response to turbulence differs in several ways:

1. it differs in that it recognizes that people are not going to meet the challenges by pursuit of the traditional Western ideals. It postulates that adaptation is occurring because people are pursuing a transformed set of ideals that have as much in common with Eastern as with Western ideals.
2. the evangelical response is within the old concept of man, the poor worthless sinner, whose salvation lies in sacrificing himself and his identity to the bigger social thing. This scenario postulates that adaptation, where we can see such signs, is arising from a reversal of the traditional man-organization relation; from greater involvement and participation as *separate* individuals.

In both of these respects evangelicism would lead people back into greater dependence on the past. Dependence on existing institutions that have followed historically the traditional western ideals and on the regressive patterns of mob behaviour that have characterized earlier periods of social turbulence.

The ideals of 'the adaptive response' are already challenging not reinforcing the great institutions. Economic institutions are being challenged to be responsible; universities are being challenged to be relevant; churches are being challenged to understand the people's message; governments are being challenged to listen, not legislate. The practices associated with 'the adaptive response' are reflected in such ways as democratized work places and local action groups and in general with the demise of manipulatory mass ideological movements.

13. Communication requirements in an adaptive society

13.1. Social design theory

Our scenario for an adaptive society is presented in *Futures We're In*. We still think that this scenario presents Australia's most probable future. Short of some natural calamity we do not think Australia will be turned from this course, during the next quarter-century. (In appendix A we explain why we discard the prospect, not of war itself, but of a war reversing this basic trend.) That scenario did not focus on communication. To try to unravel that thread we follow two guide-lines:

1. communications technology is the leading part in technological development *but* in human society human communication is a secondary property. It is and has always been a *necessary* condition for human beings to act socially. Not, however, a *sufficient* condition. Many situations can be observed where communication channels exist but are not used. In many situations communications can reduce social activity;
2. the most important of the sufficient conditions for human communication lie in a society's choice between the two basic designs for social organization.

These two designs are so basic to an understanding of the transformation taking place in Australian society that we will repeat what we stated in *Futures We're In*.

As this spelling out has to be detailed and may be a bit tedious, we will state our conclusions first. A choice in basic organizational design is inevitable so there is no question but that men will make choices (even if they are not conscious of doing so); the choice is between whether a population seeks to enhance its chances of survival by strengthening and elaborating special social mechanisms of control or by increasing the adaptiveness of its individual members. The latter is a feasible strategy in a turbulent environment and one to which western societies seem culturally biased.

Choice seems unavoidable. What makes it unavoidable is a design principle. In designing an adaptive self-regulating system, one has to build in redundancy or else settle for a system with a fixed repertoire of responses that are adaptive only to a finite, strictly identified set of environmental variations. This is an important property of any system as an arithmetical increase in redundancy tends to produce a logarithmic increase in reliability (Pierce, 1964, p. 61). Redundancy may be achieved by having redundant parts, but then there must be special control mechanisms (specialized parts) that determine which parts are active or redundant for any particular adaptive response. If the control is to be reliable it must also have *redundant parts* and the question of a further control emerges. In this type of system, reliability is bought at the cost of providing or maintaining the redundant parts, hence the tendency is toward continual reduction of the functions, and hence cost, of the individual part. The social system of an ant colony relies more upon this principle than does a human system, and a computer more so than an ant colony. The alternative principle is to increase the *redundancy (multiplicity) of functions* of the individual parts. This does not entail a pressure toward higher and higher orders of special control mechanisms, but it does entail effective mechanisms within the part for setting and re-setting its functions – for human beings *shared values* are the most significant of these self-regulating devices. Installing these values of course increases the cost of the parts. The human body is the classic example of this type of system although it is becoming more certain that the brain operates by means of overlapping assemblies based on similar sharing of multi-functional parts (Tomkins, 1962, vol. 1, p. 120).

Whatever wisdom one attributes to biological evolution, the fact is that in the design of social organization, we have a genuine choice between these design principles. When the cost of the parts is low (in our context, the cost of labour or of individual life), the principle of redundant parts is attractive. The modern Western societies are currently raising the value of individual life, although a change in reproductive rates and investment rates could reverse this. There is, however, a more general principle that favours the western ideal. The total error in a system can be represented as equal to the square root of the sum of the squares of all the component errors. It follows that a reduction in the error of all the components produces a greater increase in reliability than does an equal amount of reduction that is confined to some of them (*e.g.* to the special control parts). We are certainly not suggesting that this principle, per se, has been or is even now a conscious part of western

ideologies. Some sense of it does, however, seem to have reinforced our prejudice toward democratic forms of organization and our prejudice against
elitism.

Two further factors operate in the same direction.

When the sources of error are not independent, *i.e.* they are correlated,
then the tactic of overall reduction in error is even more advantageous. In
human systems, communication is a necessary and potent factor and hence
the advantages are considerable. In such systems where interdependence of
the functioning parts is significant the relevant theorem implies that 'it is
generally best to allocate costs in order to improve the strength of the *weakest
link* in order to give each function the same probability, of failure, regardless
of the relative cost of the parts.' (Pierce, 1964, p. 61).

By contrast when the alternative design principle of redundant parts is
adopted, there are strong reasons for investing in reducing the correlation of
parts (*e.g.* anti-unionist practices, the censorship of the mass media in totali-
tarian societies and the management of concentrations camps).

The second factor also happens to be our basic concern – *environmental
complexity*. The second design principle allows for a much greater range of
adaptive responses than does a redundancy of parts. Although its tolerance
for error in any particular response is less, this is a condition for greater
learning. We do not think that man can hope to actively adapt to turbulent
environments without restructuring his major institutions along the lines of
the second design principle, redundancy of the functions of individual parts.
Bureaucracies are based on the first principle and the individual is an instrument of the system. *An instrument functions as a lower order of system than the
system that uses it* (Ackoff and Emery, 1972, 31-32). Quite simply, using an
analogy from mathematical statistics, an instrument is always going to operate with one degree of freedom less than the system using it. Thus, although
a social system is a purposeful system whose members are purposeful there is
a constant tendency towards *increasing* or *decreasing variety* in the range and
level of the behaviour of the individual members. In systems based on the
first principle the tendency will be toward *variety decreasing*; the range of
purposeful behaviour will be restricted and increasingly behaviour will be at
a lower level of multi-goal-seeking or goal-seeking behaviour. The assembly
line has been the epitome of this process but the same phenomenon appears
in the bureaucratic organization of scientific and engineering work. Systems
designed on the second principle will tend to be *variety increasing*: to maintain and extend the multi-functionality of their members they will seek to

extend the range of their purposeful behaviours and increase the opportunities and support for ideal-seeking behaviour. That is, such systems will be founded on the assumption that they are best served by serving as an instrument to the potentially higher system capabilities of their individual members.

13.2. Communication in a social system based on redundancy of its parts i.e. bureaucratically arranged

The bulk of communication in these social systems takes place between individuals operating at different system levels; the majority are not operating at more than the level of goal directed systems, a minority with varying degrees of purposefulness. The mass of people are parts who are rendered maximally redundant and hence have to be minimally relied upon or trusted for their performancy. They are put in a situation where if they don't perform as specified they can be readily replaced by some other.[1] A minority, as supervisors, bosses and heads of varying description, have some involvement as systems. They have some degree of participation in choosing the goals that are to be pursued. At the lower levels even these special controlling parts are not usually very purposeful. The teacher in the school feels very circumscribed, in his freedom to choose teaching goals, by curricula, time-table, senior subject master, head-master, inspectors and the Department or Board. The work supervisor feels very constrained by production programmers, job estimators, M.T.M., superintendents, work managers and so on.

The ubiquity of this communications context could be demonstrated by similar paradigms running down from the senior decision makers through various more numerous cogs to the multitudes at the receiving end as ratepayers, viewers, servicemen, customers, pensioners, subscribers, voters, laymen.

This context is that of persons who are able to operate at the higher levels of their potential for self determination trying to communicate with persons of similar potential but unable to contribute at other than goal-directed systems (sometimes enables to select means, rarely able to select goals).

This context has a number of very characteristic features. These are as follows:

---

1. In a recent survey of the Australian urban work force 53 per cent saw themselves as 'quite or very easily replaceable'.

1. *Asymmetrical,* not a two-way symmetrical communication like a discussion between equals. The balancing effect of question and answer of or 'I will tell you because you have told me' is absent. Instead each communication is a potential threat to the hierarchical relation. There is no reciprocity or reflection in the choice structures of recipient and sender involved in the communication between them.This asymmetry is reflected in the relative absence of discussion and the dominance in communication of orders to 'do this', 'buy that', 'fill this form in'. Orders that require responses not replies. The other way flow reports which again do not invite discussion. It will be noted that this is the characteristic 'communication' between a machine operator and his machine.

2. *Egocentric* Flowing on from the first point, communication tends to be of the form, 'I want this'. 'I think this'. In the social climates experiments this use of the language, versus 'we want'. 'we think', was one of the most distinctive differences between autocratic and democratic organizations (Lippitt, 1943). The building block of bureaucracy is the pinning down of the individual to specific personal responsibilities for task performance. Tasks themselves get split up into one-man-shifts units to enable this allocation of personal responsibility. In this way an individual's interests are best served by looking out for himself. It is no concern of his to communicate information that is mainly of benefit to others, laterally or up-and-down. It is of no concern to him to attend to, let alone remember, communications directed to him unless there is some obvious benefit to him. The tangle that this egocentricity can create is beautifully illustrated in Wertheimer's analysis of 'A girl describes her office' (1945, 136-148). In our work, we time and again come across senior managers of large bureaucracies who are convinced that their organizational troubles would be over if only they could improve communications. This is like a native spearman saying his aim would improve if the water did not refract the light.

3. *'Them and us'* Between each of the essential points in the communication chain is a difference in status, and in interest in the effects of what is being communicated. The person of superior status wants the truth if he thinks he can do something about it, or a doctored report if he just wants to look good to his superiors (as governors of British prisons, at least up until the recent past, had a marked proclivity toward 'not wanting to know' about considerable areas of life in their prison). The inferior is naturally prepared to doctor his communication to make himself look good or blameless, or to

make his case look good. A status gap between communicants is always a potential barrier to communication. *It constitutes an inherently unstable medium: always ready to amplify or attenuate messages in ways that have nothing to do with a truthful correspondence of source events and message.* Compare this state of affairs with the properties of a good medium: docile, in the sense of creating minimum distortion between message in – message out. At the interface of organization and environment, docility, as a communications medium, would be reflected in allowing the selection and transmission from the set of possible messages of the 'truest one' that evidence and understanding allows. Put this way it is evident that troubles begin at the very point of origination of the message in the bureaucratic setting. And this, regardless of whether the point of origination is the general with 'a message to the troops' or with Smith at the bottom with, 'Smith reporting, sir.'

These three features describe a social communications medium that we will describe as 'seriality', because those features so closely approximate to what is in formal logic defined as a serial relation (Feibleman and Friend, 1969). Asymmetry, ego-centrism and the 'them – us' syndrome define the communications context of a bureaucratic organization, a bus queue, a supermarket and some kinds of sick families. What is absent in this communicative process is some point of reference whereby the communicants can see themselves as relating as part-to-part within a whole; relating with respect to their differing activities and concerns but with reference to some third mediating factor such as common interests (Chapter 8, *Futures We're In*).

A society that is bureaucratically arranged creates its *'shadow society'*. Within a bureaucratic organisation, as distinct from a society, it has been amply documented that shadow, informal structures are well nigh inevitable. We suggest that the phenomenon exists at a societal level and is identifiable as the same phenomenon.

The multitudes at the end of the multiplicity of bureaucratic chains in such a society have their rights (to choose, or to effect decisions that will influence their ability to choose) so fragmented that they can, in respect to them, act only as goal directed systems. They have however, the potential to act as purposeful systems and they are, by their own nature, better rewarded (enjoyed, excited) by acting as purposeful systems. Their desire to act as free agents tends to out-weigh the fear and distress that arises from their inadequacies and lack of learning.

The re-assertion of individual purposefulness can range from gardening, to sport, to mob action, to the 'Clockwork Orange' scenario. The mis-direction of individual objectives is a social system property not some genetic defect.

In a bureaucratised society of n persons there are $n(n-1)/2$ interstices. There is a strain to fill those interstices if there is any promise that these people can achieve a higher order of personal system functioning or even the appearance of such. For those who wish to sell goods of status – raising significance, or millenarian ideas, this is the cheap power system: a self financing system of secondary communications. Unlike the seriality of the bureaucratised organizations this shadow world is an agglutinative field, an aggregate, a mass market.

What we have described is a medium with its own characteristics; a medium in the same way that the telephone is a medium that has its distinctive characteristics compared with radio, press, lecture, TV.

In stating this we do not think that we are just using analogies. A large bureaucratic organisation is a medium. Policies made at the top have to filter through to actions at the counter, the output desk, the outgoing warehouse. Complaints about service and quality have to be fed back through the same system of diverse and partial responsibilities. We have stated that the basic characteristics of communication in a bureaucratic context are asymmetry, ego-centricity and the 'them – us' syndrome. We have further stated that this constitutes a social *medium* of communication. We now state that 'this medium is the message'. This is not stated in this way in order to get some McLuhan type shock-effect. It is stated this way because messages flowing through the medium of a bureaucratic social system undergo a transformation that is created by the medium, and relatively independent of the message. When a message enters a bureaucratised social field it is refracted just as surely as is light when it enters water.

Both Marcuse and Orwell ('Newspeak') have drawn attention to what bureaucratization of society has done to the shape of message:

'the established universe of discourse bears throughout the marks of the specific modes of domination, organization, and manipulation to which the members of a society are subjected. People depend for their living on bosses and politicians and jobs and neighbours who make them speak and mean as they do; they are compelled, by societal necessity, to identify the 'thing' (including their own person, mind, feeling) with its functions. How do we know? Because we watch television, listen to the radio, read the newspapers and magazines, talk to people.

Under these circumstances, the spoken phrase is an expression of the individual who speaks it, *and* of those who make him speak as he does, *and* of whatever tension or contradiction may interrelate them. In speaking their own language, people also speak the language of their masters, benefactors, advertisers.' (Marcuse, 1964, p. 193).

'In part, Orwell's durability is due to his central obsession. It was not politics or personalities that concerned him so much as language itself. In the '30s he saw words bent; in the

'40s he chronicled the result: 'whole governments twisted out of shape'. His best work was an attempt to restore the meaning to words, to prove that 'good prose is like a window pane'. 'One ought to recognize', he wrote, 'that the present political chaos is connected with the decay of language, and that one can probably bring about some improvement by starting at the verbal end'.' (Kanfer, 1975).

The single most pervasive effect is, we think, the bifurcation of two of the primary functions of communication; to *inform* and to *instruct*. When messages both inform and instruct they *enlighten*. When they only inform or only instruct they do not enlighten.

These distinctions derive from our theory of purposeful systems and in particular, of choice and decision making (Ackoff and Emery, 1972). Communication cannot be said to have taken place unless 'a message produced by *B* produces a change in one or more of the parameters of *A*'s purposeful state' (*Ibid.* p. 142, definition 9.9).

A message that *informs* changes the 'probability of choice' of the possible paths in a choice situation. It changes the receiver's map. What was unfamiliar seems familiar; what seemed familiar takes on strange aspects; what seemed consonant or straight forward seems dissonant or ambi-valent. (These two broad effects have been studied in depth by field theorists in psychology under the headings of 'cognitive differentiation' and 'overlapping cognitive fields' (Deutsch, 1954).

A message that *instructs* changes the receiver's perception of the Probable Effectiveness of the different courses of action open to him. Of course the instruction might produce a false confidence in one's capabilities or other aspects affecting relative effectiveness, but it would still be a communication.

'A single communication may, of course, both inform *and* instruct. A message that does both can be said to enlighten the receiver. The joint effect of information that changes probabilities of choice and instruction that changes efficiencies (sic) of choice is a change in probabilities associated with the possible outcomes. Thus whereas information relates to familiarity and instruction to knowledge, *enlightenment relates to understanding*.' (Ackoff and Emery, 1972, p. 155-156.)

These distinctions are not a deviance with dictionary definitions, only sharper more rigorously mutually exclusive and parts of a logically exhaustive set.

We are not alone in seeing the significance of these distinctions. In developing their communications theory of culture Hall and Trager, quite independently, found it necessary to make the same distinctions. 'The special meanings they indicate for formal, informal, and technical closely approximates our definitions of familiarity, understanding and knowledge. Thus the formal level of culture is what is traditional and communicated by information; the technical level is what is knowledge and communicated by instruction; the informal culture is what somehow or other has to be comprehended or understood (as, 'when you grow up you will understand' or 'when you get the hang of it')' (*Ibid.* p. 229).

For us a very significant feature of the Hall and Trager development is that their conceptualization stemmed from a concern about the Americans' ideas about time, and this when American society was thoroughly bureaucratized. The spatialization of time is an inherent feature of bureaucratization and properly symbolized by the stop watch of the time-and-motion job analysor.[2]

In that bureaucratized context Hall and Trager thought it most fitting to call 'enlightening' communication 'informal', something that happened in the interstices of the 'formal' and the 'technical'. This at a time when there had never been so many people in school, college or university for such a large proportion of their lives!

We think their conceptualization has quite inadvertently made our point: in a bureaucratized society messages automatically tend to inform *or* instruct. It is accident, almost, if they enlighten. This point we now come back to.

Where people are related bureaucratically then it is irrelevant or pointless to send messages calculated to increase understanding, enlightenment. When messages are sent down they are primarily to instruct as one would instruct or programme a bit of machinery. It is 'do this' or 'do that', 'don't do the other thing': 'fill in the form this way', 'queue here'. 'go to the store with the X sign up'. Not, *why* they should but *what* they should do. If the employees are restless, the voters uncertain, the customers wary, then they must be 'informed' (shaped as by a potter) that this is the way of life, the natural thing to do, the product that just happens to fit their style of life. Enlightenment is rarely relevant in communicating from super-ordinates to subordinates. The latter are not expected to be concerned with, experienced of, or educated to understand 'the bigger picture'.

As if to prevent any misunderstanding about this fundamental difference in concerns, the mandarins of bureaucracy typically have their deepest thoughts clothed in esoteric language by ideologues, economists, planners. A typical example, but just one picked at random, is the speech on the first budget of the first Wilson government in the U.K. Four full pages of the 'Times' were filled with esoteric economic theory about this proposed measure and the other. In the last couple of columns the reader learnt that the

2. Which is also why the rapid spread of 'flexi-time' – flexible working hours determined by the individual – within the Australian Public Service is a surer indication of intent to de-bureaucratize than any of their public statements.

budget was going to be balanced by raising excise on booze, cigarettes, petrol and increasing charges on medicine bottles dispensed under the National Health scheme. There was no essential difference between this and Stalin's famous 5-7 hour speeches. In a bureaucratized society communication is already Newspeak.

Let us now look at upward communication in a bureaucratized society. This can originate from a person in the position of being a lower-order cog or from being one bit of what we have termed the shadow world. In the first case there are some obvious constraints that will tend to shape any message.

First, even to initiate a message is to suggest that one's superior is behaving wrongly, is less than omnipotent or is not on his toes. Once the plunge is decided on, the message must be shaped so that it carries no such connotation even if the reason for the message is precisely because the superior is behaving badly, is ill-informed or is somewhat less than conscientious. The distortion, the refractive index is that the real source of the message must be hidden. The source must appear to be in some variance that was quite unpredictable, or some outside treacherous hostile, or the shortcomings of 'your humble servant' (Military history is a gold mine of such techniques). Distortion is natural even when the communication from below is in response to a demand from above to know the facts. The subordinate's first concern is that he should look good or blameless from whatever he communicates. So long as this is ensured he has but a varying degree of concern with the success of the overall enterprise of which he is a part, a cog. The second concern of the subordinate is that his lot in life be not worsened, hopefully improved by his message. If his lot in life is tied up with the lot of his peers then he may inform on them. The unreliability of such information has long been recognized in courts of law.

The general point we wish to make is that these particular forces toward distortion of communication also operate to bi-furcate informing and instructing. The message going up will tend to be hard, factual or instructing e.g. the motor is burnt out, so and so was late, this order was not delivered by this date, this part of this form was not filled, or it will be a whinge or a whine ('under these conditions we cannot . . .;' 'without extra staff we cannot . . .' etc.). Messages going upwards in this system will only rarely seek to tell the boss how to do his job. Special third parties are usually needed for this: trade unions and, in a trivial way, works councils. Even these bodies must act on the understanding that any message that enlightens the boss about how his subordinates operate threatens their chances of exercising choice; of behaving like purposeful systems.

Looking at how people are actually related in bureaucratized organizations one can only wonder why Lord Brown, noted British industrialist and management theorist, could wonder 'why such special communication bodies as Works Councils were needed when management and workers were in contact on the shop floor daily, every working day?' (Brown, 1965, p. 205).

Messages to and from the shadow world of the mass markets deserve special consideration. These messages bulk very large in the mass media. In fact they have been the decisive force in shaping the scale and character of radio and television; as the demands of business determined the shape and scale of telegraph, telephone, telex and now computer.

In this world the bifurcation of informing and instructing is almost complete. The TV cannot do much more than inform and hardly tries to do more. Even Sesame Street appears to do no more than familiarize children with the alphabet. Teachers then strike something akin to the sound barrier. Sheer familiarity with the elements of the alphabet becomes a barrier to teaching analytical use of these elements, to placing these elements in messages – 'what else exciting is there to learn?'

A multitude of small circulation, interest journals cater for horticulturalists, car fiends, do-it-yourself handymen, professionals and the like. A section of the press and the weekly magazines try to stay afloat in a world of readers who are already smugly acquainted with what is going on from their TV viewing.

The bifurcation we are writing about is probably greatest for the children, adolescents and young adults. Their life is to a large degree spent between being *instructed* by the educational institutions and *informed* by the mass media. It is accidental if they are enlightened as to why their world works as it does. Little wonder that they devour Tolkien and astrology.

What happens to the adult as consumer, pensioner, rate-payer, voter etc.? We suggest that, for the most part they can only vote with their feet (instruct) or emit howls of anguish or joy (inform). The individual, as a member of a mass of similarly placed individuals in a bureaucratized society is very hard placed to find the appropriate recipient for his message. When services to a public have been bureaucratized the organization's picture of the individual customer or claimant does not even start to come together till you are at least two steps removed in the hierarchy from the clerk at the counter. At the lower levels he is just bits and pieces. If the person who is moved to send a message finds the level where he exists as a person then he is in for a surprise. When he is put together within the organization it is an abstract him. The bits of him that belong to other departments are not there. The bits of him

that have independent existence, that belong to an aged mother, to the life
of his street etc., these are not in the bureaucratic picture of him. We are not
suggesting that they should be. (Although we are not above suggesting that
such decisions about him ought to be shifted to parts of the society where he
is seen as a whole person). We are suggesting that as the individual gets that
message he will cast his own messages accordingly.

We have dealt at some length with bureaucratized society as a medium of
communication. Such attention seems justified.

*Telecommunications practically grew up with the bureaucratization of western
society. It seems highly probable that the shape of the telecommunications as we
know it is the shape imposed by bureaucratization and its shadow society. It seems
highly probable that if the key organizations of society are being de-bureaucratized, democratized, then, in the future, telecommunications will have a very
different shape to what would be projected from its last seventy years of growth.*

Those, like Pawley, who think that the past trends will inexorably shape
the future are people who are unaware of what has been happening in the
key area of work relations.

Is it possible to identify the sorts of distortion that may have occurred in
telecommunications because it happened to grow up with bureaucracy?

The major particularized effects of bureaucratization on social communication would appear to be the following:

1. Bifurcation of the functions of informing and instructing and the subsequent decline of social institutions or institutional arrangements for communication of enlightenment and understanding.

It is claimed by some that McLuhan's thesis about the demise of the book
is rubbish (Bagdihian, 1971). However, the figures quoted against the thesis
are unsatisfactory. They give no indication of what proportion of books
produced and what proportion of new titles are cook books, text books or
are destined for technical service libraries or coffee tables.

A better guide seems to be the demise or transformation of the book shops
in all Australian cities. The book as a silent enlightening dialogue seems to
be doing what McLuhan predicted. Our thesis would likewise seem to be
contradicted by the great growth in institutions of tertiary education. Surely
these are not just instruction centres but centres of enlightenment? Centres
where young and old minds together endlessly grapple with and debate with
a view to achieving deeper understanding and greater enlightenment? Masha
Eisenberg's four year study of Sydney University students and staff amply

confirms our thesis. 'This university is too formal, structured, bureaucratic
. . . a huge impersonal even hostile campus . . . the majority came to regard
any reading that was not set as an indulgence, and a guilty one. But, as they
maintained, there was little time for reading. Indeed, it appears there is little
time at university for anything more than the mechanics – lectures, essays,
tutorials – of a nine-to-five existence.' (1975).

2. An insatiable demand for technical means of clear and unambiguous information and instructions to the subordinates. Management literature is
full of advice on communication. They are not wrong in the sense that if
communication was effective then bureaucratic organizations could probably be made to work efficiently. They are fundamentally wrong in assuming
that any improvement in the message could offset the nature of the medium.
The receivers of the messages have the capabilities of purposeful systems.
When the system motivates them to twist the message to their purposes they
will soon enough find a way to so twist the message that it serves their purposes, no matter how clever the original communications expert. We said
that this need to communicate to subordinates was insatiable. We meant this.
The need to communicate is always there. No conceivable means of achieving
this in a bureaucracy for more than the short run is conceivable. The need is
insatiable.

There is the same insatiable demand to *inform* people as members of the
shadow society. In that world people are simply an agglutinative mass, an
aggregate. They cannot be instructed, they may be informed. Why they make
a choice is irrelevant. That they should make a choice is critical otherwise
certain myths about free markets and democratic 'freedoms to be represented' would wither away.

3. An insatiable demand for information about the lower orders, their feelings and the facts about their behaviour. By the nature of the social media
such information does not come through. The mandarins will be constantly
on the search for such information or means of gaining such information.
When the super-ordinates organize an attitudinal survey of their subordinates
the latter are not likely to be slow in grasping what that means – a means for
better controlling them. A recent round of inteviews with more than 200
hundred of the top urban decision makers of Australia is instructive. They
were asked what was going on in their cities. The overwhelming response was
'don't ask us, we do not know, we don't even know what the citizens are thinking.' In today's bureaucratised cities the fog is as thick as the 'fog of battle'.

4. An inhibition of *lateral communication*. If a message comes from below it will often be of the form 'We feel . . .'. If it is of the form 'We know . . .' it is mutiny. If a message comes from above it is that 'you separately, in your individual areas, do this, that or the other'. The messages that are strange to the system are of the kind 'We consider that . . .' '*We* would like you to consider that . . .'.

The inhibitions on lateral communication are so inherent in bureaucratized organizations that they can only function by instituting a welter of special communication channels. (*e.g.* the Public Service I.D.C.'s – inter-departmental committees).

These demands and these inhibitions did not arise today. They have had time to shape telecommunications. These demands have led to a demand for a telephone on every desk, they have led to computerization so that no transaction will take place at the periphery of an organization that is unknown to the centre, they press us toward the computer data banks, they press us toward cable TV, more channels and yet longer hours for televiewing. And so on.

What this has done to society is vividly illustrated by what it did to the U.S. Army as described by Marshall, official war historian. Between World War I and World War II the American infantryman fell mute. 'This last one was about the mutest army that we ever sent to war . . . Impressed by the completeness and efficiency of our channels, we tended to forget that no mechanical means of communicating ever given man can ever become a substitute for the spoken word, and none can amplify thought.' (1947, p. 136). This army of civilians drawn out of a bureaucratized society demonstrated time and again in combat, as Marshall documents, that they had forgotten the basic rule that to survive in the turbulent environment of the battlefield 'You must prepare to talk. You must learn that speech will help you save your situation. You must be alert at all times to let others know what is happening to you. You must use your brain and your voice any time that any word of yours will help you *or others*.' (*Ibid.* p. 137).

One gets a strange sense of *deja vue* when one hears today's adolescents pleading for drop-in centres, places where they can just sit and talk.

It is their future world that we now wish to turn to.

13.3. Communication in a society based on the multi-functioning of its parts i.e. democratized

We can now come back to the main theme of this Part. What happens to communications as the Australian society gradually democratizes its organizations, communities and families? It should be obvious by now that we mean much more by 'democratizing' than extending the right to be represented by someone else. We will, however, come back to that shortly.

As a first approximation let us take the points we have made about the influences of bureaucratized society on communications and see if we can hazard some ideas about comparable effects in democratized society.

After that we can go into details.

The shape of communications

In a bureaucratized society	*In a democratized society*
1. bifurcation of *informing* and *instructing*: inhibition of enlightening messages.	demand for messages that both inform *and* instruct
2. insatiable demand for technical means to inform and instruct subordinates/masses. (mass media, offset . . .)	demand for *mutual* enlightenment and the cultural or technical means to serve this end.
3. insatiable demand for information *about* the lower orders (surveys, data banks . . .)	
4. inhibition of lateral communication.	maximizing means for lateral communication

This looks almost too simple to be true. However, this is usually what happens when one looks at media. They tend to have a small number of generalized characteristics that have tremendous effect because they are so pervasive and yet so transparently obvious that they are not always seen. We have been trying to look at societies as not just source and destination of messages but also as media.

Simple as it may look the implications are significant. If true, then the fantastic rate of growth that has made telecommunications and computers the leading part of technology will lose its head of steam.

The most significant developments in human communications in the next quarter century are much more likely to be in cultural innovations than in technical innovations.

The import and impact of such innovations can already be seen in the cases of the 'search conference', 'the participative design workshops', 'learning centres', 'video-access centres'.

Within communications technology the disappearance of 'insatiable demands' will be paralled by shifts in emphasis. The demand will grow most for technologies that facilitate one-one, many-many, us-us communication; least for the technologies that facilitate one-many, many-one communications. As the latter include press, radio, film, television and surveys the effect would be substantial.

Of all the media there is none that approaches the capability of face-to-face communication between equals for handling and generating enlightening communication. There is no other that can even begin to make a significant contribution to *directly* influencing motivations, the parameter of choice called 'Relative Intentions'. There is no other media that can so well take the printed word as its content and so realize the potential of the printed word. We strongly incline to the view that it has been the decline of conversation that killed the book. TV only aided its transformation into the coffee table item, *Bedside Esquire* and *Playboy*. At one remove, however, TV powerfully re-inforced the bureaucratic effects on conversation.

The technical factors that people will favour in order better to converse, more often, have more to do with transport and the spatial arrangements of life than with communications technology.

The medium of face-to-face contact is also critical to the fourth point about lateral communication. Lateral communication is most commonly a pressing requirement between persons who are in physical contact – but, in a bureaucratized world, have a fence between them. Their physical contiguity is negated by the fact that each has his own separate concern with *his* task, *his* department or unit, *his* world.

The *ABX* situation of face-to-face communication has such strikingly different salience in the bureaucratized world and the emergent world that we should look more closely at it. Such a look might tell us more about the emergent society.

The first thing to note, going back to Chapter IV, is that the rich potential of the *ABX* situation is based on deeply held assumptions that people implicitly bring to the situation. Experimental studies, notably by Asch, have demonstrated how deeply people suffer when these assumptions are rendered untenable.

The four assumptions we noted were:

1. that the face-to-face situation presents an objectively ordered field open to both of the participants;
2. the mutual confrontation of A and B attests to their basic psychological similarity;
3. the ABX situation leads to the emergence of a mutually shared field;
4. within mutually shared psychological fields individuals become more open.

One has only to spell out these assumptions to realize how frequently they would be abrogated in a bureaucratized society; and hence how much face-to-face exchange becomes a course of humiliation, shame, anxiety and contempt, something to be avoided. The natural course of face-to-face communication is mutual positive stimulation, joy and excitement, and mutual understanding. In a bureaucratized society it is safer to restrict such situations to those that only inform *or* instruct, that are culturally defined as content-less (pubs, cocktail parties and dinner parties) or are mere simulations on television.

As we have implied, we shall not spell out the ways in which a bureaucratized society operates to abrogate these assumptions and thus leads the individual to constantly feel that he is dealing with something that is inhuman. It is more important to try to see how the face of society will change as these assumptions are increasingly met and people increasingly meet their communication requirements in this face-to-face manner.

As the first assumption is better met, by people not having to confront over bureaucratic fences, two general effects can be expected:

1. a de-mystification of discourse about social and psychological matters and matters of nature. Where this assumption is met in face-to-face discourse 'the ruling attitude of persons is a sort of naive realism that sees no problem in the fact of perception of knowledge of the surroundings. Things are what they appear to be; they have just the qualities they reveal to sight and touch' (see p. 20). In these circumstances discussion about social matters might come down to what is experienced and be less obfuscated by discourse about 'stagflation', 'reflation', 'recession' and the like. 'Psy-

chology', 'sociology', 'psycho analysis' and 'anthropology' will also look very strange aberrations of the last hundred years.

2. where this assumption is met the fundamental operation in the event of apparent differences is to point or demonstrate, it is not to verbalize . . . (see p. 21). The successful emergence of the video-tape in Australia as a finger or hand, not an eye, has already been alluded to. In general we would expect a reversal of the past and current trend toward a stifling over-verbalization of everything. This could not but be beneficial. As Angyal noted many years ago '. . . the ability to have a symbolic grasp of things is the greatest power which nature has given to some of its creatures, but it is also the deepest source of error and suffering.' (1941, p. 76). This trend would spell the end of text-books, BBC II and teaching as we know it.

The most important feature of the second assumption is that when it is abrogated 'These circumstances fostered an oppressive sense of loneliness which increased in prominence as subjects contrasted their situation with the apparent assurance and solidity of the majority' (Asch, 1956). The most radical change when face-to-face communication between A and B attests to their basic psychological similarity is that in this perception of others is the awareness that they too can establish directive correlations with parts of the environment i.e. they too appear in the environment as action centres. (see p. 22). It has been widely noted that the spoilt darlings of bureaucracy, the young professionals, have been the 'action centres' of recent community protest movements. We are predicting that as this assumption is more frequently met in face-to-face situations there will be many more such 'action centres'. If they are short on the verbal skills, the yak of the young professional, they always have the video-pack.

About the third assumption that people bring into the ABX situation it is only when this is met that people are able to grasp, from their own experience (not the media), the primary social fact, that without some such mutual representation, and some such correspondence between the representations so ordered, intentional interaction can take place with others – not even relations of competition or slavery (see p. 24). In these circumstances we may expect a situation where the social order of things is not only de-mystified but might even be understandably related to the day-to-day life of the citizen; the corporate policies to the workers. Where such understandings emerge people are not only likely to be 'active agents' (see discussion of assumption 2) but potentially effective agents.

The last assumption, that continued interaction at the ABX levels leads to greater personal openness, is critical for our whole analysis of where communications are going. If the first three assumptions are found by people to be commonly observed, to be the coinage of the realm, then they will naturally expect the openness we are referring to, and act on the assumption that it is happening. They will assume that the boundary conditions for (the other and themselves) are increasingly defined by directive correlations that involve others as independent sources of action. At the same time the control over these boundary conditions will entail the pursuit of purposes that refer equally to the requirements he shares with others as to his own particular requirements. Put another way, the *sufficient* conditions for changes of attitudes, beliefs, motives and behaviour will more frequently have the locus in events which take place outside the individual-in-his-phenomenal-field (see p. 25). Cutting across the esoteric language we have felt it necessary to use, the point is clear. Insofar as a democratized society allows the assumptions of human face-to-face communication to be met then dissociation is dead; it is not longer a viable or necessary personal strategy.

14. Human communications in work

The purpose of this chapter is to look at three specific areas of social life and to see whether the changes taking place in these areas fit the general changes we have predicted. The three chosen areas are those of work, leisure and community life. In these matters we will be basically reporting what observations we have already made, not projections from the conclusions in the preceding chapter.

14.1. The world of work

A great mass of communication between people is generated by their need to co-ordinate and control their joint efforts. The manner in which they attempt to co-ordinate and control is very much a function of the organizational forms they adopt. In attempting to adapt to turbulent environments people will necessarily move toward democratized matrix type organization. The question we can ask is 'what effect will this have on types and amount of communication channels they need.'

As we noted earlier bureaucratized organizations seem to have insatiable demands for formalized information up and orders down the structure, and inhibiting effects on lateral communication and dialogue. In summing up his World War II studies of the U.S. Army in combat Marshall gives a clear if extreme view of how communications work in a bureaucracy.

'The flow of orders and instructions is toward the front. But the prevailing flow of information . . . is ever towards the rear (the top) and the volume of it seems to increase according to the square of the distance from the fighting line . . . it is a little bit absurd . . . To reverse the flow, or rather to equalize it, so that all levels may be served according to their necessity – there truly, is the real problem . . . complicated unnecessarily by the blindness and the indifference of men.' (1947, p. 100-101).

We would suggest that 'blindness and indifference' are induced by the form of organization but would not in any way disagree with his conclusion:

'It is a truth beyond all argument that full and accurate information becomes most vital at the point of impact for unless it is correctly applied there, the wisest plan of the ablest general will likely fail. But the organization of tactical information in combat runs directly counter to this principle almost as if it followed an unwritten law – the lower the rank of the commander, the less he is entitled to know about his own affairs.' (*Ibid*, p. 101).

A couple of diagrams will help show the radical change in the communication patterns when organizations shift from bureaucracy to democratization. The solid connecting lines in these diagrams represented formal reporting channels.

The first of these diagrams represents a typical formal organization of a bureaucracy. The second probably comes closer to the real flow of communications as additional lines of reporting to specialist functions are imposed and informal channels are opened up.

The third diagram represents a typical transformation to a democratized form. The reduction in numbers of levels is usual and not exaggeration. Depending on the nature of the task and people the number of work-face groups might have been six to eight instead of four. As we will see that would not much effect the difference.

A little bit of simple arithmetic will indicate that we are confronted with two different worlds of communication.

Table 14.1.1. Formal reporting channels and task mediated relations.

Steps removed from policy maker	Bureaucratic (diagram I)	Democratized (diagram III)
1 step	3	1
2 steps	4	1
3 steps	18	4
4 steps	26	–
5 steps	34	–
Total of formal reporting channels	85	6
Task mediated hierarchical relations (formal reporting channels)	85	6
Task mediated relations between peers (max.)	–	744
Paper generating function*	339	15

* See p. 166.

The sheer difference in the number of 'formal reporting channels' is highly significant. In the bureaucratic model everyone is at some time involved in this mode of communication, and usually more often than he would think necessary. And, in that model, the value of the communication is attenuated because the reporting relation tends to be asymmetrical, egocentric, and 'them-us'. Net result? A mass of communication that leaves people feeling they need more. In the democratic model very few are necessarily engaged in formal reporting relations. When they are there will still be some degree of asymmetry and 'them-us'. Less, however, as they will be reporting a considered group view with that much more relative weight and much less suspicion of self serving ego-centricity.

Several processes are operating in the democratized organization to dampen down the incessant hunting for information so typical of a bureaucratized organization. First, most of the information and advice a person needs for his current operations tends to be held by those who are working on other aspects of the same tasks or on similar tasks. The semi-autonomous group enables such information to be gained and understood through face-to-face dialogue (Marshall's principle, see p. 166). Second, a group that is experienced with the many facets of its task is able to sift and process what gives relevant information about their progress and their difficulties. It becomes possible to have effective 'management by objectives,' and 'management by exceptions.' What is recorded and reported upwards and what is required for instructions are correspondingly simplified. Thus there are improvements in quality as well as reduction in sheer quantity of communications.

The picture of communication flows is, of course, more complicated as can be illustrated by two simple examples. Hunsfoss Pulp and Paper Mill was the first Norwegian organization to democratize, as a way of life. It had a well run, well rewarded Suggestion Scheme. This had averaged one worthwhile suggestion per year, 1958-1964. With democratization, 1966 produced 53 such suggestions, none being put up through the Scheme for direct personal reward. Another measure of communications pattern is given by 'time span of responsibility' – how frequently formal reporting back is required. At Hommelwik metal fabrication plant the time span shifted with democratization from a daily check-up to 'a 3 monthly production planning and wage agreement with built-in productivity forecasts' (Emery and Thorsrud, 1975, p. 83).

The bottom statistic in Table 14.1. needs some comment. We do *not* know how to measure 'the paper generating function'. Marshall was simply ex-

Figure 14.1. Three types of organizational information networks.

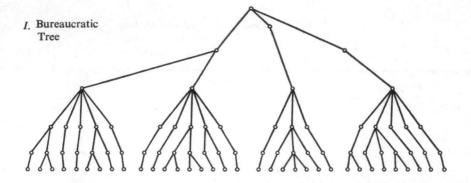

I. Bureaucratic
Tree

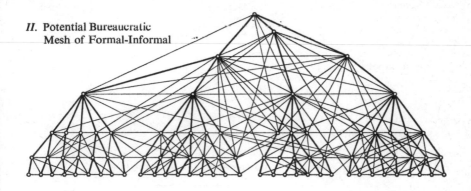

II. Potential Bureaucratic
Mesh of Formal-Informal

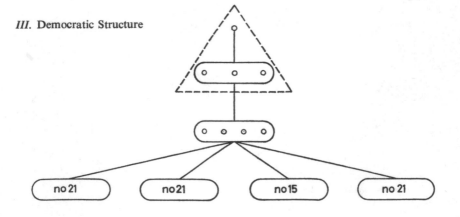

III. Democratic Structure

no 21   no 21   no 15   no 21

IV. Ahmedabad Textiles.
    Management hierarchy before change

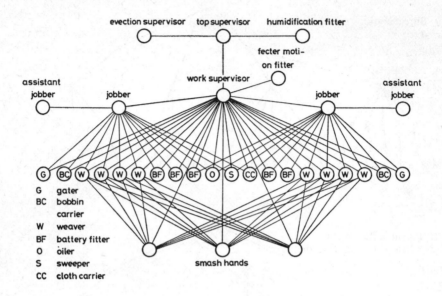

G   gater
BC   bobbin
       carrier
W   weaver
BF   battery fitter
O   oiler
S   sweeper
CC   cloth carrier

V. Management hierarchy after change

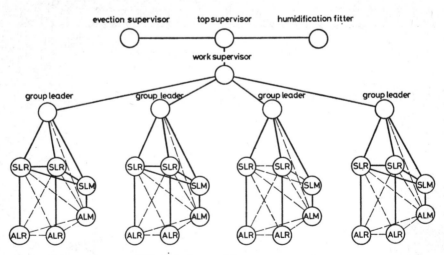

SLR   senior loom runner   SLM   senior loom maintenance
ALR   assistant loom runner   ALM   assistant loom maintenance

pressing his feelings when he wrote that it goes up by the square of the distance from the frontline. Parkinson had much the same feeling. Our estimate is probably as low as one can go in trying to guess the effect of numbers of people and numbers of level (unless the bottom ones are practically slave labourers). We simply multiplied numbers by steps removed – allowing nothing for anxiety in higher positions. Nevertheless the results are instructive.

The main point of our argument should be clear. In organizations, as in society at large, there should appear in the next decades a very significant reduction in demands for communication at a distance.

To short circuit arguments arising from our working with idealized diagrams (*i.e.* diagrams I, II, III) let us conclude with two diagrams of an actual transformation in an Indian textile mill, 1955-1956. The position of 'group leaders' was simply to provide a contact man and it could have been occupied by any one of many in the group but in reality only the fully skilled workers would know enough to be able to represent the group or interpret and check on incoming instructions.

14.2. Matrix organizations and organizational values

The most critical single change in our society's ability to cope with turbulence is democratization of work. This is able to flow rather directly into the social areas of family, school, community and leisure. These changes do not flow so simply and directly into the arrangements of power in the society. It is not possible to democratize those arrangements in any form of society of which we know. It is possible that they can so arrange their exercise of power that it is consonant with a democratized society.

It is with respect to this that we refer to 'matrix organizations and organizational values'.

The concept of 'matrix organization' has been trivialized in its American useage. Kingdon gives a full enough description of this process. In its American application it was merely a means of mobilizing the enthusiasm of scientists and engineers, usually on space programmes, whilst keeping them encapsulated in a bureaucratic organization. It was a pretty halfbaked way of democratizing work when multi-skilling was not possible (Emery and Emery, 1974).

The concept of matrix organization as it emerged in the Tavistock Institute, before the U.S. space programme existed, had a rather broader referent.

There and then the concept of matrix organization referred to the *organiza-tion of organizations* (Emery and Trist, 1968, Chap. 12). The notion that survival of organizations required some 'organization of organizations' was not new. Well back into modern history companies secured their future by taking charters from the Crown. After the bureaucratization of work and the successful establishment of large and widespread corporations this be-came a prominent strategy for survival. It was a strategy of organizing organi-zations to weaken the relative strength of the consumer, the purchaser. It evoked in the U.S.A., the Sherman Act. By the mid thirties it was becoming evident that something more was at stake. Today it is clear that much more is at stake.

There has been a reversal of figure-and-ground as the society has moved from type III to type IV environments. In the new turbulent social environ-ments security for organizations does not arise from the old forms of mono-polistic arrangement. Those arrangements only invite nationalization. The reversal lies, in a very real sense, in moving from organizing against the potential consumer to organizing with him. How is it possible that existing organizations can effect such an about face?

The keys are quite simple:

1. they explicitly organize the management of the resources they use around the principle that whatever the rights of access they have to these re-sources, they are still social resources and as such they have to be main-tained and developed, to the level the society requires;
2. where there are 'common users' of these resources they ensure that they are operating within common policies. To ensure this they must have some way of coming together and searching for relevant common policies and guidelines.

These may be simple keys but our thinking about organizations is so rooted in the past that they are easily misapprehended. Even Shirley Terreberry, after recognizing that coalitions and mergers may be inadequate responses to environmental turbulence, then proceeds to look for strategies that *individual* organizations could pursue. Our point is that such strategies do not exist. The only adaptive strategies are joint ones. But not the sort of joint strategies we have seen in the past. In the past the objective, the focus of the joint strategies was directly to benefit the individual organizations: just like a gambling syndicate. However, *the strategic objectives of matrix organizations would be directly focused on their shared environment*. Individual organizations would benefit indirectly. The objectives would stabilize, protect and enrich the *social habitat* they share. Insofar as these objectives are successfully pursued then the individual organizations have a quicker more predictable and supportive environment in which to pursue their own ends. In effect each individual organization is helped to find its appropriate *niche* in the social environment.

We need to adjust our thinking about the world of organizations and people in the way Rachel Carson led us to adjust our thinking about nature. Barry Commoner has suggested an 'informal set of laws' about ecological systems which underwrite the stress we place on matrix organizations.

'*First law*: everything is related to everything else by processes that can result in large amplification and attenuation effects. Thus a small perturbation in one place may have large, distant, long-delayed effects.'
'*Second law*: everything must go somewhere – there is no such thing as disposable 'waste'. If social resources are spoilt at one place in the system they are going to turn up somewhere else.'
'*Third law*: any large unilateral change that is introduced will almost certainly be detrimental to the system.'
'*Fourth law*: there is no such thing as a free lunch– someone foots the bill.' (1972, pp. 33-46).

These principles seem equally relevant to the management of our social ecology.

We do *not* for one moment think that a single matrix organization mapping the whole social ecology would ever be feasible. What we see emerging are many *incomplete*, *temporary* and *overlapping* assemblies. They would not, as in the past, be composed of similar but competitive organizations having a temporary but joint interest in defence or exploitation. The matrices would contain dissimilar organizations whose fates are positively correlated by matrical dependence on the resourcefulness or otherwise of their particular part of the social environment. The problem is not unlike that confronting the management of community and regional development in present day Australia.

Such matrix organizations would not tend to evolve supra-organizations because participating organizations would not be involved in surrendering their own individual objectives. What would evolve are rules which allow everyone a chance to play, and such means for protecting and developing social resources as enrich the total field.

In one further way matrix organizations differ fundamentally from the joint organizations of the past. In the latter the intent was to agree on joint *objectives*, that were clearly specified and achievable within a definite period.

For matrix organizations to 'tame' turbulent environments it seems essential that they go beyond objectives to the identification of ideals they can commonly hold by.

What is necessary is that they jointly agree to certain ideals: ideals that would encompass the various purposes they were pursuing or could probably wish to pursue. At the same time this set of ideals should be seen to exclude purposes which, if pursued by any party would place them all in jeopardy.

The shift from achievable objectives to ideals is critical:

1. Insofar as no one can achieve an ideal then no one can take it from some one else. An objective, *e.g.* share of market, can set up a zero-sum game where for every winner there is a loser.

2. Setting of 'realistic' objectives implies setting up a model of what the environment will be like, what resources will be available, what responses will be effective, what reactions will be expected. No matter how realistic the model it is still a model, an abstraction. However, once the objective is accepted everyone in the matrix is expected to act as if the model was reality.

If each organization were to restrict itself to objectives we would have as many models of reality as there are parties and each is locked into its own 'reality'.

3. Setting ideals as the overriding concern puts no such emphasis on substituting model for reality. In any situation no matter how novel, one can ask of the apparent courses of action 'what direction will this take us with respect to the ideal(s)'. Just as no conceivable course of action can achieve an ideal all courses of action could conceivably approach or go away from an ideal. The novel situation does not have to be reduced to some prior model of reality. Instead the novel situation has to be probed to find ways of testing where different courses of action lead with respect to the relevant ideals. The emergent strategies for learning to learn from novel situations constitute the *distinctive competence* of a matrix organization in a turbulent environment.

4. The objectives that emerge in the middle ground between ideals and learning are then but the temporary landmarks shifting in relevance as one proceeds, or as the ideal is seen to lie in a different quarter. And, like the ancient Pacific navigators, we must be prepared to navigate, in the absence of landmarks or sky marks, by the faintest of wave patterns attesting to happenings far beyond the horizon. Management by objectives is nice if you can get it

but fatal if the organizations in the matrix are so dependent on having objectives that they start to see mirages. The organizations must learn to manage their relations during periods when clear objectives are absent. This adds
a trial and error quality to matrix development but no more than is needed
for learning what is happening 'out there'.

5. With the introduction of ideals the relation within an individual organization, and its interfaces with the environment, change radically. With a hierarchy of objectives each sector of the boundary, *e.g.* sales, purchasing, personnel, has its own subordinate objectives and its own model of its 'real'
world. As ideals come to dominate the orientation of an organization such
variation in boundary conditions is not tolerable. Environmental uncertainty
means that one cannot predict where a message will come from or in what
form, how an action will be interpreted or by whom. Hence the same ideals
must prevail at all interfaces to the environment and the same ideals must
mediate the inflow as *guide* the outflow.

If the organizational boundaries do not have a unitary character then
messages from the outside will get misdirected within the organization. If
sectors of the boundary are strongly committed to abstract models of reality
they will act less as a good medium, either for in-or-out-flows, than as a
structuring, coding mechanism. This simply spells out some implications of
Ashby's 'Law of Requisite Variety.' If an organization cannot detect the
relevant variety present in its environment then it cannot mobilize corresponding variety in its own behaviour: it will fail to adapt.

In this emergence of matrix organizations we find once again that the future
seems to depend on innovations in social communication rather than on
technical innovations.

This discussion of matrix systems has been generalized and abstract
although it was built up from actual cases. To make the notions more concrete let us consider that set of organizations that constitute the Australian
manufacturing industry. About what matters could these organizations come
together in matrix fashion to form 'incomplete, temporary, overlapping assemblies?' What values would lay down the sides or dimensions of the matrix?
One has only to ask the simplest of questions to see the extent to which
manufacturing organizations that are involved with very dissimilar types of
organizations and publics are concerned with common supportive functions.
Let us assume a product that is currently being manufactured in Australia.

1. Is this particular product necessary?
   a. are better models being produced elsewhere and could they be imported?
   b. is the need irrelevant?
2. If it fulfils a need can the same be said of all of its attributes and appurtenances (packaging etc.)?
3. Are the costs of its assembly and distribution justifiable?

This is not a logically ordered or exclusive set of questions. They are just probes. They serve only to raise the sorts of concrete issues we are concerned with. How often is an individual manufacturing organization going to pose these questions in its policy meetings? If the questions were raised by an individual in such a policy meeting is it hard to imagine the reception? Let us try a script.

Q: We should not be selling X, Y is an obviously superior product.
A: Our product happens to be selling well and with good margins.

Q: We should not be producing X, the Swedjap version is so much superior we should be importing it.
A: We do not care what they are achieving there. The money is in keeping them out and manufacturing ours.

Q: Do we have to make it in so-hard-to-make shapes and spend so much on the packaging and the advertising?
A: It sells them.

Q: Is assembly line production necessary; and door-to-door salesmen?
A: That is the way the leading manufacturing organizations do it.

Thus does pragmatism prevail.

To keep this scenario short we have made it sharp. Our concern is not to criticize. It is to highlight the elementary point that if each party to an interdependent chain of contributions is constrained to considering his own bit in isolation then the total gets lost sight of. We only have to go back to Barry Commoner's 'laws' to see that that probably benefits none of the parties (although, as in gambling, the occasional person will make good winnings).

To look back over just those questions it is clear that in a country like Australia there needs to be:

1. feelers out for what others are able to produce, at home and abroad. To be fruitful they could not be organizationally bound.
2. means of evaluating and standardizing product performance, against *consumer requirements*, not against the in-grown criteria that the manufacturers have. Again, they could not be fruitful if bound to organizations.
3. criteria for judging when to import. If others provide a better-value-for-cost solution to consumer needs what is the higher *purpose* served by underwriting a lesser solution? It cannot be employment per se as obviously such employees and the society would be better off if they were back at school being paid to learn a still better solution.
4. some greater acceptance of 'value analysis', and some greater involvement in design of those who actually make and those who actually use the product. These are after all the people closest to the costs and pay-offs of products.
5. some greater concern with the costs to others, that is others than the organizational leaders and financial backers, of the ways and places they choose to produce the product. These matters must take them into issues of physical, mental and community welfare.
6. some greater concern with what their choice of product means for its transportation, handling and sale.

We have deliberately gone into the particulars. At this level it is obvious that the individual organization is hard put even to begin to properly use the *social* resources it employs as its resources. These are nevertheless starting points for organizations of very different kinds coming together in various forms of matrix organization. Forms within which overriding values might be identified by not just employers and employees but also by consumers, citizens and residents.

On the question of values and ideals we can also go some distance in particularizing. It is clear that all manufacturers must at some stage stop to ponder that 'the product of production is people'. (Herbst, 1974). Whatever an organization produces this day or the next day they are, as sure as anything, producing people who are shaped, or mis-shaped, by the mode of production. And this applies to workers, white collar staff and management. (The novelist Arthur Hailey, has put this well enough in his novel *Wheels*). Manufacturers may not realize or may not want to know what they are doing. As they seek less turbulence in their environment they will have to confront this issue, and work with others to keep it within bounds.

Even more specifically. Australian manufacturers already have to concern themselves with the social values that centre on:

1. 'the human use of human beings'
2. 'the sickliness of urban communities'
3. 'the vulnerability of natural environments'
4. 'the all too pervasive ugliness of manufacturing places and their products'.

Deeper and more concrete than these concerns there is the matter for the manufacturing industries of what they do with the 'base grade labourer' (*i.e.* what they do to lessen poverty in otherwise affluent societies).

Again, this is not a matter they can alone confront even though it may be a matter they can alone solve. This is a deeper issue because the employment conditions for 'base grade labourers' and 'base grade clerks' seem to set something as rigid as a gold standard. The variations above that standard are *relative* improvements in condition. Skilled workers can even look better if their 'relativities' are improved by keeping the base grade worker down.

These value issues are only the likely points at which matrix organizations in Australian manufacturing come to grips with what they are about.

Coming together in appropriate ways about these issues does not seem to require any communication technology that is not already in existence. Only new forms of social intercourse (chapter 9, Jackson, 1975).

15. Human communication and community life

15.1. Revival of community life

The revival of community life was only the romantic ideal of some town planners so long as society was largely bureaucratized. In such a society the overwhelming trend was towards privatization of existence, dissociation.

People will gain a new sense of dignity and self assurance from de-bureaucratization of work and education. As this happens they will increasingly assert their right to participate in decisions that affect their locality and increasingly seek common ground for face-to-face interaction with others. We have moved so far away from community life that it is worth reminding ourselves of what a community is:

'*Community*: a social group that provides its members with, or provides them with access to, instruments for the satisfaction of some of their analogous objectives – instruments that some of its members are responsible either for producing and maintaining or for providing the group with the means of acquiring and maintaining them, and that all its members are responsible for using in a way that does not reduce access to them by any others in the group.' (Ackoff and Emery, 1972, definition 13-15).

It is this sense of community that we have been spelling out in our discussion of matrix organization. However, this kind of sharing, usually requires geographical contiguity both for ease of access and for sharing responsibility. Just how many people can be so involved depends on what is being shared but without such sharing geographical contiguity can imply no more than a potential community. An important sub-set of community interests are the cultural means available to them. By cultural we do not mean 'high culture' but the historical evolved forms of group problem solving. Thus the questions one would ask are, do these people have a way of articulating and identifying their community problems? Do they have ways of tackling them as a community? In the revival of community life people will be concerned to make them *variety increasing* for their members; to increase the choices open to people. The basic directions in which this can be done, and hence we predict will be done, are those directions that modify the parameters of everyone's choices:

1. *Probability of Choice.*
   That is, increase the likelihood that members choose as a matter of custom or personal preferences the same courses of community action. An observable consequence would be more co-operativeness and what is usually referred to as community spirit.
2. *Probability of Production.*
   That is, increase the effectiveness of the community's instruments, facilities and services and reduce the proportion of members with inadequate access to these facilities.
3. *Probability of Outcome.*
   Increase the outcomes that are possible and probable for members of the community; in particular by increasing the range of probable outcomes for those unduly constricted.
4. *Relative Values of Different Courses of Action.*
   Increasing the range of relative values would by itself create a 'tower of Babel': dissociation into a multiplicity of private worlds. Community benefit would follow only if there were increasing unity in the increasing range of specific valuations: if the specific motivation were embedded in the pursuit of wider objectives and ideals that were commonly and explicitly shared. Such a development would reflect itself in a community which was both more tolerant *and* supporting of ideal seeking members.

There seems to be little in these directions of development that would suggest a new mass market for the mass media to replace the decline of the individual home as a market.

It could be that communities would want to project themselves to distant communities by access radio and access television. We suggest that this is unlikely for two reasons:

1. the dominant pressures for development will be centripetal, at most engaging in specific areas like sport with neighbouring communities.
2. the most attractive means for the occasional distant communication will be the video tape.

Already the Canadian experience with community access radio has revealed these drawbacks. The area served tends to cover a number of communities and they have not shown much desire to get entangled with each others affairs. The volunteers find their time and efforts increasingly sucked into doing a professional radio job and away from community affairs.

In the early stages of community revival it is the governmental bodies that might make greater use of mass media than in the past (*i.e.* work within the bureaucratic model).

At all levels of Australian government there has been serious concern with raising the quality of urban life. There is awareness that many Australian communities, particularly in industrial towns and the new working class suburbs are:

1. markedly lacking in community spirit and organized efforts at community self-help;
2. poorly served by community facilities;
3. served by an inadequate range of facilities;
4. characterised by high rates of vandalism, delinquency, suicide, mental ill-health, broken families and other such signs of dissociation of the motives of community members.

There is also an awareness that there is a sort of threshold effect in community development. Up to a certain level the community resources seem so pitiful that they are not worth caring about (we are not referring to the rich suburb where private resources are so great that there is little felt need to attend to the community). So long as they are so poor it seems a waste to add to them. Put in a public phone booth – it is busted. Put in public bus shelters – they are busted, and so on. Vandalism and delinquency are sound measures of level of community spirit. However, beyond a certain stage there is a take-off point where community pride fosters even more community action.

The governments have started to allocate large sums of money to get community life off the ground (rural and urban). It is this that raises the possibility of extensive use being made of the mass media to inform and instruct the public about the government programmes. However, it is unlikely that this will be other than a short run influence on the communication pattern in Australia.

The most critical factor in community life taking off is the community's own involvement – not in government handouts or persuasion. The greatest value for money in development of shared community resources is in developments that the community understands and shapes.

Both of these principles have been recognized in the Australian Assistance

Plan and the establishment of video-access centres. The latter is of special significance in several ways.

The portable video-pack was a technical breakthrough that made it possible for people to record experience in a visual *non-conceptual way*. It thus made it possible for people to share experiences that they had not all shared or of which they now may have different memories. Technically, video also made it possible for ordinary people to go from recording what they wanted to record, to replaying it for themselves or others. There was no dependence in the communication chain on any specialists who were not necessarily 'one of us'.

As a medium, *video must not be associated with T.V., radio or film*, each of which is characterized by a refining process by 'experts' (such as journalists, technicians, film makers), leading to a professional product tied up with professional pride in the product. As a medium, video is a truer medium than any of the mass media in that it imposes less structuring on the messages. There may be a lot of noise in terms of low quality but any deliberate distortions are those that users themselves produce by pointing the porta-pak here rather than there. The immediate recording, play-back, erasing nature of video without the intervention of specialists is as much a communication utility as is passing notes in a meeting. The relevant life of the video message is only the life of the face-to-face processes of which it is a part.

Thus this technology supports and enriches the very trends that we identified with democratization.

The centres themselves provide any community or citizens, even if they are not much good with the pen, with a potent means of:

1. informing public agencies of what their programs are doing to themselves and other people: such as freeways, mining leases, housing, transport, police, schooling etc; potentially leading to social organization and action;
2. informing other people and public agencies of social needs that are currently being unattended to; potentially leading to social organization and action.

As such this influence of the centres is double-edged. On the one side they provide a catalyst to community development, on the other they erode organizational bureaucracy.

Resurgence of community life is likely to assist and to grow from several other social trends. As increasingly both parents are in employment and more jobs are in information handling (rather than materials handling) we can expect more people will work at home, a lot more of the time. One British estimate put it at about 25% of jobs by the year 2,000. With more adults in the home and neighbourhood during the day and with the growing irrelevance of compulsory school attendance we expect that an increasing proportion of children's learning will be done in the neighbourhood of home, not school. With more work and learning being done at home groups of neighbours may well start to develop shared communication facilities for receipt and transmission of documents. It is hard to envisage that they would normally have much call for more technology than that. Computational requirements of such neighbourhood groups could probably be met in the near future by owned or shared mini or micro computers.

As children grow up in such multi-purpose home clusters and communities, with parents freed from the depersonalization of bureaucratized work, we think it highly likely that they will wish to spend much more time using the shared resources with other children. Much less time tele-viewing. The strains on children of the nuclear family are also likely to be much less when they have so many friendly people and homes in their immediate neighbourhood. When real people are friendly and available, television will lose much of its attractiveness.

Richard Sennett (1970) has argued that there are three positive directions toward change that are necessary if community life is to be revived in our cities:

'The first of these directions is to increase the visible density of urban areas.' (p. 128).
'second . . . a concerted effort to effect socio-economic integration of living, working and recreational spaces.' (p. 129).
'third, and most important . . . the removal of central bureaucracies from their present directive power.' (p. 132).

We believe that the first will, in the first instance, flow largely from the second and that movement in the second and third directions is the most probable future for Australian cities and towns.

15.2. Development in rural communities

Our preceding discussion has been largely about urban communities. Australia has a rural society. It is not now large in numbers but it carries a big part of the national history and identity. In this section we try to assess what has happened and is likely to happen to the rural sector. From this we may be able to infer changing communication requirements.

Rural society in Australia is essentially that part of society that is located in the wheat-sheep areas and the high rainfall areas (as defined in the Report on the Australian Wool Industry (R.A.W.I.) 1971-1972). The arid pastoral areas are more by way of being a scatter of families than a rural society.

The quality of life that can be expected in this rural society is what we shall be concerned with: and we mean this in the same broad encompassing sense that has been used to debate the future of our cities. More specifically we are concerned about whether the quality of life we can expect will be a sore or a strength to our national well-being.

Let us first see from where we start:

1. We have no peasantry locked into rural squalor. World War II basically saw us out of the social disasters of the first post-war settlement programme and the subsequent closer settlement schemes. Thanks to Wadham and like minded spirits, the second post-war settlement was rational and since then average farm incomes have generally stood higher than those of the self-employed in the urban areas, and considerably higher than average wages.

2. We have no mass of landless farm labourers. The required labour inputs, per unit of capital, have markedly declined with mechanical and chemical innovations and the spread of internal combustion engines and electrification. The plight of the few we have is no credit to us but their numbers are so few that their continuance or their disappearance from that role would little affect the viability of rural industries. Consequently it is a matter on which urban and rural sectors can be expected to collaborate to improve their lot, not conflict. The essential non-farm family labour inputs are being increasingly met by contract labour who can stand free of the individualistic, paternal supervision that can so taint the lot of the farm labourer; who are mobile enough to enforce decent rates of economic exchange; who can offer their families the benefits of town living and who have some chance of capitalizing on their own efforts for future security and status.

3. We have passed the stage that one might term 'the primitive accumulation of farm capital'. Land clearing, fencing, water storage and even the building up of soil fertility are the achievements that basically lie behind us in the wheat-sheep and high rainfall areas. As noted in R.A.W.I. this gives a built-in flexibility that augurs well for the rural economy riding with fluctuations

in the world markets. It also lessens dependence on political decisions at the national level for major investments in the primary industries at a time when these decisions are increasingly difficult to come by.

4. We have a well developed, but not necessarily adequate, physical infra-structure of rural towns, transport facilities, electrification, communications, and an institutional infra-structure of legislative and organizational arrange-ments. Enough of these have been going long enough to have considerable reserve capabilities for doing new things, if required. They are no longer in the ad hoc mode of frontier living.

5. The decline in rural population has about reached the point where the forces that produced it are spent. The moral effects of the steady attrition of the rural population are still with us but, except for some of the hamlets of 500 or under, not the spectre of dissolution.

6. The way of life that is offered by farming and, to a lesser extent by rural towns, is increasingly that which people at large are seeking. In a rural population that is urbane this is not a trivial matter. In Fox's study of why farmers (graziers) did not wish to leave the desolation of west of Cobar it stood out as a matter that was not affected by their wealth or family tradi-tion – they knew the city life and they were not about to trade their way of life for one of coercion. From the city we see the stream of city farmers, and it is very doubtful that tax relief is their only purpose, and the would-be commune dwellers (often, we guess, children of the former). The points made in the previous section are by no means exhaustive but they do suggest that the Australian rural society (excluding the special case of the purely pastoral areas) might be self-determining about the shape of its course in the seventies.

Now let us consider some of the features of the present situation that render it less likely that the rural society will properly use the chances that are open. We will ignore those difficulties that arise from the historical happenstance of agriculture shifting from being nationally critical, to being important or to being in the maybe category. It seems to us that that is the sort of thing for which leaders are supposed to emerge to cope with. Some of the things that seem to us to make the future something other than what the rural population want are the following:

1. At the *family* level. Our farms are mostly family managed and worked and passed on to a son (Schapper puts the figure at about 80%). The questions we wish to raise are, where does the farmer get a wife who will put up with farm life and actively support him in his activity, and how does he get a son to take over with the necessary increment in managerial acumen? Quite apart from gradual disappearance of the one-teacher schools, with their offerings of nubile women to farmers, there is a much more serious problem due to the general changes in women's expectations of life. The problem is no easier regarding sons who might succeed to ownership. Higher general education offers them a choice of occupations with apparently similar degrees of self-determination to that of the farmer and, for the less gifted there is an almost automatic but painfully long transition to ownership. For the latter the 'apprenticeship' is so long that special schooling is not particularly attractive, except as an excuse to be away from home.

2. At the *community* level. Here we feel most unsure of what we wish to say, even to make guesses. I (*F.E.*) have not had a chance to go back into any of the half dozen small communities that I studied in the fifties. Bearing this in mind we will nevertheless try a guess. Our hamlets, of about 500 population, were built around very sharp age and sex role definitions. Just the sort of thing which is now inclining women and youth to get out of the rural society. The car and the macadamised road are reducing the relevance of the hamlet and its forced social life. The TV is making it almost indefensible except as a simple point of commercial exchange. Maybe social life in our rural society has already transcended the hamlets.

3. At the *industry* level. On both its input and its output sides the primary industries have been geared to massive, undifferentiated economic exchanges. Variations in quality due to the individual producer have been next to irrelevant. This seems to be the attitude of mind of most primary producers. Only a few are market-oriented. Most hide beyond the commodity boards and their equivalent.

4. At the *national* level. Historically the role of the rural sector has been plagued by being cast between the images of the wealthy pastoralists and the worthy farmers. These images encourage others to try political manipulation and seduce members of the rural sector to rely on political solutions. This seems to me to be one of the difficulties in the way of the rural society making its own way into the seventies.

Where can our rural society go in the future? We are not much interested in where they would go if nothing was done. As stated earlier the rural sector has a degree of potential self-determination that could be a major factor in where they actually go. Let us proceed on the assumption that the rural sector will try to make its own future and will be so allowed by the urban sector. We will make the following suggestions about where our rural society might go in the seventies:

1. The critical changes are those that can be made in our rural townships. We do not think it will be possible to provide an acceptable quality of life to farmers' wives and children, let alone farmers, unless something is done about these places. The only real possibility of enlivening our rural township is the cooperative leisure organization based on the local taxation device of the poker machine. We know of no other way of bringing together the sorts of money that can give a town of 5-10,000 the cultural and recreational facilities that might be expected by suburban dwellers. For this size of town we can expect, as for example we have with Deniliquin and Narrandera, a number of so-called Registered Clubs and hence a fair range of freedom for people to fall out with each other and still find attractive ways to be in the social life of the community. This is not the future in New South Wales but what is already happening. Concern with the drunkenness/gambling problem that characterized the wretched state of our labour force (urban as well as rural) seems to have prevented people from recognizing the genuine novelty of what has been achieved by the Registered Clubs movement.

We aware that we are running two ideas together. On the one hand the minimal size of the communities we need and on the other hand how we get out of the penny-scraping of bazaars and raffles without falling into reliance on uncertain funds from some national decentralization scheme. Our feelings are that these two things ought to be considered together because the right size for a town depends on whether it can raise the funds needed to provide its people with an adequate quality of life. Maybe there is some way in which we can extend the life of the hamlets. We would personally like to think so. Most of them have a lot of history and a lot of character. But we do think that:

a. they are so small that the resultant narrow minded, status conscious meanness is not going to meet the needs of the farming people nor the townspeople,

b. they grew up in the horse age and now they are hindering the concentration of purchasing power and loyalties that might give vitality to the 110 odd communities of 5,000 to 50,000 inhabitants (in toto about one and a quarter million townspeople) that are so strategically placed throughout the wheat-sheep and high rainfall areas.

Very few of our farm families are so far removed that they could not plan on visiting these population centres twice a week to do business, shop and enjoy the recreational and leisure facilities with others.

If we take 50 miles as the extreme distance we would want farmers to be from a town of at least 5,000 inhabitants then we find that this pretty well exists throughout Australia. To come up to that standard requires de-centralization on a very much smaller scale than that envisaged by the planners. The following table indicates all that would be needed:

NSW	population increase of 7,000 over	5 communities
Qld	population increase of 8,000 over	4 communities
Vic. & SA.	population increase of 15,000 over	7 communities
WA.	population increase of 8,000 over	4 communities
	Total + 38,000 over	20 communities

Of course, a population of 5,000 odd might not enable a community to come alive if it lacks institutions like the NSW Clubs to raise real money for community needs.

2. Even if we can provide a proper focus for rural social life, *i.e.* other than the cities, there remains a weak link in the heart of the venture. Where do we get the necessary growth in managerial capabilities to run farms, to co-operate about commercial interests, to do with the townspeople what is needed to provide a better life in the rural society? The studies by Crouch, myself (*F.E.*) and others have shown how central this quality is to the adaptiveness and vitality of our farming. We did not say anything much about how this factor of production might be changed. We still cannot think of anything in the ordinary run of things that would make much difference. We think that something very different from the ordinary run of things should be done, and we think it is within the power of our rural society to do it. What we wish to suggest is that the notion of 'continuing education' be taken seriously by our rural society. The Danish Folk Colleges come to

mind. We think it is pointless trying to drum management theory into a lad of 17-20 when he is not about to take over the property till he is 30 plus. Let us look at it another way. As the lad gets older the father will be wishing that he could talk to him about the farm. More than that, most of the important managerial activities of the property are not muscle-bound, they can be done equally well by a woman. The evidence is clear that it makes a real difference to a farmer's work whether his wife and sons are involved, and interested in what he is doing. It is my belief that this is obvious to all concerned and that we will generate our own version of the Danish Folk Colleges to bring the farmers, their wives and sons together for a couple of weeks a year – for discussion of farm management.

3. The organization of the rural industries is likely to see the emergence of a significant degree of cooperative activity. We are not predicting a return to the cooperative retail stores of the thirties but something like the developments we are seeing with the National Farmers Union in the U.K. That is, cooperative bulk buying groups to seek economic advantages against the increasingly monopolistic forces controlling the major inputs into agriculture (fuel, chemicals etc.) and group contracts to exploit the increasing segmentation of consumer markets. A very hard look at individual margins and potential marketing efficiencies will be needed before this trend does become significant. We think it is possible because of the shakeup that is occurring with our traditional bulk markets. The present North-Western (NSW) Co-op Pig Marketing Group is marking out this trail.

4. The interface between the rural and urban sectors of our society are likely to change radically with the growth of internal tourism, caravanning etc. What we see already in the New South Wales South Coast dairying area is very likely to extend to the older inland towns. People are becoming interested in their own history and have the leisure and money to pursue that interest. Such intermingling may seem a mixed blessing to some but in the longer run it could contribute significantly to the prosperity and quality of life of the rural towns.

5. In the context of a declining rate of growth of the national population an alliance of the rural towns about their common interests may counter the tendency to see the future in terms of further urban growth and the replication of these urban complexes, e.g. the Albury-Wodonga, Orange-Bathurst growth centre proposals. Such an alliance might also be expected to foster a

pattern of inter-town transportation at variance with the radial patterns currently imposed by the big cities.

6. With the emergence of the Australian Assistance Plan (or its successor, because even if that is killed another such would have to be created) we see the potential of new forms of self government at the local level. Forms of matrix organization in which local authorities, regional authorities, the Clubs and Farmer co-operatives' would provide an amalgam of community wisdom and money to ensure continued enrichment of community life.

Reviewing these possible developments we do not see much demand for new technologies of communication. The need to improve reception and increase available channels particularly to the outback might well warrant satellite coverage. The cheaper, more flexible and localized coverage offered by the Westinghouse Electric tethered balloon seems on the other hand ideally suited to the broadcast communication needs of the emerging regions. The objection that they would constitute a hazard to aviation hardly stands serious consideration. The potential benefits to rural regions are of an entirely different order of magnitude.

However, again we see that it is in the development of their social institutions that people are most likely to get the sorts of social communication they want. They already have most of the technical means they require.

16. Leisure: recreation or the pursuit of beauty?

Let us look at the future of leisure, recreation and physical education. Let us seriously question what we pretty well take for granted.

Over the past fifty years, since World War I, we in Australia have evolved a great complex of organizations, social expectations and cultural practices to cope with our leisure time. Some of the organizations were for all practical purposes social institutions *e.g.* the Surf Life Saving clubs, cricket, football, bowls, tennis, yachting and the R.S.L. clubs. And not least, our pubs and betting shops. Social expectations were so strong that failure to participate in these organized forms of recreation was counted as a sign of doubtful moral character. For those who could not participate there was special dispensation if they showed themselves to be keen interested followers of a major sport. Culturally the 'week-end break' was as much a fact of Australian life as night and day. Even in our highest educational institutions there seemed to be no thought given to the fact that work could be done over week-ends. Sometime during Friday afternoons the Australian minds switched off thoughts of work and entered another world.

Two features appeared to give this pattern great strength and flexibility. Compulsory school sports and an endless round of competitive sporting activities for children, indoctrinated the young into a love of sport or, at least, a healthy respect for its ultimate value to individual and society. The cultural dispensation to the spectator, follower, the barracker, gave the society flexibility which permitted those who could not afford to participate or were otherwise disabled to share the illusion of all being in it; in the great Australian classless dream.

We will return to this pattern but let us first ask a question. Is it likely that the next 25 years will be just a further development and extension of this pattern of leisure usage? If so, then the deep roots of this pattern give us a very firm basis on which to build. If not then this strength may well be our greatest weakness; the source of our worst mistakes in the future. Putting the question as bluntly as this seems to beg for the negative answer; of course not! But need it? It could be that the trends we are seeing toward more leisure time and greater affluence would simply see more people moving from 'the pub-betting-shop, television' pole to the middle class pole of active participation. Even this shift would have its interesting sides. We think it likely that the overwhelming role of sport in defining our ideas of how to use our leisure time arose from the times when week-ends and public holidays were too short or the people were too impoverished to do anything significant with them. With a shorter and less exhausting working week we do not think that people will be filled with the same urgency to make the week-end count by participating in or following the sports. With longer annual leave, that they are financially able to use, people are more likely to think of ways of using their leisure times other than by attending or participating in sports. If they follow the middle class example they will move away from the mass oriented large team sports toward tennis, squash, golf, yachting and the multitude of more individualized sporting activities that can be more easily geared to one's own time table and matched to one's own abilities and requirements. As annual holidays become a serious proposition, thoughts will turn away from sport per se to forms of recreation that serve family needs. Caravans, small boats, off-road vehicles and holiday homes would continue to multiply.

Thus even the least surprising future for leisure in Australia will confront us with problems that we have not previously had to face. 'Will confront us' is a bit too optimistic. We think we are already confronted with some of these new problems. The multiplicity of new sports like water skiing, parachute jumping, gliding etc. is not a problem. We have ample experience with writing consitutions for bodies to govern such sports, control their membership, train and classify skill levels and organize competitive events. Our problems lie with how to gracefully run down sports that have had their heyday and avoid the artificial respiration now being provided by professionalized players and TV contracts for organized sporting events.

Our problems are at least three fold:

1. How to gracefully run down sports that have had their heyday.
2. How to provide facilities that will enable people to pursue the multitude of more individualized pursuits.
3. How to accommodate the rapidly growing pressure on our natural resources for leisure; the beaches, waterways, forests and parklands.

The first problem will only slowly be solved. As we mentioned earlier, some of the traditional sports have practically become institutions in our society. That is, they have come to be the very embodiment of some core social values like that of the masculine hero figure, and to claim an indispensable right to existence; with the social support that that entails. They are deeply entrenched in the establishment of the society right through from the compulsory school sports to the old men on the selection board and governing bodies. For these reasons we can expect the organizations built around cricket, football and surf-lifesaving to be major obstacles to adaptive change. These bodies will be forced to adapt to change as there is a decline in compulsory sport in schools and as at the same time the leisure facilities in schools are developed as joint school and community complexes. The South Australian proposals for Angle Park and Thebarton are examples of this. Furthermore, subsidies to these sports in the form of artificially low ground rents will probably be brought into line with subsidies for the minor sports. Lastly, efforts will increasingly be made to prevent these sports being artificially supported by commercialization (*e.g.* advertising for those manly products of tobacco and alcohol), TV contracts or the excessive siphoning off of poker machine funds which is so characteristic of NSW Rugby League Football. As the so-called major sports have to find their own level in the future one would expect them to start dismantling the upper and most expensive levels of the pyramid of international and interstate competitions. The focus might even get back to the local and district level where participation is highest and the identification of the followers least spurious. If this means the virtual end of Test Matches, Sheffield Shield, Cup Finals and the like, then what will the society feel it has lost? A phoney test of state or national superiority? An equally phoney mechanism for creating national heroes? Perhaps more than anything the mass media will suffer.

We are well aware that the first steps of change will be the most difficult. We are also aware that they are directly contrary to the advice John Bloomfield recently gave to the federal minister for Tourism and Recreation in his report on '*The Role, Scope and Development of Recreation in Australia*' (1973). Bloomfield endorsed what he called 'the recreation pyramid' (p. 10). His pyramid is clearly only a sporting pyramid, passing through district, state, and national levels of competition to Olympics, Commonwealth Games, World Championships, etc.

This is the pyramid of competitive sport that automatically creates champion sportsmen and women. We say automatically because that is precisely the nature of the process: someone must win and at each higher level more must drop-out than remain in. Bloomfield is sufficiently sensitive to the change in our culture to emphatically advise that this narrowly defined 'pursuit of excellence' *must never* become the major aim of a department of recreation' (p. 9). Despite this he recommends a programme of governmental support for sport that would do credit to East Germany. In his programme for our future, government monies would underwrite the emergence of professional administrators. As he put it, via the words of one of his informants, 'the kitchen table era of sport administration would cease and that the government would support the administration of sporting associations as was done in many other countries through the world' (p, 34). As the superior sportsmen and women emerge from the ruck there would be sporting scholarships in order 'to make it worthwhile to compete for their countries in international competition' (p. 39).

Bloomfield's reason for so encouraging sport as a way of life for the selected few are:

1. the pursuit of excellence in sport, which must be fostered . . .;
2. that the excellence of Australian Sportsmen in international competitions fosters the image of Australia; and
3. the hero-worship accorded to these selected few keeps the whole process going by creating similar ambitions in our children (p. 40) (one could add, 'and in their parents').

This is by no means all of the scenarios that Bloomfield presents.

As he sees it the present commercial support for national and international competitions would not be simply withdrawn, as we have suggested it probably would; it would be replaced by government monies. Far from asking why there is not enough grass roots support for this expensive top end of the sports pyramid he recommends a further addition of 'The Australia Games', another sort of Commonwealth games but between the States; financed by government money, of course.

Even more important as an indicator of where the Bloomfield scenario would take us in the future are the recommendations to bring into being a professional, university qualified establishment to reinforce the declining relevance of the traditional sporting establishment. This new professional establishment would have even less motivation to let the old sports die gracefully. He proposes 'a massive infusion of money' to create top jobs in training physical educationists (p. 64); a National Institute of Sport and Recreation to train the leading coaches of all states and conduct final training for national teams before they leave for overseas competitions (p. 94-95); professionalization of coaches (p. 66); professional accreditation of occupations from community recreation officers and above, and of course, government monies to support the rest of the professional bit with research programmes, research centres, computerized libraries, and the like. We started off suggesting that one of Australia's big problems in the years immediately ahead was to de-institutionalize our major mass-oriented sports. Bloomfield proposes that we do the opposite, and in fact enshrine a few more sports if needs be, and bolster the lot with another self-serving but professionally certified establishment. Obviously we cannot walk away from why there can be such contradictory scenarios of our future. We will, however, come back to this later as there are the other two problems mentioned. Let us deal with these and then return to this dilemma.

The other two problems need no detain us long. Ways of coping with these are already emerging.

If people are to be given a chance of genuinely choosing forms of recreation that suit their particular needs then some community support is needed to bring the necessary physical facilities into being. When the minor sports were a prerogative of the rich few they could well afford to provide and maintain their own facilities. Thus a rich man with a waterfront home could afford his own boat shed, launching ramp and mooring facilities. If a majority of the society are to exercise such a choice of recreation then we have to start thinking in terms of marinas. The emerging concept of community recreation complexes starts to meet these sorts of needs. The sharing of capital costs and overheads enables many recreational activities to exist where individually they would not get off the ground.

Similarly with the third problem. In the last five years we have had a revolution in the way we think about our natural resources, our National Estate. We have become acutely conscious of the impact on our environment as we have shifted ourselves from regularized mass concentrations on and around our urban sporting fields to more individualized pursuits at the coasts, waterways, forests, etc. We have not just become conscious of the problems; we have begun to make inroads on the problem. Greatly increased powers have been given to State and Federal authorities to plan and develop the use of our natural resources for recreational purposes. Party political differences have been negligible in this matter and hence there is no reason to believe that we shall not continue to make further constructive inroads into the problem. Now all of this seems fine.

The future creates some clearly distinguishable problems. These problems have been generally recognized and we already have some very promising solutions to some. There is some disagreement about how to resolve the problem of the declining social relevance of the traditional major sports. Need that worry us? It may be just a question of the values of those proposing the different solutions. After all, there has always been a small minority in Australian society who have failed to appreciate the social value attached to organized sport.

At this point we beg to differ. We do not think it is just a question of personal differences between people like Bloomfield and ourselves.

Up to now we have worked on the assumption that the next 25 years will be so much like the past 25 years that we could adapt by doing more of the same. More money and more regulatory power and hey presto – we have more champion sportsmen and women, more community recreation facilities and control over the degradation of our national recreational resources.

Well we think that all of that is simply wrong-headed; a case of looking down the wrong end of the telescope.

Over the past ten years we have had ample warning that we are not confronted just by a change in the allocation of social resources. Greater affluence and increased leisure time are important but they do not tell us what our future is about to be.

We are blind to the future if we fail to recognize the shift in human values that characterizes the past ten years. Bloomfield projects a future as if we were still going to be hung up on striving for national superiority, public identification of individual excellence through competitive matches of person-against-person; the certified expert lording it over the amateur; national standards of individual physical fitness. Are these values orientations real? Do they reflect the last ten years? The answer is obviously no.

Recreation does not exist in and of itself. Recreation is a function of work, family and school – of man-in-society. In *Futures We're In* we looked closely at the expected changes in work, family and school. We simply restate the conclusions we then reached about the ideal people are likely to pursue.

The significance of leisure, per se, in future western societies seems to have been grossly overestimated because the people specializing in studying leisure have made simple assumptions about the evolution of the rest of the society. The most gross assumption, that had considerable airing, was that automation would render redundant the great mass of unskilled and semi-skilled workers. Western societies would then be faced with the 'circuses and bread' problem of later day Rome. By the end of the sixties this scenario seemed strikingly irrelevant. There was no sign of a relentlessly increasing mass of unrequired labour. It was obvious that the great majority of people would be continuing to work.

A new scenario emerged that recognized that the mass of unskilled and semi-skilled work was not going to go away, in either manual or mental work. It predicted that we could and would use our growing affluence to automate out those tasks which were especially dangerous or brutalizing, reduce the hours of work, raise incomes and seek to enhance the quality of leisure life. The shorter working hours and higher incomes would enable individuals compensatory areas of choice in their lives: to choose between a wide range of leisure-oriented products. This is a pretty good prediction of the present. Hours worked per-lifetime are declining, incomes are increasing and the 'leisure market' from electronic gear to second homes – is probably the fastest growing market in western economies. To organize this market there is an emerging profession of 'recreationalists', displacing in significance the older skills of the physical educationalist. In line with this way of thinking the question is being asked whether education will not have to become 'education for leisure'. A great deal of this new leisure is organized about the increased mobility offered by car, jet aircraft and cruise ships (Patmore, 1972). Working on trend lines from 1955 it would seem an easy matter to project the future of leisure. More and more of the same, only increasingly sophisticated and more capital intensive. The main cloud on the horizon of this scenario is the emerging paradox that the more people are free to choose their leisure the more they spoil it for each other. We are not here referring to the modern gladiatorial spectacles of football because these are increasingly for the viewer, not the spectator. We refer to the more affluent forms of leisure that require access to, and use of outdoor areas. However well planned and developed and managed these outside resources are it seems inevitable that leisure choices will become more and more restricted, and hence less compensatory.

We do not think that the future of leisure will simply be the outcome of war between those concerned with exploiting the environment in pursuit of individual pleasure and those concerned with the continuing potential of the environment to give pleasure.

The problem for us is to try to see what men do with their leisure as worklife and schooling are increasingly democratized and the family changes to exploit the new possibilities.

Leisure is in its nature free, relative to the other roles in work, family and education which always retain some core of commitments. To that extent it is even harder to predict what might happen. The amount of genuine novelty is likely to be too great. What is not likely to happen is easier to predict because of what we know about how current and past forms of leisure are embedded in their social contexts. Thus, there seems little reasons to believe that we are moving to the classic utopian situation; to the Big Rock Candy Mountain. Commitments remain too many. Similarly, we do not see a real possibility of the second leisure scenario working its way by bureaucratizing leisure. We think that what the 'surfies' did to undermine the almost para-military Surf Life Saving Clubs of Australia is evidence of the hopelessness of this solution even before de-bureaucratization has hardly begun. Technological solutions, such as colour television, are not viable solutions. People who feel themselves to be growing by way of meaningful involvement in work, family and education are not likely to be seduced even by a techno-logical opiate as rich as that envisaged by the science fiction writer Ray Bradbury in *The Illustrated Man* (1967).

Thus we do not feel able to make the more specific predictions that we made in other areas because there is so little that must necessarily carry over to the future. There is, however, a clue as to what may well be the overriding ideal that will tend to guide men to the choice of their leisure purposes. This clue is given, in pretty obvious form by de Grazia in trying to predict 'Leisure's Future' at the end of his classic study of *Time, Work and Leisure*:

'Leisure, given its proper political setting, benefits, gladdens and beautifies the lives of all. It lifts up all heads from practical workaday life to look at the whole high work with refreshed wonder. The urge to celebrate is there. Felicity, happiness, blessedness. Certainly the life of leisure is the life for thinkers, artists, and musicians.' (1962, p. 415).

The conclusion we draw from de Grazia's clue is this: the pursuit of the ideals of homonomy, nurturance and humanity are unavoidably those that will engage men in their involvement in work, education and family, it is only in leisure that men will be able to whole heartedly pursue the ideal of beauty, without which harmonious social and personal development is un-likely.

In our discussion of the ideal of beauty in *Futures We're In* we identified it as that dimension of choosing between purposes that concerned 'Relative value of intention'. What we are saying now is that in his leisure man has a chance to lift his eyes above the level of better fulfilment of his commit-ments to ponder on whether there may not be more, namely, that no matter how much men may shape their leisure to allow of pursuit of other ideals, they will be increasingly concerned in their leisure with the pursuit of beauty. Their concern with this will be enhanced as they are able in work etc. to pursue the other ideals and hence realize that approach to the overriding ideal the meta-ideal of omnipotence of man, in the image of God, is not possible without some concurrent ability to pursue the ideal of beauty. As a side comment, we feel that those in higher intellectual pursuits will probably be able to reach the same conclusion and hence be desirous of making a place in their lives for leisure – despite the dire predictions about these people being headed for a seventy-two hour week whilst the ordinary folk head for the twenty-seven hour week.

Thus we expect that people will structure their leisure hours around creativity, not re-creation of what has been stifled and thwarted.

Epilogue

We started with the question of what telecommunication facilities the Australian people would be demanding, and presumably willing to pay for, in the 1990's.

We did not go out and ask the people what they thought they would require. It seemed to us from the earlier study that the circumstances contributing to their currently felt needs might well have changed radically before the 1990's. We did not go and ask the scientists and technologists about when the next technical revolution could be expected. Changes in Probable Effectiveness of means of communication would obviously modify the choices people would make in the 1990's. It seemed to us that the psychological nature of man and his intentions would have much more to do with his future choices.

We did go out of our way to see what people are currently doing to better realize their own nature and values. We took the view that we were probably already into our future; but in such a small way that it was not easily recognized. What people are now looking for in their lives can no longer provide a human driving force for the proliferation of mass media.

What we have stated so far in Part III are essentially our answers to the question we confronted.

Apendix A

War and the stability of Australia's future

We think several quite basic trends can be taken for granted as extending to and through the year 2,000.

1. continued growth in productivity. There seems no reason that the rate of 3.0% per annum achieved through the sixties should not be sustained. It was not a demanding rate of growth.
2. continued growth in personal wealth; more than doubling in the period.
3. increased range of productive capabilities paralleling the continued up-grading of the education of the workforce (including management).
4. increasing indirectness of the human contribution to productive processes. The proportion of the workforce in manufacturing and transport will decline in the way that it has in agriculture.

A lot of attention has been given to conditions that could limit such growth, particularly to population explosion, depletion of non-renewable resources and pollution of our ecological system. We do not think these limits will become critical for Australia in the period we are considering. These conditions are not independent of social action and hence cannot be predicted by extrapolating from their past trend lines. Our population growth rate has already shown that it is self adaptive and the society has shown some alacrity in moving toward pollution controls and conservation. Our reserves of non-renewable resources continue to grow faster than we deplete them (except, at the time of writing, of oil but this is an eminently tradeable commodity as so many of the world's producers have so little use for their oil – except to trade).

The potentially serious external limiting conditions (*i.e.* external to our social structure) are in Asia; not in rocks, babies or smog. These are only potential but it will do no harm to discuss them as we can quickly come to the point. War on Australia could seriously upset the trends predicted above, and much more beside. The only two countries that could and might make war on Australia in the period are Indonesia and Japan. We would have had some doubt about attributing the capability to Japan but for the revolution in overseas logistics brought by containerization. Let us explain this.

There has been a quiet revolution in conventional warfare. Quiet because it has not been heralded by the emergence of a radically new weapon; another factor has been at work. The revolution has been in the exchange ratio of mutual destruction[1] that now characterizes battle between two formally constituted armies. Kursk was the scene of the greatest battle of material of World War II, Verdun of World War I and probably Austerlitz in the Napoleonic Wars. The difference in exchange ratios between Kursk and Austerlitz was very much less than the difference between Kursk and the Israeli-Arab war of 1974. At Austerlitz it was the guns, for the first time the dominant weapon. At Kursk it was the tanks with ground attack aircraft and guns as major supplements. In the Sinai desert and the Golan Heights the new element was the electronic battlefield; still in embryo but still no longer the mechanical and chemical ingredients of past battles. The striking characteristics of the new battlefield are the speed of target acquisition and of response capability, and the rapid selective, adaptive nature of response to changing target characteristics. Thus if 10,000 antiaircraft shells were an average requirement to knock out one hostile aircraft in World War II then we are now talking of 2 to 3 surface-to-air missiles. To use the systems language of Ackoff and Emery the military scene is crowding over from '1A, passive functional', e.g. the bayonet, sword etc. with one function and one structure in all environments, to '3B active multi-functional' (1972, Fig. 2.2. p. 29). Electronic sensors, computers and cybernetic systems have given an entirely new lethality to existing mechanical and chemical ingredients of war. What took weeks to destroy at Kursk and months at Verdun, was done in the first two days in the Arab-Israeli war. They could only continue their war because of massive airlifts of new equipment and munitions.

To come back to our point. Only the contemporaneous revolution in containerization enables Japan to sustain a materials-gobbling war of modern dimensions on Australian soil. It is only thus that the transmit time across the beaches to the ultimate consumer could be fast enough to meet the requirements of combat units engaged in present day rates of exchange.

War with Indonesia poses a threat at the other end of the spectrum. Whereas a hostile Japan could conceive of exerting maximum military force in the heartland of Australia the only feasible strategy for Indonesia would be a

---

1. The nature of the exchange being an exchange of energy for structures: the purpose being to increase the state of entropy in opposing forces.

protracted war on the periphery until the sheer strain bent Australian national purposes to the ends the Indonesians wanted. If they attempted the intensive assault role they would simply re-enact the fiascos of the Egyptian armed forces. They would not have the industrial depth to follow through, and always the Australian resources could be mobilized to last the next round because the Indonesians would have to crack, at some point short of where the Australian nation could recoup.

Neither of these two war scenarios predicate an end to an independent Australian nation. We could probably survive both wars with an intact independent nation. In the Japanese scenario the critical fact favouring Australian defence is that they could not blackmail all the other major defence material suppliers into non cooperation with us. Unlike the Arab nations Japan does not have a throttle hold over any strategic commodity. Thus we could expect that if suddenly confronted with such a war, *e.g.* in 2-3 years, we could get by with externally supplied credit and materials. On the human side, the threat of a strike into the heartland would adequately mobilize our own resources. The so-called Indonesian scenario offers no more of a threat. Their only chance of success would lie in basing themselves on their own relative strengths. Their greatest strength is in low mobility, low powered infantry. Our industrial basis is such that we could confront them with high mobility, high powered fighting men. Our geography is such that the approach lines to the heartland could easily be too long for their concept of protracted war.

These are negative scenarios. However, even if these came to be we do not think the war aims would include annihilation of the Australian nation. In neither the Indonesian or Japanese cases do we think there would be a determination on genocide. Even in the extreme case of an overwhelmingly successful outcome for them of a war against us it seems more than likely that their interests would be adequately served by letting the Australian nation grow as the Czech nation has grown throughout centuries of foreign control.

Reference
Emery, F. E., *Australia's defence posture for the '70's*, April 1971. Paper prepared for Centre of Continuing Education Conference on Defence Supply and Procurement.

Appendix B

Computers and communication

We started off by doing a lot of study of computers, on the assumption that computer development would have a major influence on human communications.

Two things emerged from our studies that relegated the topic to this appendix:

1. the dominating trend in computer development up to the present carried ingredients of Orwell's 1984 but did not seem to be indicative of the future;
2. the de-bureaucratization of human affairs seemed to radically change dependence upon integrated computer-communications networks.

A few words on these matters seems to be in order.

On the first point, it has become clear that this development of massive centralized computer facilities did *not* emerge in response to the requirements of civil society. It seems very clear that the I.B.M. and Control Data Corporation would never have been launched on this course if it had not been for the demands of the super-war technologies – for nuclear and then ballistic war.

The first computer arose from the need for ballistic tables (UNIVAC, 1946). The developments from this, through SAGE, to the computer requirements for the Anti-Ballistic Missile placed a constant pressure, and provided astronomical sums of money, for the R & D of the big 'number crunchers'. As an interesting aside we can note that the development of these great machines demonstrates Mumford's thesis of the *Myth of the Machine*. The principles of design in general followed those of a bureaucratic organization. Reliability of operation was sought in the *redundancy of parts* and the development of overriding supervisors. The CS – control system – has now become their nightmare. Gobbling up a higher and higher proportion of total machine capacity as the machine gets larger and less and less open to human control and correction. The programming of such super systems has shown the same bureaucratic characteristics. Within the very big systems a programmer cannot be counted on to produce as many valid machine instructions in a month as he could do in half a day on a small system.

The realization of the alternative design principle based on *redundant functions* has emerged with LSI chips (large scale integrated chips) as the building blocks. These provide a radically different answer to computer-aiding what human beings require in production, education, libraries etc.

Our second point about de-bureaucratization points in the same direction. If our future lay with bigger and more powerful bureaucracies and Perlmutter's world of 300 multinational corporations then the future would indeed be secure for IBM and Control Data. It does not lie there and we are more likely to see the dismantling of existing centralized data banks than their further growth. The communication pattern of data links is most likely to parallel the pattern shown in diagrams (see p. 169).

One development that is likely to be demanded is that where local data banks exist there will need to be good facilities for instructing people on how to interrogate the data bank. And more than this. If for instance the data bank is a regional land registry then a member of the public who tries to check on the status of a block of land he would like to buy, should, on getting nowhere, be able to go to an instructional module (a learning machine) to check out where he went wrong and what he should do instead. That sort of thing is simple and well within our present capabilities to provide. It happens to provide, like the mini computers, the sort of enhanced facility that a 'face-to-face' society will require and hence what they will most likely demand.

There may need to be massive communications systems to allow technical systems to 'talk' to each other. That has not been our concern. For man to talk to man, or man to 'talk to technical systems', there appears to be no such need. The needs that have been forecast are falsely predicted on the persistence and growth of bureaucracy. The chequeless, cashless society is based on the same premise.

Appendix C

Computers, communications and containerization

As was the case with computers we looked closely at transportation as a technology that might radically change what was required of communications.

The conclusion was that these technologies needed each other, together they could and probably would change the possibilities open to human action. Together they could give us a new socio-technical system. However, the net effect would be to give people more 'organizational choice; to enable people to better do more of the things they would wish to do.'

The technological revolution in transport is effectively over. There might be some radical change in inter-city person transit (*e.g.* Boston to Washington vaccum tube trains). They are not likely. Just about everything in transport from width of trucks, speed of aircraft and size of ships has got to limits beyond which it will not be economically possible to go for many foreseeable decades ahead.

There is, however, a revolution under our very eyes. This revolution is at the interface of transport, communications and computerization. It has not, for this reason, we suggest, been readily seen. It was in no-man's land.

This revolution is the containerization of cargo. The move to containerization of sea cargo makes the shift from sail to steam look like a change in skirt hems. With the introduction of containerization it became, overnight, practical to build cargo ships with a speed of 20-30 knots as against the leisurely 11-15 knots that had been standard for cargo ships. With the introduction of container ships the docks and the world of dock labourers became obsolete. The car had already destroyed the communities of dock labourers.

The effects of containerization do not stop with the design of ships and port facilities. As Julius Stuhlman has pointed out they create an entirely new basis for commodity accounting between nations. This sort of accounting makes the gold standard look primeval. In simplifying communication flows containerization makes it possible to greatly enhance the use of computers in the field of distribution. It is, however, primarily a communication flow between technical systems.

Our task was to consider communication between purposeful systems, human beings. Hesketh has argued that 'Institutional changes will, to an increasing extent, replace technological changes as the major sources of productivity increases in transportation, warehousing, inventory control and order processing activities in the intermediate future' (p. 132). Finding new matrix forms of organization that will involve at least managements, unions and governmental authorities is what Hesketh sees as the key to the future. If, as he argues, productivity lies in this direction it seems a very probable development.

For the movement of people within cities we do not see the emergence of 'futuristic', centralized, computerized, public transport systems. We would expect public bus systems to move toward being decentralized and de-bureaucratized, radically changing the present unstable relation between staff and management. We would also expect a very significant decline in multiple car ownership and in useage patterns, as work, leisure and learning move back to the neighbourhood and as flexi-time becomes more general.

References
Allen, J. E. and J. Bruce (ed.): *The future of aeronautics*, Hutchinson, London, 1970.
Hesketh, J. L.: Sweeping changes in distribution, *Harvard Business Review*, March, 1973, 123-132.
Phillips-Birt, D.: *The Future of ships*, Imray, London, 1970.
Stuhlman, J.: The third revolution, *Fields*, No. 10, 1973, p. 83-94.

Bibliography

Ackoff, R. L. and F. E. Emery: *On purposeful systems*, Tavistock, London, 1972.

Angyal, A.: *Foundations for a science of personality*, Commonwealth Fund, Cambridge, Mass., 1941.

Arons, L.: *Advertising and the dynamics of mass media*, Television bureau of advertising inc., New York, 1960.

Arnheim, R.: *Films as art*, Faber, London, 1935.

Arnheim, R.: *Radio*, Faber, London, 1936.

Arnheim, R.: *Art and visual perception*, Faber, London, 1956.

Arnheim, R.: *Film*, 2nd revised edition, Faber, London, 1958.

Aries, Philippe: *Centuries of childhood*, Penguin, Harmondsworth, 1960.

Asch, S. E.: *Social psychology*, Prentice-Hall, New York, 1952.

Asch, S. E.: Studies in independence and conformity, *Psychological monographs*, 1956, 70.

Atkinson, Richard C. and Richard M. Shiffrin: The control of short term memory, *Scientific American*, 1971, 25.2, 82-90.

Bagdikian, B. H.: *The information machines*, Harper, New York, 1971.

Barratt, P. E. H. and Jean M. Herd: Subliminal conditioning of the alpha rhythm, *Australian journal of psychology*, 1964, 16.1, 9-19.

Bion, W. R.: *Experiences in groups*, Tavistock, London, 1961.

Bloomfield, J.: *Recreation in Australia*, Department of tourism and recreation, Canberra, 1973.

Booker, Christopher: *The neophiliacs*, Collins, London, 1969.

Bradbury, Ray: *Fahrenheit 451*, Ballantine Books, New York, 1953.

Breznitz, Shlomo: A critical note on secondary revision, *International journal of psycho-analysis*, 1971, 52, 409-412.

Brown, W.: *Exploration in management*, Pelican, Harmondsworth, 1965.

Cannon, W. B.: Voodoo death, *J. psychosomatic medicine*, 1957, 152.

Carr, Terry: The answer, *Tomorrow's alternatives*, 1973, 165-168.

Carsons, R.: *The silent spring*, Hamish Hamilton, London, 1963.

Carter, Thomas N.: Group psychological phenomena of a political system as satirized in 'Animal farm': An application of the theories of W. R. Bion, *Human relations*, 1974, 27.6, 525-546.

Chein, I.: Environment as a determinant of behaviour, *J. social psychol.*, 1954, 39, 115-127.

Cleghorn, J., C. Neblett, E. Sutter, G. Farrel and I. Kraft: The effect of drugs on hyperactivity in children with some observations of changes in mineral metabolism, *Journal of nervous and mental disease*, 1971, 153, 118-125.

Commoner, B.: *The closing circle*, Jonathan Cape, London, 1972.

Creutzfeldt, O., G. Grunewald, I. Simonova and H. Schmitz: Changes of the basic rhythms of the EEG during performance of mental and visuomotor tasks, *Attention in neurophysiology*, Butterworths, London, 1969.

Crichton, M.: *The terminal man*, Corgi, New York, 1972.

Dember, W. N.: *Psychology of perception*, Holt-Dryden, New York, 1960.
Deutsch, M.: An experimental study of the effect of co-operation and competition upon group processes, *Human relations*, 1949, 2, 199-232.
Deutsch, M.: Field theory in social psychology, Chapter 5 in G. Lindzey (ed.), *Handbook of social psychology*, Vol. 1, Addison-Wesley, Cambridge, Mass., 1954.
Disch, T. M.: *334*, Sphere Books, New York, 1974.
Drabman, R. S. and Margaret H. Thomas: Does media violence increase children's toleration of real-life aggression?, *Developmental psychol.*, 1974, 10.3, 418-421.
Ellis, D. A. and F. J. Ludwig: *Systems philosophy*, Prentice-Hall, Englewood Cliffs, N.J., 1962.
Emery, F. E.: Psychological effects of the western film: a study in television viewing, *Human relations*, XII, 1959, 195-213, 215-232.
Emery, F. E. et al.: Report on environmental pollution, *Doc. T387*, Tavistock Institute, London, 1964.
Emery, F. E.: Reactions to an abstract film, *Doc. 5-36*, Tavistock Institute, London, 1959.
Emery, F. E.: *Freedom and justice within walls*, Tavistock Publications, London, 1970.
Emery, F. E. and E. L. Trist: Socio-technical systems, Chap. 14 in Emery, F. E. (ed.), *Systems thinking*, Penguin, Harmondsworth, 1968.
Emery, F. E. and E. L. Trist: The causal texture of organizational environments, Chap. 12 in Emery, F. E. (ed.), *Systems thinking*, Penguin, Harmondsworth, 1968.
Emery, F. E. and R. Cass-Beggs: Irritation and informativeness of a TV commercial, *Doc. T35*, Tavistock Institute, London, 1962.
Emery, F. E. and M. Emery: *Participative design: work and community life*, CCE., A.N.U., Canberra, 1974.
Emery, F. E. et al.: *Futures we're in*, CCE., A.N.U., Canberra, 1974.
Eisenberg, M.: quoted *National times*, 6 April 1975.
Fabun, D.: *The children of change*, Glencoe Press, 1969.
Fast, Irene: Some relationships of infantile self boundary development to depression, *International journal of psycho-analysis*, 1967, 48, 259-266.
Feibleman, J. and J. W. Friend: The structure and function of organization in Emery F. E. (ed.), *Systems thinking*, Penguin, Harmondworth, 1969.
Gazzaniga, M. S.: *The bisected brain*, Appleton-Century-Crofts, New York, 1970.
Gibson, J. J.: Visually controlled locomotion and visual orientation, *British journal of psychology*, 1958, 49, 182-194.
Goldmeier, E.: Similarity in visually perceived forms, *Psychological issues*, monograph 29, 1936, reprinted 1972.
Greco, M. C.: *Group life*, Philosophical Library, New York, 1950.
Grey, Walter W.: Human frontal lobe function in sensory-motor association, in *Psychophysiology of the frontal lobes*, Academic Press, New York, 1973.
Grossman, S. P.: *A textbook of physiological psychology*, John Wiley, New York, 1967.
Guyton, Arthur C.: *Function of the human body*, Saunders, London, 1964.
Hartmann, Ernest (ed.): *Sleep and dreaming*, Little, Brown & Co. (inc.), New York, 1970.
Head, H.: *Studies in Neurology*, Oxford University Press, London, 1920.
Hebb, D. O.: The mammal and his environment, *American journal of psychiatry*, 1955.
Heider, F.: Attitudes and cognitive organization, *J. of psychol.*, 1946, 21, 107-112.
Heider, F.: *The psychology of interpersonal relations*, Wiley, New York, 1958.
Heider, F.: Thing and medium, 1926, The function of the perceptual system, 1930, both reprinted in *Psychol. issues*, monograph 3, 1959.
Herbert, Frank: Introduction to *Tomorrow's alternatives*, 1973.
Hernandez, P.: A neurophysiological and evolutionary model of attention, *Attention in neurophysiology*, Butterworths, London, 1969.
Heron, Woodburn: The pathology of boredom, *Scientific American*, January, 1957.

Hess, E. H.: Shadows and depth perception, *Scientific American*, March, 1961.
Himmelweit, H. et al.: *Television and the child*, O.U.P., London, 1958.
Horwitz, M.: The recall of interrupted group tasks, *Human relations*, 1954, 7, 3-38.
Huxley, Aldous: *Brave new world*, Penguin modern classic, Harmondsworth, 1932.
Illich, Ivan D.: *Tools for conviviality*, Harper & Row, New York, 1973.
Jackson, R. G. et al.: *Policies for development of manufacturing industry*, Australian Govt. publishing service, Canberra, 1975.
James, William: *The principles of psychology*, Dover publications, 1890.
John, E. R. and K. F. Killam: Electrophysical correlates of avoidance conditioning in the cat, *Pharmacol. exp. therap.*, 1959, 125, 252-274.
Jus, A. and D. Jus: Studies on photic driving conditioning in man, *EEG in clinical neurophysiology*, 1959, 11, 178.
Kanfer, S.: Orwell 25 years later: future imperfect, *Time*, 24 March, 1975.
Kaufman, L. and I. Rock: The moon illusion, *Scientific American*, July, 1962.
Kimball, P.: People without papers, *Public opinion quarterly*, 1959, 23, 389-398.
Kingdon, D. R.: *Matrix organization*, Tavistock, London, 1973.
Kohler, I.: The formation and transformation of the perceptual world, *Psychological issues*, monograph 12, 1970.
Krugman, Herbert E.: *Electroencephalographic aspects of low involvement; implications for the McLuhan hypothesis*, American association for public opinion research, New York, 1970.
Lang, K. and G. E. Lang: The unique perspective of television and its effects: a pilot study, *Amer. sociol. rev.*, 1953, 18, 3-12.
Liebert, R. M. et al.: *The early window*, Pergamon, New York, 1973.
Lippitt, R. and R. K. White: The 'social climate' of children's groups, in Barker, R. G. et al., *Child behaviour and development*, McGraw-Hill, New York, 1943.
Lippold, O.: *The origin of the alpha rhythm*, Churchill Livingstone Longman group, London, 1973.
Lorand, Sandor: Adolescent depression, *International journal of psycho-analysis*, 1967, 48, 53-60.
Luria, A. R.: The frontal lobes and the regulation of behaviour, *Psychophysiology of the frontal lobes*, Academic Press, New York, 1973.
Lynch, James and David A. Paskewitz: On the mechanisms of feedback control of human brain wave activity, *Journal of nervous and mental disease*, 1971, 153, 4, 205-217.
MacLean, Paul D.: Psychosomatic disease and the 'Visceral Brain': recent developments bearing on the Papez theory of emotion, *Basic readings in neuropsychology*, Robert L. Isaacson (ed.), Harper & Row, 1964.
Marshall, S. L. A.: *Men against fire*, Morrow, New York, 1947.
McLuhan, M.: *The mechanical bride*, Vanguard, New York, 1951.
McLuhan, M.: *Culture is our business*, Ballantine Books, New York, 1970.
McLuhan, M.: Playboy interview, *Playboy*, 1969.
McLuhan, M. (with G. Leonard): Learning in the global village, in R. and B. Gross (eds.), *Radical school reform*, Pelican, London, 1969.
McLuhan, M. (with Q. Fiore and J. Agel): *War and peace in the global village*, Bantam Books, New York, 1968.
McLuhan, M.: *Understanding media*, Routledge and Kegan Paul, London, 1964.
McLuhan, M. (with Q. Fiore): *The medium is the massage*, Bantam Books, New York, 1967.
McLuhan, M.: *Gutenberg galaxy*, Routledge and Kegan Paul, London, 1962.
McLuhan, M. (with H. Parker): *Counterblast*, Harcourt Brace, New York, 1969.
Marcuse, H.: *Eros and civilization*, Routledge and Kegan Paul, London, 1956.
Marcuse, H.: *One dimensional man*, Routledge, London, 1964.

Marcuse, H.: *An essay on liberation*, Pelican Books, Harmondsworth, 1969.
Marien, Michael: The discovery and decline of the ignorant society, 1965-1985, *Educational planning in perspective*, 1974, 80-89.
Maruyama, Magoroh: Hierarchists, individualists and mutualists, *Futures*, April, 1974.
Mendels, J. and D. R. Hawkins: Sleep and depression. IV longitudinal studies, *The journal of nervous and mental disease*, 1971, 153/ 4, 251-272.
Mendelson, Wallace, Noel Johnson and Mark A. Stewart: Hyperactive children as teen-agers: a follow-up study, *Journal of nervous and mental disease*, 1971, 153.4, 273-279.
Meissner, W. W.: Dreaming as process, *International journal of psycho-analysis*, (a), 1968, 49, 63-79.
Meissner, W. W.: Notes on dreaming: dreaming as a cognitive process, *International journal of psycho-analysis*, (b), 1968, 49, 699-708.
Merton, R. K.: *Social theory and social structures*, Free Press, New York, 1948.
Miller, G. A., E. Galanter and K. H. Pibram: *Plans and the structure of behavior*, Holt, New York, 1960.
Miller, B. and L. Taylor: Right hemisphere superiority in tactile pattern recognition, *Neuropsychologia*, 1972, 10, 1-15.
Mulholland, T. B.: The concept of attention and the electroencephalographic alpha rhythm, *Attention in neurophysiology*, Butterworths, London, 1969.
Newcomb, T. M.: An approach to the study of communicative acts, *Psychol. rev.*, 1953, 60, 393-404.
Olds, James: Pleasure centres in the brain, *Scientific American*, October, 1956.
Olds, James and Peter Milner: Positive reinforcement produced by electrical stimulation of septal area and other regions of rat brain, *Basic readings in neuropsychology*, (ed. by Robert L. Isaacson), Harper & Row, New York, 1964.
Orme & Johnson: *Psychosomatic medicine*, 1972.
Pawley, Martin: *The private future*, Thames and Hudson, London, 1973.
Pearlin, L. I.: Social and personal stress and escape television viewing, *Public Opinion quarterly*, 1959, 23, 255-259.
Peper, E.: Localized EEG alpha feedback training: a possible technique for mapping subjective, conscious and behavioral experiences, *Kybernetik*, 1972, 11, 166-169.
Pierce, W. H.: Redundancy in computers, *Scientific American*, February, 1964.
Posner, Michael I.: Short term memory systems in human information processing, *Information-processing approaches to visual perception*, 49-60, (ed. R. N. Haber), Holt, Rinehart & Winston inc., New York, 1969.
Rosenthal, R.: *McLuhan: Pro and con*, Pelican Books, Harmondsworth, 1969.
Rosenzweig, Mark R., Edward L. Bennett and Marian C. Diamond: Brain changes in respond to experience, *Scientific American*, 1972, 226.2, 22-29.
Russell, B.: *The analysis of mind*, Allen & Unwin, London, 1949.
de Saussure, Janice: Some complications in self-esteem regulation caused by using an archaic image of the self as an ideal, *International journal of psycho-analysis*, 1971, 52, 87-97.
Schachtel, E. G.: *Metamorphosis*, Basic Books, New York, 1959.
Schaffer, Frank: *The new town story*, Paladin, London, 1970.
Seeman: *Journal of counseling psych.*, Nidich and Banta, 1972.
Sennett, R.: *The uses of disorders*, Pelican, Harmondsworth, 1970.
Solomon, P. et al.: Sensory deprivation: a review, *American journal of psychiatry*, 1957, 114.
Sommerhoff, G.: *Analytical biology*, Oxford University Press, London, 1950.
Sperry, R. W.: Hemisphere deconnection and unity in conscious awareness, *American psychologist*, 1968, 23.10, 723-733.
Spinrad, N.: *Bug Jack Barron*, Panther, London, 1972.

Stearn, G. E. (ed.): *McLuhan: hot and cool*, Dial Press, New York, 1967.

Stewart, Mark A: Hyperactive children, *Scientific American*, 1970, 222.4, 94-98.

Swinehart, J. W. and J. M. McLeod: News about science, *Public opinion quarterly*, 1960, 24, 583-589.

Szekely, Lajos: The creative pause, *International journal of psycho-analysis*, 1967, 48, 353-367.

Thompson, R. J.: *Television crime drama*, Cheshire, Melbourne, 1959.

Tomkins, S.S.: *Affect, imagery, consciousness*, Vols. I and II, Springer, New York, 1962.

Vernon, M. D.: *Perception through experience*, Barnes and Noble, 1970.

Wallace, Robert Keith and Herbert Benson: The psychology of meditation, *Scientific American*, 1972, 226.2, 84-90.

Wertheimer, M.: *Productive thinking*, Harper, New York, 1945.

Wyndham, J.: *The midwich cuckoo*, Penguin, Harmondwsorth, 1960.

Wynne-Edwards, V. C.: *Animal dispersion in relation to social behaviour*, Oliver and Boyd, Edinburgh, 1962.

Zurif, E. and A. Ramier: Some effects of unilateral brain damage, *Neuropsychologia*, 1972, 10, 103-110.